MICROFILM RESOURCES

for Research

A Comprehensive Catalog

NATIONAL ARCHIVES TRUST FUND BOARD

NATIONAL ARCHIVES AND RECORDS ADMINISTRATION

WASHINGTON, DC

2000

LIBRARY OF CONGRESS CATALOGING-IN-PUBLICATION DATA

United States. National Archives and Records Administration.
    Microfilm resources for research: a comprehensive catalog.
        p. cm.
    Includes index.
    ISBN 1-880875-22-5
    1. United States. National Archives and Records Administration—Microform catalogs.
2. United States—History—Sources—Bibliography—Microform catalogs. 3. United
States—Civilization—Sources—Bibliography—Microform catalogs. 4. Documents on
microfilm—Catalogs. I. Title.

CD3026 2000
016.973—dc21   00-057883

Contents

THE NATIONAL ARCHIVES AND RECORDS ADMINISTRATION is responsible for administering and making available for research the permanently valuable noncurrent records of the Federal Government. These archival holdings, now amounting to more than 2 million cubic feet, date from the first days of the Continental Congress in 1774 and preserve the basic records of the legislative, judicial, and executive branches of Government from that time to the present. The National Archives also administers the Presidential libraries.

These research resources document significant events in our nation's history, but most of them are preserved for their continuing practical use in ordinary processes of Government. All non-restricted records are available for the use of scholars, students, genealogists, and others.

THE NATIONAL ARCHIVES MICROFILM PUBLICATIONS PROGRAM

Microfilm has been and continues to be an important way of distributing and preserving records. Since 1941 the National Archives has microfilmed Federal records of high research interest to make the records available for researchers while preserving the originals from deterioration and damage from handling. Copies of these microfilmed records are sold to the public, making these Federal records accessible to libraries, research centers, and individuals.

The National Archives microfilm publications program provides ready access to records for research in a wide variety of fields, including history, economics, political science, law, and genealogy. This program emphasizes microfilming groups of records relating to the same general subject or to a specific geographic area. For example, many of the compiled military service records and accompanying indexes for 19th-century volunteer soldiers are on microfilm. Microfilmed State Department records, such as consular despatches and notes, provide almost complete coverage of relations between the United States and other countries during the 19th and early 20th centuries.

TYPES OF MICROFILM PUBLICATIONS

The National Archives reproduces records in two forms: microfilm and microfiche. Rolls of film are wound on plastic reels, and each frame reproduces one or two single pages or items. A microfiche is a sheet of film containing multiple microimages in a grid pattern, and each microimage is a copy of one or two pages or items.

National Archives microfilm publications are divided into five types: M, A, T, P, and C publications. Most M publications reproduce an entire series of records. Usually, at the beginning of the first roll (frequently on every roll) and on the first fiche, an introduction is reproduced that contains explanatory material to help researchers use the records. Each introduction consists of a general and brief history of the originating agency, a description of the records' content, and an explanation of the arrangement of the records. Some introductions also include special aids, such as indexes and appendixes. A table of contents of the microfilm publication follows the introduction.

Many introductions and tables of contents are printed as accompanying descriptive pamphlets (DPs). DPs that are available (as shown in this catalog) may be requested by contacting the National Archives and Records Administration, Research Support Branch (NWCC1), Room 404, 700 Pennsylvania Avenue, NW, Washington, DC 20408 (telephone 1-800-234-8861 or 202-501-5235; fax 202-501-7170).

A, T, P, and C publications are numbered in the same sequence and, unlike M publications, do not always reproduce a complete series of records. They may contain only segments, by date or subject, of a larger series. In addition, A and T publications may be copies of microfilm produced by other Federal agencies and accessioned by the National Archives. A and T publications are reproduced and sold exactly as they were filmed; they may contain no introductions and have no accompanying descriptive pamphlets. P publications are reproduced for preservation purposes. C publications are produced by private contractors and are available through the National Archives after 7 years of publication.

This catalog, which lists more than 2,000 microfilm publications available from the National Archives, supersedes *National Archives Microfilm Resources for Research: A Comprehensive Catalog* (1996). The catalog is arranged by numbered record group, a system that groups records according to the agency that created them, generally at the bureau level. Donated materials and miscellaneous records are listed last.

Within each record group in this catalog, the microfilm publications are arranged to make them easy to use:

1. Similar records for various date spans, such as census records, are in chronological order:

M637 First Census of the United States, 1790. 12 rolls.

M32 Second Census of the United States, 1800. 52 rolls.

M252 Third Census of the United States, 1810. 71 rolls.

2. Related records concerning foreign countries, such as despatches from U.S. ministers, are arranged alphabetically by country or city:

T158 Despatches From U.S. Ministers to Cuba, 1902–1906. 18 rolls.

M93 Despatches From U.S. Ministers to the Dominican Republic, 1883–1906. 15 rolls.

T50 Despatches From U.S. Ministers to Ecuador, 1848–1906. 19 rolls.

3. Indexes and other users' tools generally precede the records they accompany. For example, the indexes to compiled service records of volunteer Union soldiers precede the compiled service records.

4. If no particular arrangement seems logical, the publications are listed in their own numerical order, with the M publication numbers preceding the A, T, P, and C publication numbers.

Each entry gives the M, A, T, P, or C publication number; the full title of the publication; the number of rolls; and whether there is an accompanying descriptive pamphlet ("DP" signifying that a descriptive pamphlet exists). The film is on 35mm rolls unless the entry specifies 16mm or microfiche. Entries marked with a * have been published since 1996. A typical entry appears as follows:

M1375 Records of the U.S. Morgan Horse Farm, 1907–1951. 12 rolls. DP.

The catalog does not include administrative histories, roll-by-roll lists, or descriptions of what is on the microfilm. Roll lists are available in DPs, in select catalogs, and from reference services at the Washington, DC, and College Park, MD, National Archives facilities and regional archives across the country.

HOW TO GET MORE INFORMATION

For more information on specific publications and roll lists, please contact the National Archives and Records Administration, Research Support Branch (NWCC2), Room 1000, 8601 Adelphi Road, College Park, MD 20740-6001 (telephone 1-800-234-8861 or 301-713-6800 x366; fax 301-713-6169).

OTHER CATALOGS OF MICROFILM PUBLICATIONS

Individual microfilm publications are described in more detail in a series of catalogs of select microfilm publications. These catalogs, which relate to subjects of high research interest, provide roll-by-roll lists and contain detailed descriptions of the records. The following catalogs comprise the series.

Most titles are also available on NARA's web page, *www. nara.gov.*

1790–1890 Federal Population Censuses (1997)
1900 Federal Population Census (2000)
1910 Federal Population Census (2000)
1920 Federal Population Census (1998)
Immigrant & Passenger Arrivals (1991)
Military Service Records (1985)
Black Studies (1996)
American Indians (1998)
Diplomatic Records (1986)
Federal Court Records (1987)

For information about fees and the ordering of catalogs, please contact the National Archives and Records Administration, Research Support Branch (NWCC2), Room 1000, 8601 Adelphi Road, College Park, MD 20740-6001 (telephone 1-800-234-8861 or 301-713-6800 x365, fax 301-713-6169).

Most of NARA's microfilm publication roll lists and descriptive pamphlets are not online. By searching for microfilm publications in the NARA Archival Locator (NAIL), however, you will be able to find out if a roll list or descriptive pamphlet is available for use. This microfilm locator allows you to search for microfilm publications via keywords, microfilm IDs, record group number, and/or NARA viewing location. Each description indicates *all* NARA units which have copies of a microfilm publication in part or in full.

HOW TO ORDER MICROFILM

All microfilm publications of National Archives records are for sale. An individual roll or fiche or a complete set (all rolls or fiche), can be purchased. The prices as of November 1, 2000 are $34 a roll and $4.25 a fiche (U.S. orders), but these prices are subject to change without advance notice. The prices for foreign orders are $39 a roll and $4.65 a fiche. Shipping is included in these prices. The minimum order is $6 for fiche.

A check or money order made payable to the "National Archives Trust Fund" (NAT) must accompany each order. Orders may also be charged to VISA, MasterCard, American Express, and Discover (Novus) accounts. Government agencies, educational institutions, and businesses may purchase microfilm on an accounts-receivable basis but must submit purchase orders. Mail orders to the National Archives Trust Fund (NAT), P.O. Box 100793, Atlanta, GA 30384-0793.

When ordering microfilm, please state the microfilm publication number; if you are not buying a complete set, also state the specific roll or fiche number(s) you wish to purchase.

If you need more information on how to order, details of specific shipping charges, or help identifying which rolls of a publication you wish to purchase, please contact the National Archives and Records Administration, Research Support Branch (NCCC2), Room 1000, 8601 Adelphi Road, College Park, MD 20740-6001 (telephone 1-800-234-8861 or 301-713-6800 x366; fax 301-713-6169).

Copies of National Archives microfilm publications may also be purchased from Scholarly Resources, Inc., 104 Greenhill Avenue, Wilmington, DE 19805 (telephone 302-654-7713; fax 302-654-3871; email: sales@scholarly.com). Copies available for sale from other sources have not been authorized or duplicated by the National Archives and may be one or more generations removed from the master materials. This can adversely affect the quality and legibility of each image.

MICROFILM SPECIFICATIONS

Roll-based microfilm sold through the National Archives publications program is silver-halide film. Rolls are 35mm or 16mm reel microfilm on plastic reels. Reduction ratios range from 12:1 to 20:1; the number of frames on each reel varies.

Microfiche products are diazo copies. Each fiche measures 105mm by 148.75mm (approximately 4 by 6 inches). Reduction ratios range from 24:1 to 32:1; the number of images on each fiche varies.

In some instances, it is possible to obtain microfilm in a different form (e.g., duplicate negative rather than positive). If you desire such services, please contact the National Archives and Records Administration, Research Support Branch (NWCC2), Room 1000, 8601 Adelphi Road, College Park, MD 20740-6001 (telephone 1-800-234-8861 or 301-713-6800 x366; fax 301-713-6169).

RG 7 Records of the Bureau of Entomology and Plant Quarantine

M864 Letters Received by the Bureau of Entomology From W. D. Hunter, May 5, 1902-Nov. 23, 1908. 3 rolls. DP.

RG 9 Records of the National Recovery Administration

M213 Document Series of the National Recovery Administration, 1933-1936. 186 rolls. DP. 16mm.

T692 National Recovery Administration's *Blue Eagle*, a Weekly Newspaper, June 11, 1934-May 17, 1935. 1 roll.

RG 11 General Records of the U.S. Government

M337 Enrolled Original Acts and Resolutions of the U.S. Congress, 1789-1823. 17 rolls.

M338 Certificates of Ratification of the Constitution and the Bill of Rights, Including Related Correspondence and Rejections of Proposed Amendments, 1787-1792. 1 roll.

M668 Ratified Indian Treaties, 1722-1869. 16 rolls. DP.

M1118 Executive Orders, 1-7521, 1862-1936. 17 rolls. DP.

M1247 Perfected International Treaties ("Treaty Series"), 1778-1945. 56 rolls available.

M1326 Enrolled Acts and Resolutions of Congress, 1893-1956. 139 rolls.

M1331 Numerical List of Presidential Proclamations, 1-2317, 1789-1938. 1 roll.

M1518 Ratified Amendments XI-XXVI to the United States Constitution. 16 rolls. DP.

T279 Index to Presidential Proclamations, 1789-1947. 2 rolls.

T1223 Presidential Proclamations, 1-2160, 1789-1936. 11 rolls.

RG 12 Records of the Office of Education

M635 Letters Sent by the Commissioner of Education, 1870-1909. 71 rolls. DP.

RG 15 Records of the Veterans Administration

M123 Schedules Enumerating Union Veterans and Widows of Union Veterans of the Civil War, 1890. 118 rolls.

M313 Index to War of 1812 Pension Application Files. 102 rolls. DP.

M804 Revolutionary War Pension and Bounty-Land Warrant Application Files. 2,670 rolls. DP.

M805 Selected Records From Revolutionary War Pension and Bounty-Land Warrant Application Files. 898 rolls. DP.

M850 Veterans Administration Pension Payment Cards, 1907-1933. 2,539 rolls. DP.

M910 Virginia Half Pay and Other Related Revolutionary War Pension Application Files. 18 rolls. DP.

M1274 Case Files of Disapproved Pension Applications of Widows and Other Dependents of Civil War and Later Navy Veterans ("Navy Widows' Originals"), 1861-1910. Approx. 8,500 cards (microfiche). DP.

M1279 Case Files of Approved Pension Applications of Widows and Other Dependents of Civil War and Later Navy Veterans ("Navy Widows' Certificates"), 1861-1910. Approx. 40,000 cards (microfiche). DP.

M1391 Lists of Navy Veterans for Whom There are Navy Widows' and Other Dependents' Disapproved Pension Files ("Navy Widows' Originals"), 1861-1910. 15 cards (microfiche). DP.

*M1749 Historical Registers of National Homes for Disabled Volunteer Soldiers, 1866-1938. 282 rolls.

M1784 Index to Pension Application Files of Remarried Widows Based on Service in the War of 1812, Indian Wars, Mexican War, and Regular Army Before 1861. 1 roll.

M1785 Index to Pension Application Files of Remarried Widows Based on Service in the Civil War and Later Wars and in the Regular Army After the Civil War. 7 rolls.

M1786 Record of Invalid Pension Payments to Veterans of the Revolutionary War and the Regular Army and Navy, March 1801-September 1815. 1 roll.

*M2035 Selected Military Service and Pension Records Relating to Ulysses S. Grant. 1 roll.

T288 General Index to Pension Files, 1861-1934. 544 rolls. 16mm.

T289 Organization Index to Pension Files of Veterans Who Served Between 1861 and 1900. 765 rolls. 16mm.

T316 Old War Index to Pension Files, 1815-1926. 7 rolls. 16mm.

T317 Index to Mexican War Pension Files, 1887-1926. 14 rolls. 16mm.

T318 Index to Indian War Pension Files, 1892-1926. 12 rolls. 16mm.

T1196 Selected Pension Application Files Relating to the Mormon Battalion, Mexican War, 1846-1848. 21 rolls.

RG 16 Records of the Office of the Secretary of Agriculture

M122 Letters Sent by the Assistant Secretary of Agriculture, 1889-1894. 16 rolls.

M440 Letters Sent by the Secretary of Agriculture, 1893-1929. 563 rolls. DP.

RG 17 Records of the Bureau of Animal Industry

M1375 Records of the U.S. Morgan Horse Farm, 1907-1951. 12 rolls. DP.

RG 18 Records of the Army Air Forces

M1065 Mission and Combat Reports of the Fifth Fighter Command, 1942-1945. 9 rolls. DP.

M1380 Missing Air Crew Reports of the U.S. Army Air Forces, 1942-1947. 5,990 cards (microfiche).

RG 19 Records of the Bureau of Ships

M1157 Index to the General Photographs of the Bureau of Ships, 1914-1946. 9 rolls. 16mm.

M1176 Captured Japanese Ships' Plans and Design Data. 10 rolls.

M1222 General Photographs of the Bureau of Ships, 1914. 1,100 rolls.

RG 21 Records of District Courts of the United States

M1241 Indexes to the Naturalization Records of the U.S. District Court for the District and Territory of Alaska, 1900-1929. 1 roll. DP.

M1539 Naturalization Records of the U.S. District Courts for the State of Alaska, 1900-1924. 5 rolls.

*M1966 Bankruptcy Case Files of the U.S. District Court for the District and Territory of Alaska, Second Division (Nome), 1901-53. 6 rolls. DP.

*M1967 Admiralty Case Files of the U.S. District Court for the District and Territory of Alaska, Second Division (Nome), 1899-1950. 13 rolls. DP.

*M1788 Indexes to Naturalization Records of the U.S. District Court for the District, Territory, and State of Alaska (Third Division), 1903-1991. 22 rolls. DP.

M1615 Naturalization Records of the U.S. District Court for the Territory of Arizona, 1864-1915. 5 rolls.

M1616 Naturalization Records of the U.S. District Court for the District of Arizona, 1912-1955. 7 rolls.

M1249 Admiralty Case Files of the U.S. District Court for the Northern District of California, 1850-1900. 401 rolls. DP.

*M1744 Index to Naturalization in the U.S. District Court for the Northern District of California, 1852-ca. 1989. 165 rolls. DP.

M1741 Index Cards to Bankruptcy, Civil, and Criminal Case Files of the U.S. District Court for the Southern District of California, Southern Division (San Diego), 1953 to 1954. 1 roll.

M1735 Index Cards to Civil Case Files of the U.S. District Court for the Southern District of California, Southern Division (San Diego), January 1955 to June 1962. 1 roll.

M1737 Index Cards to Civil and Criminal Case Files of the U.S. District Court for the Southern District of California, Southern Division (San Diego), July 1962 to August 1966. 3 rolls.

M1736 Index Cards to Criminal Case Files of the U.S. District Court for the Southern District of California, Southern Division (San Diego), January 1955 to June 1962. 2 rolls.

T1220 Selected Indexes to Naturalization Records of the U.S. Circuit and District Courts, Northern District of California, 1852-1928. 3 rolls.

T717 Records of the U.S. District Court for the Northern District of California and Predecessor Courts, 1851-1950. 125 rolls.

M1607 Index to Naturalization Records of the U.S. District Court for the Southern District of California, Central Division, Los Angeles, 1887-1937. 2 rolls.

M1525 Naturalization Index Cards of the United States District Court for the Southern District of California, Central Division, Los Angeles, 1915-1976. 14 rolls. DP.

M1606 Index Cards to Overseas Military Petitions of the U.S. District Court for the Southern District of California, Central Division (Los Angeles), 1943-1945, 1954, 1955-1956. 2 rolls.

M1524 Naturalization Records of the United States District Court for the Southern District of California, Central Division, Los Angeles, 1887-1940. 244 rolls. DP.

T1216 Index by County to Private Land Grant Cases, U.S. District Court, Northern and Southern Districts of California. 1 roll.

T1214 Index to Private Land Grant Cases, U.S. District Court, Northern District of California, 1853-1903. 1 roll.

T1207 Private Land Grant Case Files in the Circuit Court of the Northern District of California, 1852-1910. 28 rolls.

T1215 Index to Private Land Grant Cases, U.S. District Court, Southern District of California. 1 roll.

M1192 Naturalization Records Created by the U.S. District Courts in Colorado, 1877-1952. 79 rolls.

*M1827 Index to Naturalization Records of the U.S. Supreme Court for the District of Columbia, 1802-1909. 1 roll

*M1753 Records of the U.S. District and Circuit Courts for the District of Connecticut: Documents Relating to the Various Cases Involving the Spanish Schooner *Amistad*. 1 roll.

*M2012 Appellate Case File No. 2161, *United States* v. *The Amistad*, 40 U.S. 518 (15 Peters 518), Decided March 9, 1841, and Related Lower Court and Department of Justice Records. 1 roll. DP.

M1649 Index to Naturalization Petitions for the U.S. Circuit Court, 1795-1911, and District Court, 1795-1928, for the District of Delaware. 1 roll.

M1644 Naturalization Petitions of the U.S. District and Circuit Courts for the District of Delaware, 1795-1930. 19 rolls.

M433 Records of the U.S. District Court for the District of Columbia Relating to Slaves, 1851-1863. 3 rolls.

M434 Habeas Corpus Case Records, 1820-1863, of the U.S. Circuit Court for the District of Columbia. 2 rolls.

M1021 Minutes of the U.S. Circuit Court for the District of Columbia, 1801-1863. 6 rolls. DP.

*M2011 Indentures of Apprenticeship Recorded in the Orphans Court, Washington County, District of Columbia, 1801-1811. 1 roll. DP.

M1360 Admiralty Final Record Books of the U.S. District Court for the Southern District of Florida (Key West), 1828-1911. 19 rolls. DP.

M1172 Index Books, 1789-1928, and Minutes and Bench Dockets, 1789-1870, for the U.S. District Court, Southern District of Georgia. 3 rolls. DP.

M1184 Minutes of the U.S. Circuit Court for the District of Georgia, 1790-1842, and Index to Plaintiffs and Defendants in the Circuit Courts, 1790-1860. 3 rolls. DP.

*M2074 Index to Naturalization in the U.S. District Court for the District of Hawaii, 1900-1976. 23 rolls.

M1530 Lincoln at the Bar: Selected Case Files from the United States District and Circuit Courts, Southern District of Illinois, 1855-1861. 7 rolls. DP.

M1082 Records of the U.S. District Court for the Eastern District of Louisiana, 1806-1814. 18 rolls. DP.

M1115 Land Claim Case Files of the U.S. District Court for the Eastern District of Louisiana, 1844-1880. 16 rolls.

M931 Minutes of the U.S. Circuit Court for the District of Maryland, 1790-1911. 7 rolls. DP.

M1010 Criminal Case Files of the U.S. Circuit Court for the District of Maryland, 1795-1860. 4 rolls. DP.

M1031 Act of 1800 Bankruptcy Case Files of the U.S. District Court for the District of Maryland, 1800-1803. 2 rolls. DP.

M1168 Indexes to Naturalization Petitions to the U.S. Circuit and District Courts for Maryland, 1797-1951. 25 rolls. DP.

M1640 Naturalization Petitions of the U.S. District Court for the District of Maryland, 1906-1930. 43 rolls.

M1545 Index to Naturalization Petitions and Records of the U.S. District Court, 1906-1966, and the U.S. Circuit Court, 1906-1911, for the District of Massachusetts. 115 rolls.

M1368 Petitions and Records of Naturalization of the U.S. District Court and Circuit Courts of the District of Massachusetts, 1906-1929. 330 rolls.

M1111 Records of the Territorial Court of Michigan, 1815-1836. 9 rolls. DP.

M1236 Indexes to Naturalization Records of the Montana Territorial and Federal Courts, 1868-1929. 1 roll. DP.

M1538 Naturalization Records of the U.S. District Courts for the State of Montana, 1891-1929. 3 rolls.

T928 Records of the U.S. District Court for the District of New Jersey and Predecessor Courts, 1790-1950. 186 rolls. 16mm.

M854 Minutes, Trial Notes, and Rolls of Attorneys of the U.S. Circuit Court for the Southern District of New York, 1790-1841. 3 rolls. DP.

M855 Appellate Case Files of the U.S. Circuit Court for the Southern District of New York, 1793-1845. 8 rolls. DP.

M882 Judgment Records of the U.S. Circuit Court for the Southern District of New York, 1794-1840. 8 rolls. DP.

M883 Law Case Files of the U.S. Circuit Court for the Southern District of New York, 1790-1846. 43 rolls. DP.

M884 Equity Case Files of the U.S. Circuit Court for the Southern District of New York, 1791-1846. 23 rolls. DP.

M885 Criminal Case Files of the U.S. Circuit Court for the Southern District of New York, 1790-1853. 6 rolls. DP.

M886 Minutes and Rolls of Attorneys of the U.S. District Court for the Southern District of New York, 1789-1841. 9 rolls. DP.

M919 Admiralty Case Files of the U.S. District Court for the Southern District of New York, 1790-1842. 62 rolls. DP.

M928 Prize and Related Records for the War of 1812 of the U.S. District Court for the Southern District of New York, 1812-1816. 9 rolls. DP.

M933 Act of 1800 Bankruptcy Records of the U.S. District Court for the Southern District of New York, 1800-1809. 11 rolls. DP.

M934 Judgment Records of the U.S. District Court for the Southern District of New York, 1795-1840. 16 rolls. DP.

M937 Law Case Files of the U.S. District Court for the Southern District of New York, 1795-1844. 15 rolls. DP.

M938 Records of the Clerk of the Court, 1746-1932, and of the U.S. Commissioners, 1837-1860, of the U.S. District Court for the Southern District of New York. 1 roll. DP.

M948 Case Papers of the Court of Admiralty of the State of New York, 1784-1788. 1 roll. DP.

M965 Case Files in Suits Involving Consuls and Vice Consuls and the Repeal of Patents of the U.S. District Court for the Southern District of New York, 1806-1860. 2 rolls. DP.

M1164 Index to Naturalization Petitions of the United States District Court for the Eastern District of New York, 1865-1957. 142 rolls. DP.

M1674 Index (Soundex) to Naturalization Petitions Filed in Federal, State, and Local Courts in New York, New York, Including New York, Kings, Queens, and Richmond Counties, 1792-1906. 294 rolls.

M1675 Alphabetical Index to Declarations of Intention of the U.S. District Court for the Southern District of New York, 1917-50. 111 rolls.

M1676 Alphabetical Index to Petitions for Naturalization of the U.S. District Court for the Southern District of New York, 1824-1941. 102 rolls.

M1677 Alphabetical Index to Petitions for Naturalization of the U.S. District Court for the Western District of New York, 1906-1966. 20 rolls.

T842 Records of the Vice Admiralty Court of the Province of New York. 1 roll.

M436 Confederate Papers of the U.S. District Court for the Eastern District of North Carolina, 1861-1865. 1 roll.

M1425 Minute Books, U.S. District Court, Eastern District of North Carolina, Albemarle Division at Edenton, 1807-70, and at Elizabeth City, 1870-1914. 1 roll. DP.

M1426 Minute Books, U.S. District Court, Eastern District of North Carolina, Cape Fear Division at Wilmington, 1795-96 and 1858-1911. 2 rolls. DP.

M1427 Minute Books, U.S. District Court, Eastern District of North Carolina, Pamlico Division at New Bern, 1858-1914. 2 rolls.

M1428 Minute Books, U.S. Circuit Court, Eastern District of North Carolina, Raleigh, 1791-1866. 2 rolls. DP.

C0017 Records of the U.S. Circuit Court, North Carolina Division at Raleigh, 1790-1897. 70 rolls.

M1429 Admiralty Final Record Books, U.S. District Court, Eastern District of North Carolina, 1858-1907. 1 roll. DP.

M1430 Confederate Court Records, Eastern District of North Carolina, 1861-1864. 1 roll. DP.

M1242 Index to the Naturalization Records of the U.S. District Court for Oregon, 1859-1956. 3 rolls. DP.

M1540 Naturalization Records of the U.S. District Court for the District of Oregon, 1859-1941. 62 rolls.

M932 Minutes of the U.S. Circuit Court for the Eastern District of Pennsylvania, 1790-1844. 2 rolls. DP.

M966 War of 1812 Prize Case Files of the U.S. District Court for the Eastern District of Pennsylvania, 1812-1815. 2 rolls. DP.

M969 Law and Appellate Records of the U.S. Circuit Court for the Eastern District of Pennsylvania, 1790-1847. 26 rolls. DP.

M985 Equity Records of the U.S. Circuit Court for the Eastern District of Pennsylvania, 1790-1847. 23 rolls. DP.

M986 Criminal Case Files of the U.S. Circuit Court for the Eastern District of Pennsylvania, 1791-1840. 7 rolls. DP.

M987 Records of the U.S. Circuit Court for the Western District of Pennsylvania, 1801-1802, and Minutes and Habeas Corpus and Criminal Case Files of the U.S. District Court for the Eastern District of Pennsylvania, 1789-1843. 3 rolls. DP.

M988 Admiralty Case Files of the U.S. District Court for the Eastern District of Pennsylvania, 1789-1840. 18 rolls. DP.

M992 Information Case Files, 1789-1843, and Related Records, 1792-1918, of the U.S. District Court for the Eastern District of Pennsylvania. 10 rolls. DP.

M993 Act of 1800 Bankruptcy Records of the U.S. District Court for the Eastern District of Pennsylvania, 1800-1806. 24 rolls. DP.

M1057 Law (Civil Action) Records for the U.S. District Court for the Eastern District of Pennsylvania, 1789-1844. 40 rolls. DP.

M1208 Indexes to Registers and Registers of Declarations of Intention and Petitions for Naturalization of the U.S. District and Circuit Courts for the Western District of Pennsylvania, 1820-1906. 3 rolls. DP.

M1248 Indexes to Naturalization Petitions to the U.S. Circuit and District Courts for the Eastern District of Pennsylvania, 1795-1951. 60 rolls. DP.

M1626 Naturalization Petitions of the U.S. Circuit and District Courts for the Middle District of Pennsylvania, 1906-1930. 123 rolls.

M1522 Naturalization Petitions for the Eastern District of Pennsylvania. 369 rolls.

M1537 Naturalization Petitions of the U.S. District Court, 1820-1930, and Circuit Court, 1820-1911, for the Western District of Pennsylvania. 437 rolls.

M1639 Landing Reports of Aliens from the U.S. District Court for the Eastern District of Pennsylvania, 1798-1828. 1 roll.

T819 Records of the U.S. District Court for the Eastern District of Pennsylvania Containing Statements of Fact in Forfeiture Cases, 1792-1918. 1 roll.

M1180 Pre-Federal Admiralty Court Records, Province and State of South Carolina, 1716-1789. 3 rolls. DP.

M1181 Minutes, Circuit and District Courts, District of South Carolina, 1789-1849, and Index to Judgments, Circuit and District Courts, 1792-1874. 2 rolls. DP.

M1182 Admiralty Final Record Books and Minutes for the U.S. District Court, District of South Carolina, 1790-1857. 4 rolls. DP.

M1183 Record of Admissions to Citizenship, District of South Carolina, 1790-1906. 1 roll. DP.

M1212 Final Record Books of the U.S. Circuit Court for West Tennessee, 1808-1839, and of the U.S. Circuit Court for the Middle District of Tennessee, 1839-1865. 10 rolls. DP.

M1213 Minute Books of the U.S. District Court for West Tennessee, 1797-1839, and of the U.S. District Court for the Middle District of Tennessee, 1839-1865. 1 roll. DP.

M1214 Minute Books of the U.S. Circuit Court for West Tennessee, 1808-1839, and of the U.S. Circuit Court for the Middle District of Tennessee, 1839-1864. 4 rolls. DP.

M1215 Final Record Books of the U.S. District Court for West Tennessee, 1803-1839, and of the U.S. District Court for the Middle District of Tennessee, 1839-1850; Land Claims Records for West Tennessee, 1807-1820. 1 roll. DP.

M1611 Index to Naturalization Records of the U.S. District Court for the Eastern District of Tennessee at Chattanooga, 1888-1955. 1 roll.

M1610 Equity Case Files from the Western District Court of Texas at El Paso Relating to the Chinese Exclusion Acts, 1892-1915. 34 rolls. DP.

M1401 Territorial Case Files of the U.S. District Courts of Utah, 1870-1896. 38 rolls. DP.

M1300 Admiralty Case Files of the U.S. District Court for the Eastern District of Virginia, 1801-1861. 18 rolls. DP.

M435 Case Papers of the U.S. District Court for the Eastern District of Virginia, 1863-1865, Relating to the Confiscation of Property. 1 roll.

M1645 Naturalization Petitions of the U.S. District Court for the Western District of Virginia (Abingdon), 1914-1929. 2 rolls.

M1646 Naturalization Petitions of the U.S. District Court for the Western District of Virginia (Charlottesville), 1910-1929. 1 roll.

M1647 Naturalization Petitions of the U.S. District Court for the Eastern District of Virginia (Richmond), 1906-1929. 10 rolls.

M1648 Naturalization Petitions of the U.S. District Court for the Eastern District of Virginia (Alexandria), 1909-1920. 5 rolls.

M1232 Indexes to Naturalization Records of the U.S. District Court for Western Washington, Northern Division (Seattle), 1890-1952. 6 rolls. DP.

M1233 Indexes to Naturalization Records of the King County Territorial and Superior Courts, 1864-1889 and 1906-1928. 1 roll. DP.

M1234 Indexes to Naturalization Records of the Thurston County Territorial and Superior Courts, 1850-1974. 2 rolls. DP.

M1235 Indexes to Naturalization Records of the Snohomish County Territorial and Superior Courts, 1876-1974. 3 rolls. DP.

M1237 Indexes to Naturalization Records of the U.S. District Court, Western District of Washington, Southern Division (Tacoma), 1890-1953. 2 rolls. DP.

M1238 Indexes to Naturalization Records of the Pierce County Territorial and Superior Courts, 1853-1923. 2 rolls. DP.

M1541 Naturalization Records of the U.S. District Court for the Eastern District of Washington, 1890-1972. 40 rolls.

M1542 Naturalization Records of the U.S. District Court for the Western District of Washington, 1890-1957. 153 rolls.

M1543 Naturalization Records of the Superior Courts for King, Pierce, Thurston, and Snohomish Counties, Washington, 1850-1974. 103 rolls.

M1618 U.S. District Court of Washington Rolls of Attorneys, 1890-1959. 1 roll.

M1643 Naturalization Petitions of the U.S. District Court for the Northern District of West Virginia, Wheeling, 1856-1867. 2 rolls.

*M1547 Naturalization Records of U.S. District Courts in the Southeast, 1790-1958. 106 rolls.

T265 Trial of Aaron Burr and Harman Blennerhassett, 1808. 1 roll.

T410 Records of the U.S. Civil Commission at Memphis, 1863-1864. 9 rolls.

RG 22 Records of the U.S. Fish and Wildlife Service

M720 "Alaska File" of the Office of the Secretary of the Treasury, 1868-1903. 25 rolls. DP.

RG 23 Records of the Coast and Geodetic Survey

M642 Correspondence of A. D. Bache, Superintendent of the Coast and Geodetic Survey, 1843-1865. 281 rolls. DP.

*T274 Nautical Charts: Aid Proofs & Standards. 15 rolls.

T296 Selected Tide-Staff Readings and Hydrographic Survey Soundings of Rear Adm. Robert E. Peary, USN, 1908-1909 North Polar Expedition. 1 roll.

RG 24 Records of the Bureau of Naval Personnel

M330 Abstracts of Service Records of Naval Officers ("Records of Officers"), 1798-1893. 19 rolls.

M1030 Logbooks and Journals of the U.S.S. Constitution, 1798-1934. 16 rolls. DP.

M1328 Abstracts of Service Records of Naval Officers ("Records of Officers"), 1829-1924. 18 rolls. DP.

*T508 Log Books of the USS Kearsarge, 1862-1864. 1 roll.

T576 Logbooks of PT 109 (President Kennedy). 1 roll.

*T1087 Log Books of the USS Susquehanna, January 1, 1853-March 15, 1855. 3 rolls.

*T1088 Log Books of the USS Mississippi, May 11, 1852-April 26, 1855. 4 rolls.

*T1089 Log Books of the USS Lexington, May 25, 1853-February 26, 1855. 3 rolls.

*T1090 Log Books of the USS Saratoga, June 21, 1852-October 10, 1853. 1 roll.

*T1091 Log Books of the USS Macedonian, February 24, 1853-May 16, 1855. 3 rolls.

*T1092 Log Books of the USS Vandalia, February 14, 1853-March 28, 1855. 2 rolls.

*T1093 Log Books of the USS Southampton, November 4, 1852-April 3, 1855. 2 rolls.

*T1094 Log Books of the USS Supply, April 25, 1852-February 7, 1855. 3 rolls.

*T1095 Log Books of the USS Plymouth, July 7, 1852-January 18, 1855. 4 rolls.

*T1096 Log Books of the USS Powhatan, September 2, 1852-September 18, 1855. 3 rolls.

T1098 Index to Rendezvous Reports, Before and After the Civil War, 1846-1861, 1865-1884. 32 rolls. 16mm.

T1099 Index to Rendezvous Reports, Civil War, 1861-1865. 31 rolls. 16mm.

T1100 Index to Rendezvous Reports, Naval Auxiliary Service, 1917-1918. 1 roll. 16mm.

T1101 Index to Rendezvous Reports, Armed Guard Personnel, 1917-1920. 3 rolls. 16mm.

T1102 Index to Officers' Jackets, 1913-1925 ("Officers Directory"). 2 rolls.

RG 26 Records of the U.S. Coast Guard

M63 Lighthouse Letters, 1792-1809. 3 rolls.

M94 Lighthouse Deeds and Contracts, 1790-1853. 2 rolls.

M641 Alaska File of the Revenue Cutter Service, 1867-1914. 20 rolls. DP.

M1373 Registers of Lighthouse Keepers, 1845-1912. 6 rolls.

T720 U.S. Coast Guard Reports of Assistance to Individuals and Vessels, 1916-1940. 247 rolls.

T919 Index by District to U.S. Coast Guard Reports of Assistance, 1917-1938. 19 rolls. 16mm.

T920 Index by Station to U.S. Coast Guard Reports of Assistance, 1924-1938. 9 rolls. 16mm.

T921 Index by Floating Unit to U.S. Coast Guard Reports of Assistance, 1917-1935. 5 rolls. 16mm.

T925 U.S. Coast Guard Casualty and Wreck Reports, 1913-1939. 21 rolls. 16mm.

T926 Index to U.S. Coast Guard Casualty and Wreck Reports, 1913-1939. 7 rolls. 16mm.

RG 27 Records of the Weather Bureau

M1160 The Maury Abstract Logs, 1796-1861. 88 rolls. DP.

M1379 Selected Records From Records of the Weather Bureau Relating to New Orleans, 1841-1907. 8 rolls. DP.

T298 Journal of the Lockwood Expedition on the North Coast of Greenland, Apr. 31-June 1, 1882. 1 roll.

T907 Climatological Records of the Weather Bureau, 1819-1892. 564 rolls.

RG 28 Records of the Post Office Department

M601 Letters Sent by the Postmaster General, 1789-1836. 50 rolls. DP.

M1131 Record of Appointment of Postmasters, Oct. 1789-1832. 4 rolls.

M841 Record of Appointment of Postmasters, 1832-Sept. 30, 1971. 145 rolls. DP.

M1126 Post Office Department Reports of Site Locations, 1837-1950. 683 rolls. DP.

*M2075 Record of Appointment of Substitute Clerks in First- and Second-Class Post Offices, 1899-1905. 1 roll.

*M2076 Index and Registers of Substitute Mail Carriers in First- and Second-Class Post Offices, 1885-1903. 1 roll.

*M2077 Indexes to Rosters of Railway Postal Clerks, ca. 1883-ca. 1902. 1 roll.

T268 Journal of Hugh Finlay, Surveyor of Post Roads and Post Offices, 1773-1774; and Accounts of the General Post Office in Philadelphia and of the Various Deputy Postmasters—"The Ledger of Benjamin Franklin"—Jan. 1775-Jan. 1780. 1 roll.

RG 29 Records of the Bureau of the Census

Federal Population Decennial Census Schedules

M637 First Census of the United States, 1790. 12 rolls.

M32 Second Census of the United States, 1800. 52 rolls.

M252 Third Census of the United States, 1810. 71 rolls.

M33 Fourth Census of the United States, 1820. 142 rolls.

M19 Fifth Census of the United States, 1830. 201 rolls.

M704 Sixth Census of the United States, 1840. 580 rolls.

M432 Seventh Census of the United States, 1850. 1,009 rolls.

M653 Eighth Census of the United States, 1860. 1,438 rolls.

M593 Ninth Census of the United States, 1870. 1,748 rolls.

T132 Minnesota Census Schedules for 1870. 13 rolls.

Tenth Population Census

T9 Tenth Census of the United States, 1880. 1,454 rolls.

T734 Index (Soundex) to the 1880 Population Schedules for Alabama. 74 rolls. 16mm.

T735 Index (Soundex) to the 1880 Population Schedules for Arizona. 2 rolls. 16mm.

T736 Index (Soundex) to the 1880 Population Schedules for Arkansas. 48 rolls. 16mm.

T737 Index (Soundex) to the 1880 Population Schedules for California. 34 rolls. 16mm.

T738 Index (Soundex) to the 1880 Population Schedules for Colorado. 7 rolls. 16mm.

T739 Index (Soundex) to the 1880 Population Schedules for Connecticut. 25 rolls. 16mm.

T740 Index (Soundex) to the 1880 Population Schedules for Dakota Territory. 6 rolls. 16mm.

T741 Index (Soundex) to the 1880 Population Schedules for Delaware. 9 rolls. 16mm.

T742 Index (Soundex) to the 1880 Population Schedules for the District of Columbia. 9 rolls. 16mm.

T743 Index (Soundex) to the 1880 Population Schedules for Florida. 16 rolls. 16mm.

T744 Index (Soundex) to the 1880 Population Schedules for Georgia. 86 rolls. 16mm.

T745 Index (Soundex) to the 1880 Population Schedules for Idaho Territory. 2 rolls. 16mm.

T746 Index (Soundex) to the 1880 Population Schedules for Illinois. 143 rolls. 16mm.

T747 Index (Soundex) to the 1880 Population Schedules for Indiana. 98 rolls. 16mm.

T748 Index (Soundex) to the 1880 Population Schedules for Iowa. 78 rolls. 16mm.

T749 Index (Soundex) to the 1880 Population Schedules for Kansas. 51 rolls. 16mm.

T750 Index (Soundex) to the 1880 Population Schedules for Kentucky. 83 rolls. 16mm.

T751 Index (Soundex) to the 1880 Population Schedules for Louisiana. 55 rolls. 16mm.

T752 Index (Soundex) to the 1880 Population Schedules for Maine. 29 rolls. 16mm.

T753 Index (Soundex) to the 1880 Population Schedules for Maryland. 47 rolls. 16mm.

T754 Index (Soundex) to the 1880 Population Schedules for Massachusetts. 70 rolls. 16mm.

T755 Index (Soundex) to the 1880 Population Schedules for Michigan. 73 rolls. 16mm.

T756 Index (Soundex) to the 1880 Population Schedules for Minnesota. 37 rolls. 16mm.

T757 Index (Soundex) to the 1880 Population Schedules for Mississippi. 69 rolls. 16mm.

T758 Index (Soundex) to the 1880 Population Schedules for Missouri. 114 rolls. 16mm.

T759 Index (Soundex) to the 1880 Population Schedules for Montana Territory. 2 rolls. 16mm.

T760 Index (Soundex) to the 1880 Population Schedules for Nebraska. 22 rolls. 16mm.

T761 Index (Soundex) to the 1880 Population Schedules for Nevada. 3 rolls. 16mm.

T762 Index (Soundex) to the 1880 Population Schedules for New Hampshire. 13 rolls. 16mm.

T763 Index (Soundex) to the 1880 Population Schedules for New Jersey. 49 rolls. 16mm.

T764 Index (Soundex) to the 1880 Population Schedules for New Mexico Territory. 6 rolls. 16mm.

T765 Index (Soundex) to the 1880 Population Schedules for New York. 187 rolls. 16mm.

T766 Index (Soundex) to the 1880 Population Schedules for North Carolina. 79 rolls. 16mm.

T767 Index (Soundex) to the 1880 Population Schedules for Ohio. 143 rolls. 16mm.

T768 Index (Soundex) to the 1880 Population Schedules for Oregon. 8 rolls. 16mm.

T769 Index (Soundex) to the 1880 Population Schedules for Pennsylvania. 168 rolls. 16mm.

T770 Index (Soundex) to the 1880 Population Schedules for Rhode Island. 11 rolls. 16mm.

T771 Index (Soundex) to the 1880 Population Schedules for South Carolina. 56 rolls. 16mm.

T772 Index (Soundex) to the 1880 Population Schedules for Tennessee. 86 rolls. 16mm.

T773 Index (Soundex) to the 1880 Population Schedules for Texas. 77 rolls. 16mm.

T774 Index (Soundex) to the 1880 Population Schedules for Utah Territory. 7 rolls. 16mm.

T775 Index (Soundex) to the 1880 Population Schedules for Vermont. 15 rolls. 16mm.

T776 Index (Soundex) to the 1880 Population Schedules for Virginia. 82 rolls. 16mm.

T777 Index (Soundex) to the 1880 Population Schedules for Washington Territory. 4 rolls. 16mm.

T778 Index (Soundex) to the 1880 Population Schedules for West Virginia. 32 rolls. 16mm.

T779 Index (Soundex) to the 1880 Population Schedules for Wisconsin. 51 rolls. 16mm.

T780 Index (Soundex) to the 1880 Population Schedules for Wyoming. 1 roll. 16mm.

Eleventh Population Census

M407 Eleventh Census of the United States, 1890. 3 rolls.

M496 Index to the Eleventh Census of the United States, 1890. 2 rolls. 16mm.

Twelfth Population Census

T623 Twelfth Census of the United States, 1900. 1,854 rolls.

T1030 Index (Soundex) to the 1900 Federal Population Census Schedules for Alabama. 177 rolls. 16mm.

T1031 Index (Soundex) to the 1900 Federal Population Census Schedules for Alaska. 15 rolls. 16mm.

T1032 Index (Soundex) to the 1900 Federal Population Census Schedules for Arizona. 22 rolls. 16mm.

T1033 Index (Soundex) to the 1900 Federal Population Census Schedules for Arkansas. 135 rolls. 16mm.

T1034 Index (Soundex) to the 1900 Federal Population Census Schedules for California. 198 rolls. 16mm.

T1035 Index (Soundex) to the 1900 Federal Population Census Schedules for Colorado. 69 rolls. 16mm.

T1036 Index (Soundex) to the 1900 Federal Population Census Schedules for Connecticut. 107 rolls. 16mm.

T1037 Index (Soundex) to the 1900 Federal Population Census Schedules for Delaware. 21 rolls. 16mm.

T1038 Index (Soundex) to the 1900 Federal Population Census Schedules for the District of Columbia. 42 rolls. 16mm.

T1039 Index (Soundex) to the 1900 Federal Population Census Schedules for Florida. 62 rolls. 16mm.

T1040 Index (Soundex) to the 1900 Federal Population Census Schedules for Georgia. 214 rolls. 16mm.

T1041 Index (Soundex) to the 1900 Federal Population Census Schedules for Hawaii. 30 rolls. 16mm.

T1042 Index (Soundex) to the 1900 Federal Population Census Schedules for Idaho. 19 rolls. 16mm.

T1043 Index (Soundex) to the 1900 Federal Population Census Schedules for Illinois. 475 rolls. 16mm.

T1044 Index (Soundex) to the 1900 Federal Population Census Schedules for Indiana. 253 rolls. 16mm.

T1045 Index (Soundex) to the 1900 Federal Population Census Schedules for Iowa. 212 rolls. 16mm.

T1046 Index (Soundex) to the 1900 Federal Population Census Schedules for Kansas. 148 rolls. 16mm.

T1047 Index (Soundex) to the 1900 Federal Population Census Schedules for Kentucky. 200 rolls. 16mm.

T1048 Index (Soundex) to the 1900 Federal Population Census Schedules for Louisiana. 146 rolls. 16mm.

T1049 Index (Soundex) to the 1900 Federal Population Census Schedules for Maine. 80 rolls. 16mm.

T1050 Index (Soundex) to the 1900 Federal Population Census Schedules for Maryland. 127 rolls. 16mm.

T1051 Index (Soundex) to the 1900 Federal Population Census Schedules for Massachusetts. 318 rolls. 16mm.

T1052 Index (Soundex) to the 1900 Federal Population Census Schedules for Michigan. 257 rolls. 16mm.

T1053 Index (Soundex) to the 1900 Federal Population Census Schedules for Minnesota. 180 rolls. 16mm.

T1054 Index (Soundex) to the 1900 Federal Population Census Schedules for Mississippi. 156 rolls. 16mm.

T1055 Index (Soundex) to the 1900 Federal Population Census Schedules for Missouri. 300 rolls. 16mm.

T1056 Index (Soundex) to the 1900 Federal Population Census Schedules for Montana. 40 rolls. 16mm.

T1057 Index (Soundex) to the 1900 Federal Population Census Schedules for Nebraska. 107 rolls. 16mm.

T1058 Index (Soundex) to the 1900 Federal Population Census Schedules for Nevada. 7 rolls. 16mm.

T1059 Index (Soundex) to the 1900 Federal Population Census Schedules for New Hampshire. 52 rolls. 16mm.

T1060 Index (Soundex) to the 1900 Federal Population Census Schedules for New Jersey. 204 rolls. 16mm.

T1061 Index (Soundex) to the 1900 Federal Population Census Schedules for New Mexico. 23 rolls. 16mm.

T1062 Index (Soundex) to the 1900 Federal Population Census Schedules for New York. 768 rolls. 16mm.

T1063 Index (Soundex) to the 1900 Federal Population Census Schedules for North Carolina. 168 rolls. 16mm.

T1064 Index (Soundex) to the 1900 Federal Population Census Schedules for North Dakota. 36 rolls. 16mm.

T1065 Index (Soundex) to the 1900 Federal Population Census Schedules for Ohio. 397 rolls. 16mm.

T1066 Index (Soundex) to the 1900 Federal Population Census Schedules for Oklahoma. 42 rolls. 16mm.

T1067 Index (Soundex) to the 1900 Federal Population Census Schedules for Oregon. 54 rolls. 16mm.

T1068 Index (Soundex) to the 1900 Federal Population Census Schedules for Pennsylvania. 611 rolls. 16mm.

T1069 Index (Soundex) to the 1900 Federal Population Census Schedules for Rhode Island. 49 rolls. 16mm.

T1070 Index (Soundex) to the 1900 Federal Population Census Schedules for South Carolina. 124 rolls. 16mm.

T1071 Index (Soundex) to the 1900 Federal Population Census Schedules for South Dakota. 44 rolls. 16mm.

T1072 Index (Soundex) to the 1900 Federal Population Census Schedules for Tennessee. 188 rolls. 16mm.

T1073 Index (Soundex) to the 1900 Federal Population Census Schedules for Texas. 286 rolls. 16mm.

T1074 Index (Soundex) to the 1900 Federal Population Census Schedules for Utah. 29 rolls. 16mm.

T1075 Index (Soundex) to the 1900 Federal Population Census Schedules for Vermont. 41 rolls. 16mm.

T1076 Index (Soundex) to the 1900 Federal Population Census Schedules for Virginia. 174 rolls. 16mm.

T1077 Index (Soundex) to the 1900 Federal Population Census Schedules for Washington. 69 rolls. 16mm.

T1078 Index (Soundex) to the 1900 Federal Population Census Schedules for West Virginia. 93 rolls. 16mm.

T1079 Index (Soundex) to the 1900 Federal Population Census Schedules for Wisconsin. 189 rolls. 16mm.

T1080 Index (Soundex) to the 1900 Federal Population Census Schedules for Wyoming. 15 rolls. 16mm.

T1081 Index (Soundex) to the 1900 Federal Population Census Schedules for Military and Naval. 32 rolls. 16mm.

T1082 Index (Soundex) to the 1900 Federal Population Census Schedules for Indian Territory. 42 rolls. 16mm.

T1083 Index (Soundex) to the 1900 Federal Population Census Schedules for Institutions. 8 rolls. 16mm.

Thirteenth Population Census

T624 Thirteenth Census of the United States, 1910. 1,784 rolls.

T1259 Index (Soundex) to the 1910 Federal Population Census Schedules for Alabama. 140 rolls. 16mm.

T1260 Index (Miracode) to the 1910 Federal Population Census Schedules for Arkansas. 139 rolls. 16mm.

T1261 Index (Miracode) to the 1910 Federal Population Census Schedules for California. 272 rolls. 16mm.

T1262 Index (Miracode) to the 1910 Federal Population Census Schedules for Florida. 84 rolls. 16mm.

T1263 Index (Soundex) to the 1910 Federal Population Census Schedules for Georgia. 174 rolls. 16mm.

T1264 Index (Miracode) to the 1910 Federal Population Census Schedules for Illinois. 491 rolls. 16mm.

T1265 Index (Miracode) to the 1910 Federal Population Census Schedules for Kansas. 145 rolls. 16mm.

T1266 Index (Miracode) to the 1910 Federal Population Census Schedules for Kentucky. 194 rolls. 16mm.

T1267 Index (Miracode and Soundex) to the 1910 Federal Population Census Schedules for Louisiana. 132 rolls. 16mm.

T1268 Index (Miracode) to the 1910 Federal Population Census Schedules for Michigan. 253 rolls. 16mm.

T1269 Index (Soundex) to the 1910 Federal Population Census Schedules for Mississippi. 118 rolls. 16mm.

T1270 Index (Miracode) to the 1910 Federal Population Census Schedules for Missouri. 285 rolls. 16mm.

T1271 Index (Miracode) to the 1910 Federal Population Census Schedules for North Carolina. 178 rolls. 16mm.

T1272 Index (Miracode) to the 1910 Federal Population Census Schedules for Ohio. 418 rolls. 16mm.

T1273 Index (Miracode) to the 1910 Federal Population Census Schedules for Oklahoma. 143 rolls. 16mm.

T1274 Index (Miracode) to the 1910 Federal Population Census Schedules for Pennsylvania. 688 rolls. 16mm.

T1275 Index (Soundex) to the 1910 Federal Population Census Schedules for South Carolina. 93 rolls. 16mm.

T1276 Index (Soundex) to the 1910 Federal Population Census Schedules for Tennessee. 142 rolls. 16mm.

T1277 Index (Soundex) to the 1910 Federal Population Census Schedules for Texas. 262 rolls. 16mm.

T1278 Index (Miracode) to the 1910 Federal Population Census Schedules for Virginia. 183 rolls. 16mm.

T1279 Index (Miracode) to the 1910 Federal Population Census Schedules for West Virginia. 108 rolls. 16mm.

Fourteenth Population Census

T625 Fourteenth Census of the United States, 1920. 2,076 rolls.

M1548 Index (Soundex) to the 1920 Federal Population Census Schedules for Alabama. 159 rolls. 16mm.

M1549 Index (Soundex) to the 1920 Federal Population Census Schedules for Arizona. 30 rolls. 16mm.

M1550 Index (Soundex) to the 1920 Federal Population Census Schedules for Arkansas. 131 rolls. 16mm.

M1551 Index (Soundex) to the 1920 Federal Population Census Schedules for California. 327 rolls. 16mm.

M1552 Index (Soundex) to the 1920 Federal Population Census Schedules for Colorado. 80 rolls. 16mm.

M1553 Index (Soundex) to the 1920 Federal Population Census Schedules for Connecticut. 111 rolls. 16mm.

M1554 Index (Soundex) to the 1920 Federal Population Census Schedules for Delaware. 20 rolls. 16mm.

M1555 Index (Soundex) to the 1920 Federal Population Census Schedules for District of Columbia. 49 rolls. 16mm.

M1556 Index (Soundex) to the 1920 Federal Population Census Schedules for Florida. 74 rolls. 16mm.

M1557 Index (Soundex) to the 1920 Federal Population Census Schedules for Georgia. 200 rolls. 16mm.

M1558 Index (Soundex) to the 1920 Federal Population Census Schedules for Idaho. 33 rolls. 16mm.

M1559 Index (Soundex) to the 1920 Federal Population Census Schedules for Illinois. 510 rolls. 16mm.

M1560 Index (Soundex) to the 1920 Federal Population Census Schedules for Indiana. 230 rolls. 16mm.

M1561 Index (Soundex) to the 1920 Federal Population Census Schedules for Iowa. 181 rolls. 16mm.

M1562 Index (Soundex) to the 1920 Federal Population Census Schedules for Kansas. 129 rolls. 16mm.

M1563 Index (Soundex) to the 1920 Federal Population Census Schedules for Kentucky. 180 rolls. 16mm.

M1564 Index (Soundex) to the 1920 Federal Population Census Schedules for Louisiana. 135 rolls. 16mm.

M1565 Index (Soundex) to the 1920 Federal Population Census Schedules for Maine. 67 rolls. 16mm.

M1566 Index (Soundex) to the 1920 Federal Population Census Schedules for Maryland. 126 rolls. 16mm.

M1567 Index (Soundex) to the 1920 Federal Population Census Schedules for Massachusetts. 326 rolls. 16mm.

M1568 Index (Soundex) to the 1920 Federal Population Census Schedules for Michigan. 291 rolls. 16mm.

M1569 Index (Soundex) to the 1920 Federal Population Census Schedules for Minnesota. 174 rolls. 16mm.

M1570 Index (Soundex) to the 1920 Federal Population Census Schedules for Mississippi. 123 rolls. 16mm.

M1571 Index (Soundex) to the 1920 Federal Population Census Schedules for Missouri. 269 rolls. 16mm.

M1572 Index (Soundex) to the 1920 Federal Population Census Schedules for Montana. 46 rolls. 16mm.

M1573 Index (Soundex) to the 1920 Federal Population Census Schedules for Nebraska. 96 rolls. 16mm.

M1574 Index (Soundex) to the 1920 Federal Population Census Schedules for Nevada. 9 rolls. 16mm.

M1575 Index (Soundex) to the 1920 Federal Population Census Schedules for New Hampshire. 41 rolls. 16mm.

M1576 Index (Soundex) to the 1920 Federal Population Census Schedules for New Jersey. 253 rolls. 16mm.

M1577 Index (Soundex) to the 1920 Federal Population Census Schedules for New Mexico. 31 rolls. 16mm.

M1578 Index (Soundex) to the 1920 Federal Population Census Schedules for New York. 885 rolls. 16mm.

M1579 Index (Soundex) to the 1920 Federal Population Census Schedules for North Carolina. 166 rolls. 16mm.

M1580 Index (Soundex) to the 1920 Federal Population Census Schedules for North Dakota. 48 rolls. 16mm.

M1581 Index (Soundex) to the 1920 Federal Population Census Schedules for Ohio. 476 rolls. 16mm.

M1582 Index (Soundex) to the 1920 Federal Population Census Schedules for Oklahoma. 155 rolls. 16mm.

M1583 Index (Soundex) to the 1920 Federal Population Census Schedules for Oregon. 69 rolls. 16mm.

M1584 Index (Soundex) to the 1920 Federal Population Census Schedules for Pennsylvania. 712 rolls. 16mm.

M1585 Index (Soundex) to the 1920 Federal Population Census Schedules for Rhode Island. 53 rolls. 16mm.

M1586 Index (Soundex) to the 1920 Federal Population Census Schedules for South Carolina. 112 rolls. 16mm.

M1587 Index (Soundex) to the 1920 Federal Population Census Schedules for South Dakota. 48 rolls. 16mm.

M1588 Index (Soundex) to the 1920 Federal Population Census Schedules for Tennessee. 162 rolls. 16mm.

M1589 Index (Soundex) to the 1920 Federal Population Census Schedules for Texas. 373 rolls. 16mm.

M1590 Index (Soundex) to the 1920 Federal Population Census Schedules for Utah. 33 rolls. 16mm.

M1591 Index (Soundex) to the 1920 Federal Population Census Schedules for Vermont. 32 rolls. 16mm.

M1592 Index (Soundex) to the 1920 Federal Population Census Schedules for Virginia. 168 rolls. 16mm.

M1593 Index (Soundex) to the 1920 Federal Population Census Schedules for Washington. 118 rolls. 16mm.

M1594 Index (Soundex) to the 1920 Federal Population Census Schedules for West Virginia. 109 rolls. 16mm.

M1595 Index (Soundex) to the 1920 Federal Population Census Schedules for Wisconsin. 196 rolls. 16mm.

M1596 Index (Soundex) to the 1920 Federal Population Census Schedules for Wyoming. 17 rolls. 16mm.

M1597 Index (Soundex) to the 1920 Federal Population Census Schedules for Alaska. 6 rolls. 16mm.

M1598 Index (Soundex) to the 1920 Federal Population Census Schedules for Hawaii. 24 rolls. 16mm.

M1599 Index (Soundex) to the 1920 Federal Population Census Schedules for the Panama Canal Zone. 3 rolls. 16mm.

M1600 Index (Soundex) to the 1920 Federal Population Census Schedules for Military-Naval Districts. 18 rolls. 16mm.

M1601 Index (Soundex) to the 1920 Federal Population Census Schedules for Puerto Rico. 165 rolls. 16mm.

M1602 Index (Soundex) to the 1920 Federal Population Census Schedules for Guam. 1 roll. 16mm.

M1603 Index (Soundex) to the 1920 Federal Population Census Schedules for American Samoa. 2 rolls. 16mm.

M1604 Index (Soundex) to the 1920 Federal Population Census Schedules for the Virgin Islands. 3 rolls. 16mm.

M1605 Index (Soundex) to the 1920 Federal Population Census Schedules for Institutions. 1 roll. 16mm.

Federal Nonpopulation Census Schedules

M1793 Nonpopulation Census Schedules for the District of Columbia, 1850–1870: Agriculture, Industry, Mortality, and Social Statistics, and Nonpopulation Census Schedules for Worcester County, Maryland, 1850: Agriculture. 1 roll.

*M1794 Nonpopulation Census Schedules for the District of Columbia, Montana Territory, Nevada and Wyoming Territory, 1880: Agriculture. 1 roll.

*M1795 Nonpopulation Census Schedules for the District of Columbia, 1880: General and Special Schedules of Manufacturing and Supplemental Schedules of Dependent, Defective, and Delinquent Classes. 1 roll.

T1137 Nonpopulation Census Schedules for Georgia, 1850–1880. 27 rolls.

T1133 Nonpopulation Census Schedules for Illinois, 1850–1880. 64 rolls.

T1156 Nonpopulation Census Schedules for Iowa, 1850–1880. 62 rolls.

T1130 Nonpopulation Census Schedules for Kansas, 1850–1880. 48 rolls.

M1528 Nonpopulation Census Schedules for Kentucky, 1850–1880. 42 rolls.

T1136 Nonpopulation Census Schedules for Louisiana, 1850–1880. 15 rolls.

M1799 Nonpopulation Census Schedules for Baltimore City and County, Maryland, 1850–1860: Agriculture, Industry, and Social Statistics. 1 roll.

T1204 Nonpopulation Census Schedules for Massachusetts, 1850–1880. 40 rolls.

T1164 Nonpopulation Census Schedules for Michigan, 1850–1880 (in the custody of the Michigan State Archives). 77 rolls.

T1163 Nonpopulation Census Schedules for Michigan, 1850: Mortality Schedules (in the custody of the State Library of Ohio). 1 roll.

M1802 Nonpopulation Census Schedules for Minnesota, 1860: Agriculture. 1 roll.

*M1806 Nonpopulation Census Schedules for Montana, 1870 and 1880. 1 roll.

T1128 Nonpopulation Census Schedules for Nebraska, 1860–1880. 16 rolls.

*M1810 Nonpopulation Census Schedules for New Jersey, 1850–1880: Mortality. 4 rolls.

M1792 Manufacturing Schedules Contained in the 1810 Population Census Schedules of New York State. 1 roll.

*M1805 Nonpopulation Census Schedules for North Carolina, 1850–1880: Mortality and Manufacturing. 9 rolls.

T1159 Nonpopulation Census Schedules for Ohio, 1850–1880. 104 rolls.

T1157 Nonpopulation Census Schedules for Pennsylvania, 1850–1860: Manufactures Schedules. 9 rolls.

M597 Nonpopulation Census Schedules for Pennsylvania, 1850–1880: Social Statistics and Supplemental Schedules. 23 rolls.

T1138 Nonpopulation Census Schedules for Pennsylvania, 1850–1880: Agriculture. 62 rolls.

M1796 Nonpopulation Census Schedules for Pennsylvania, 1870–1880: Industry and Manufacturing. 9 rolls.

*M1838 Nonpopulation Census Schedules for Pennsylvania, 1850–1880: Mortality. 11 rolls.

T1135 Nonpopulation Census Schedules for Tennessee, 1850–1880. 39 rolls.

T1134 Nonpopulation Census Schedules for Texas, 1850–1880. 59 rolls.

M1798 Nonpopulation Census Schedules for Vermont, 1850–1870: Agriculture and Industry. 9 rolls.

M1807 Nonpopulation Census Schedules for Utah Territory and Vermont, 1870: Mortality. 1 roll.

T1132 Nonpopulation Census Schedules for Virginia, 1850–1880. 34 rolls.

A1154 Nonpopulation Census Schedules for Washington Territory, 1860–1880. 8 rolls.

T655 Federal Mortality Census Schedules, 1850–1880 (formerly in the custody of the Daughters of the American Revolution), and Related Indexes. 30 rolls.

M279 Records of the 1820 Census of Manufactures. 27 rolls. DP.

*M2069 1935 Census of Business: Schedules of Public Warehousing. 6 rolls.

State and Special Census Schedules

T1175 Schedules of the Minnesota Territory Census of 1857. 5 rolls.

M158 Schedules of the Colorado State Census of 1885. 8 rolls. DP.

M845 Schedules of the Florida State Census of 1885. 13 rolls. DP.

M352 Schedules of the Nebraska State Census of 1885. 56 rolls. DP.

M846 Schedules of the New Mexico Territory Census of 1885. 6 rolls. DP.

*M1791 Schedules of a Special Census of Indians, 1880 5 rolls. DP.

*M1797 1935 Census of Business: Schedules of Advertising Agencies. 1 roll.

*M2066 1935 Census of Business: Schedules of Banking and Financial Institutions. 31 rolls.

*M2067 1935 Census of Business: Schedules of Miscellaneous Enterprises. 43 rolls.

*M2068 1935 Census of Business: Schedules of Motor Trucking for Hire. 103 rolls

*M2070 1935 Census of Business: Schedules of Radio Broadcasting Stations. 1 roll.

*M1803 Third Census of the United States, 1810. Population Schedules, Washington County, Ohio. 1 roll.

*M1804 Second Census of the United States, 1800: Population Schedules, Washington County, Territory Northwest of the River Ohio; and Population Census, 1803: Washington County, Ohio. 1 roll.

*M1808 Eighth Census of the United States for the Northern District of Halifax County, Virginia, 1860: Schedules of Free Inhabitants, Slave Inhabitants, Mortality, Agriculture, Industry, and Social Statistics. 1 roll.

*M1809 Wisconsin Territorial Censuses of 1836, 1842, and 1847. 3 rolls.

*M1811 First Territorial Census for Oklahoma, 1890. 1 roll.

*M1813 Kansas Territorial Censuses, 1855-1859. 2 rolls.

*M1814 1907 Census of Seminole County, Oklahoma. 1 roll.

*M2073 Statistics of Congregations of Lutheran Synods, 1890. 1 roll.

Other Census Records

M1283 Cross Index to Selected City Street and Enumeration Districts, 1910 Census. 50 cards (microfiche).

T498 Publications of the Bureau of the Census: 1790 Census, Printed Schedules. 3 rolls.

T825 Publications of the Bureau of the Census, 1790-1916. 42 rolls.

*T1224 Descriptions of Census Enumeration Districts, 1830-1950. 156 rolls.

RG 33 Records of the Extension Service

M1146 Photographs of the Federal Extension Service, 1920-1954 (S Series). 13 rolls.

M1147 Photographs of the Federal Extension Service, 1920-1945 (SC Series). 11 rolls.

T845 Extension Service Annual Reports: Alabama, 1909-1944. 115 rolls. 16mm.

T846 Extension Service Annual Reports: Alaska, 1930-1944. 2 rolls. 16mm.

T847 Extension Service Annual Reports: Arizona, 1915-1944. 22 rolls. 16mm.

T848 Extension Service Annual Reports: Arkansas, 1909-1944. 106 rolls. 16mm.

T849 Extension Service Annual Reports: California, 1913-1944. 54 rolls. 16mm.

T850 Extension Service Annual Reports: Colorado, 1913-1944. 77 rolls. 16mm.

T851 Extension Service Annual Reports: Connecticut, 1913-1944. 30 rolls. 16mm.

T852 Extension Service Annual Reports: Delaware, 1914-1944. 13 rolls. 16mm.

T853 Extension Service Annual Reports: District of Columbia, 1917-1919. 1 roll. 16mm.

T854 Extension Service Annual Reports: Florida, 1909-1944. 46 rolls. 16mm.

T855 Extension Service Annual Reports: Georgia, 1909-1944. 141 rolls. 16mm.

T856 Extension Service Annual Reports: Hawaii, 1929-1944. 7 rolls. 16mm.

T857 Extension Service Annual Reports: Idaho, 1913-1944. 47 rolls. 16mm.

T858 Extension Service Annual Reports: Illinois, 1914-1944. 82 rolls. 16mm.

T859 Extension Service Annual Reports: Indiana, 1912-1944. 80 rolls. 16mm.

T860 Extension Service Annual Reports: Iowa, 1912-1944. 195 rolls. 16mm.

T861 Extension Service Annual Reports: Kansas, 1913-1944. 186 rolls. 16mm.

T862 Extension Service Annual Reports: Kentucky, 1912-1944. 89 rolls. 16mm.

T863 Extension Service Annual Reports: Louisiana, 1909-1944. 67 rolls. 16mm.

T864 Extension Service Annual Reports: Maine, 1915-1944. 48 rolls. 16mm.

T865 Extension Service Annual Reports: Maryland, 1912-1944. 70 rolls. 16mm.

T866 Extension Service Annual Reports: Massachusetts, 1914-1944. 59 rolls. 16mm.

T867 Extension Service Annual Reports: Michigan, 1913-1944. 77 rolls. 16mm.

T868 Extension Service Annual Reports: Minnesota, 1914-1944. 105 rolls. 16mm.

T869 Extension Service Annual Reports: Mississippi, 1909-1944. 96 rolls. 16mm.

T870 Extension Service Annual Reports: Missouri, 1914-1944. 90 rolls. 16mm.

T871 Extension Service Annual Reports: Montana, 1914-1944. 64 rolls. 16mm.

T872 Extension Service Annual Reports: Nebraska, 1913-1944. 89 rolls. 16mm.

T873 Extension Service Annual Reports: Nevada, 1915-1944. 19 rolls. 16mm.

T874 Extension Service Annual Reports: New Hampshire, 1914-1944. 37 rolls. 16mm.

T875 Extension Service Annual Reports: New Jersey, 1913-1944. 45 rolls. 16mm.

T876 Extension Service Annual Reports: New Mexico, 1914-1944. 30 rolls. 16mm.

T877 Extension Service Annual Reports: New York, 1912-1944. 90 rolls. 16mm.

T878 Extension Service Annual Reports: North Carolina, 1909-1944. 144 rolls. 16mm.

T879 Extension Service Annual Reports: North Dakota, 1912-1944. 68 rolls. 16mm.

T880 Extension Service Annual Reports: Ohio, 1915-1944. 98 rolls. 16mm.

T881 Extension Service Annual Reports: Oklahoma, 1909-1944. 135 rolls. 16mm.

T882 Extension Service Annual Reports: Oregon, 1914-1944. 73 rolls. 16mm.

T883 Extension Service Annual Reports: Pennsylvania, 1914-1944. 43 rolls. 16mm.

T884 Extension Service Annual Reports: Puerto Rico, 1930-1944. 14 rolls. 16mm.

T885 Extension Service Annual Reports: Rhode Island, 1914-1944. 12 rolls. 16mm.

T886 Extension Service Annual Reports: South, 1913-1914. 1 roll. 16mm.

T887 Extension Service Annual Reports: South Carolina, 1909-1944. 91 rolls. 16mm.

T888 Extension Service Annual Reports: South Dakota, 1913-1944. 65 rolls. 16mm.

T889 Extension Service Annual Reports: Tennessee, 1910-1944. 64 rolls. 16mm.

T890 Extension Service Annual Reports: Texas, 1909-1944. 182 rolls. 16mm.

T891 Extension Service Annual Reports: Utah, 1914-1944. 30 rolls. 16mm.

T892 Extension Service Annual Reports: Vermont, 1912-1944. 31 rolls. 16mm.

T893 Extension Service Annual Reports: Virginia, 1908-1944. 82 rolls. 16mm.

T894 Extension Service Annual Reports: Washington, 1913-1944. 45 rolls. 16mm.

T895 Extension Service Annual Reports: West Virginia, 1912-1944. 47 rolls. 16mm.

T896 Extension Service Annual Reports: Wisconsin, 1913-1944. 49 rolls. 16mm.

T897 Extension Service Annual Reports: Wyoming, 1914-1944. 37 rolls. 16mm.

RG 35 Records of the Civilian Conservation Corps

M1783 Civilian Conservation Corps Newspaper, "Happy Days," 1933-1940. 6 rolls.

RG 36 Records of the U.S. Customs Service

See also Records of the Immigration and Naturalization Service (RG 85).

Passenger Lists, Vessel Lists, and Indexes

INDEXES TO PASSENGER AND VESSEL LISTS

M326 Index to Passenger Lists of Vessels Arriving at Baltimore, Maryland, 1833-1866. 22 rolls. DP. 16mm.

M327 Index to Passenger Lists of Vessels Arriving at Baltimore, Maryland, 1820-1897 (Federal Passenger Lists). 171 rolls. DP. 16mm.

M265 Index to Passenger Lists of Vessels Arriving at Boston, Massachusetts, 1848-1891. 282 rolls. DP. 16mm.

T527 Index to Passenger Lists of Vessels Arriving at New Orleans, Louisiana, 1853-1899. 32 rolls. 16mm.

M261 Index to Passenger Lists of Vessels Arriving at New York, New York, 1820-1846. 103 rolls. DP. 16mm.

M360 Index to Passenger Lists of Vessels Arriving at Philadelphia, Pennsylvania, 1800-1906. 151 rolls. DP. 16mm.

M334 Supplemental Index to Passenger Lists of Vessels Arriving at Atlantic and Gulf Coast Ports (Excluding New York), 1820-1874. 188 rolls. DP. 16mm.

PASSENGER LISTS

M255 Passenger Lists of Vessels Arriving at Baltimore, Maryland, 1820-1891. 50 rolls. DP.

M596 Quarterly Abstracts of Passenger Lists of Vessels Arriving at Baltimore, Maryland, 1820-1869. 6 rolls. DP.

M277 Passenger Lists of Vessels Arriving at Boston, Massachusetts, 1820-1891. 115 rolls. DP.

M259 Passenger Lists of Vessels Arriving at New Orleans, Louisiana, 1820-1902. 93 rolls. DP.

M272 Quarterly Abstracts of Passenger Lists of Vessels Arriving at New Orleans, Louisiana, 1820-1875. 17 rolls. DP.

M237 Passenger Lists of Vessels Arriving at New York, New York, 1820-1897. 675 rolls. DP.

M425 Passenger Lists of Vessels Arriving at Philadelphia, Pennsylvania, 1800-1882. 108 rolls. DP.

M575 Copies of Lists of Passengers Arriving at Miscellaneous Ports on the Atlantic and Gulf Coasts and at Ports on the Great Lakes, 1820-1873. 16 rolls. DP.

VESSEL LISTS

M1066 Registers of Vessels Arriving at the Port of New York, New York, From Foreign Ports, 1789-1919. 27 rolls. DP.

OTHER RECORDS

M177 Letters and Reports Received by the Secretary of the Treasury From Special Agents, 1854-1861. 3 rolls. DP.

*T1219 State Department Transcripts of Passenger Lists, ca. October 1819-ca. December 1832. 2 rolls.

M802 Alaska File of the Special Agents Division of the Department of the Treasury, 1867-1903. 16 rolls. DP.

T1189 Records of Alaskan Custom Houses, 1867-1939. 131 rolls.

*M1825 Proofs of Citizenship Used to Apply for Seamen's Protection Certificates at the Port of Bath, Maine, 1833, 1836, 1839-50, 1853-65, 1867-68; and at Portsmouth, New Hampshire, 1857-58. 3 rolls. DP.

M1162 Records of the Collector of Customs for the Collection District of New London, Connecticut, 1789-1938. 57 rolls.

*M1826 Proofs of Citizenship Used to Apply for Seamen's Protection Certificates for the Port of New Orleans, Louisiana, 1800, 1802, 1804-07, 1809-12, 1814-16, 1818-19, 1821, 1850-51, 1855-57. 12 rolls. DP.

M972 Computer-Processed Tabulations of Data From Seamen's Protective Certificate Applications to the Collector of Customs for the Port of Philadelphia, 1812-1815. 1 roll. DP.

T255 Impost Books of the Collector of Customs at Philadelphia, 1789-1804. 6 rolls.

M1633 U.S. Customs, Puget Sound District Log Books and Shipping Articles, ca. 1890-1937. 68 rolls.

RG 37 Records of the Hydrographic Office

M75 Records of the U.S. Exploring Expedition Under the Command of Lt. Charles Wilkes, 1836-1842. 27 rolls. DP.

RG 38 Records of the Office of the Chief of Naval Operations

M975 Selected Naval Attache Reports Relating to the World Crisis, 1937-1943. 3 rolls. DP.

M1332 Subject Index to Naval Intelligence Reports, 1940-1946. 20 rolls. DP.

M1752 U.S. Submarine War Patrol Reports, 1941-1945. 1155 cards (microfiche). DP.

RG 39 Records of the Bureau of Accounts (Treasury)

*T292 Account Book of Receipts & Expenditures, Temporary Loans, Estimates of Appropriations and Interests, 1793-1800. 1 roll.

*T723 Blotters of the Office of the Register of the Treasury, 1782-1810. 17 rolls.

RG 40 General Records of the Department of Commerce

M838 General Correspondence of the Office of the Secretary of Commerce, 1929-1933. 16 rolls. DP.

T10 Minutes of the Industrial Commission, 1898-1902. 1 roll.

RG 41 Records of the Bureau of Marine Inspection and Navigation

M130 Certificates of Registry, Enrollment, and License Issued at Edgartown, Massachusetts, 1815-1913. 9 rolls. DP.

M1339 Vessel Documentation Records From the Port of Pembina, North Dakota, 1885-1959. 10 rolls.

M1340 Vessel Licenses and Enrollments From the Port of St. Louis, Missouri, 1835-1944. 26 rolls.

M1632 Merchant Marine License Applications, Puget Sound District, 1888-1910. 3 rolls.

*M2034 Certificates of Registration and Enrollment Issued for Merchant Vessels at Beaufort, Edenton, Elizabeth City, New Bern, Ocracoke, Plymouth, Washington, and Wilmington, North Carolina, 1815-1902. 31 rolls.

RG 42 Records of the Office of Public Buildings and Public Parks of the National Capital

M371 Records of the District of Columbia Commissioners and of the Offices Concerned With Public Buildings, 1791-1867. 27 rolls. DP.

RG 43 Records of International Conferences, Commissions, and Expositions

M662 Records of the Department of State Relating to the First Panama Congress, 1825-1827. 1 roll. DP.

T954 Records of the Department of State Relating to the Paris Peace Commission, 1898. 3 rolls.

M1243 Records of the American Delegation, U.S.-USSR Joint Commission on Korea, and Records Relating to the United Nations Temporary Commission on Korea (UNTCOK), 1945-1948. 23 rolls. DP.

C0036 Records of the Far Eastern Commission, 1945-1952. 167 rolls.

RG 44 Records of the Office of Government Reports

T37 Minutes of the Executive Council, July 11, 1933-Nov. 13, 1934. 1 roll.

T38 Proceedings of the National Emergency Council, Dec. 19, 1933-April 28, 1936. 1 roll.

RG 45 Naval Records Collection of the Office of Naval Records and Library

Records of the Office of the Secretary of the Navy

M89 Letters Received by the Secretary of the Navy From Commanding Officers of Squadrons ("Squadron Letters"), 1841-1886. 300 rolls. DP.

M124 Miscellaneous Letters Received by the Secretary of the Navy, 1801-1884. 647 rolls. DP.

M125 Letters Received by the Secretary of the Navy From Captains ("Captains' Letters"), 1805-1861, 1866-1885. 413 rolls. DP.

M147 Letters Received by the Secretary of the Navy From Commanders, 1804-1886. 124 rolls. DP.

M148 Letters Received by the Secretary of the Navy From Commissioned Officers Below the Rank of Commander and From Warrant Officers ("Officers' Letters"), 1802-1884. 518 rolls. DP.

M517 Letters Received by the Secretary of the Navy From the President and Executive Agencies, 1837-1886. 49 rolls. DP. 16mm.

M518 Letters Received by the Secretary of the Navy From Chiefs of Navy Bureaus, 1842-1885. 33 rolls. DP. 16mm.

M528 Letters Received by the Secretary of the Navy From Navy Agents and Naval Storekeepers, 1843-1865. 12 rolls. DP.

M1029 Letters Received by the Secretary of the Navy From the Attorney General of the United States Containing Legal Opinions and Advice, 1807-1825. 1 roll. DP.

M149 Letters Sent by the Secretary of the Navy to Officers, 1798-1868. 86 rolls. DP.

M209 Miscellaneous Letters Sent by the Secretary of the Navy, 1798-1886. 43 rolls. DP.

M441 Letters Sent by the Secretary of the Navy to Commandants and Navy Agents, 1808-1865. 5 rolls. DP.

M472 Letters Sent by the Secretary of the Navy to the President and Executive Agencies, 1821-1886. 20 rolls. DP.

M480 Letters Sent by the Secretary of the Navy to Chiefs of Navy Bureaus, 1842-1886. 3 rolls. DP.

M205 Correspondence of the Secretary of the Navy Relating to African Colonization, 1819-1844. 2 rolls. DP.

M739 Letters Sent by the War Department Relating to Naval Matters, Jan. 3, 1794-June 14, 1798. 1 roll. DP.

Other Records

M88 Records Relating to the U.S. Surveying Expedition to the North Pacific Ocean, 1852-1863. 27 rolls. DP.

M118 *History of the Boston Navy Yard, 1797-1874,* by Commodore George Henry Preble, U.S.N., 1875. 1 roll. DP.

M180 Papers of Stephen C. Rowan, 1826–1890. 1 roll. DP.

M206 Letter Books of Commodore Matthew C. Perry, 1843–1845. 1 roll. DP.

M625 Area File of the Naval Records Collection, 1775–1910. 414 rolls. DP.

M875 Journal of Lt. Charles Gauntt Aboard the U.S.S. *Macedonian*, 1818–1821. 1 roll. DP.

M876 Journal of Charles J. Deblois, Captain's Clerk, Aboard the U.S.S *Macedonian*, 1818–1819. 1 roll. DP.

M902 Report of Capt. James Biddle, Commanding the U.S.S. *Ontario*, 1817–1819. 1 roll. DP.

M981 The Journals of Thomas A. Dornin, U.S. Navy, 1826–1855. 1 roll. DP.

M1034 The Journal of Lt. Comdr. William B. Cushing, 1861–1865. 1 roll. DP.

M1091 Subject File of the Confederate States Navy, 1861–1865. 61 rolls. DP.

T12 Journal of John Landreth on an Expedition to the Gulf Coast, Nov. 15, 1818–May 19, 1819. 1 roll.

T297 Log of Arctic Steamer *Jeanette*. 1 roll.

T319 Log of the U.S.S. *Nautilus*, Aug. 1–31, 1958. 1 roll.

*T829 Miscellaneous Records of the Office of Naval Records and Library. 461 rolls.

T1097 Private Journals of Commodore Matthew C. Perry, 1853–1854. 1 roll.

RG 46 Records of the U.S. Senate

M200 Territorial Papers of the U.S. Senate, 1789–1873. 20 rolls. DP.

M1196 Records of the Senate Select Committee That Investigated John Brown's Raid at Harper's Ferry, Virginia, in 1859. 3 rolls. DP.

M1251 Journal of the Legislative Proceedings of the U.S. Senate, 1789–1817. 28 rolls. DP.

M1252 Journal of the Executive Proceedings of the U.S. Senate, 1789–1823. 3 rolls. DP.

M1253 Journal of the Impeachment Proceedings Before the U.S. Senate, 1798–1805. 1 roll. DP.

M1254 Journal of the Secretary of the Senate, 1789–1845. 1 roll. DP.

M1255 Bill Books of the U.S. Senate, 1795–1845. 2 rolls. DP.

M1256 Transcribed Reports of Committees of the U.S. Senate, 1817–1827. 2 rolls. DP.

M1257 Transcribed Reports and Communications Transmitted by the Executive Branch to the U.S. Senate, 1789–1819, and Transcribed Reports of Senate Committees, 1798–1817. 4 rolls. DP.

M1258 Transcribed Treaties and Conventions Approved by the U.S. Senate, 1789–1836. 2 rolls. DP.

M1259 Registers of Documents Presented to the U.S. Senate, 1814–1828. 1 roll. DP.

M1260 Engrossed Bills and Resolutions of the U.S. Senate, 1789–1817. 5 rolls. DP.

M1261 Register of Credentials of U.S. Senators, 1789–1821. 1 roll. DP.

M1546 Petitions Submitted to the U.S. Senate Requesting the Removal of Political Disabilities of Former Confederate Officeholders, 1869–1877. 14 rolls. DP.

M1704 Unbound Records of the U.S. Senate, Fifth Congress, 1797–1799. 5 rolls. DP.

M1706 Unbound Records of the U.S. Senate, Sixth Congress, 1799–1801. 8 rolls. DP.

M1403 Unbound Records of the U.S. Senate for the Eighth Congress, 1803–1805. 5 rolls. DP.

*P2000 Unbound Records of the U.S. Senate, Seventh Congress, 1803–1805. 5 rolls.

*P2280 Senate Democratic Conference Minutes. 2 rolls.

*P2289 Office of Legislative Counsel, 1918–1969. 5 rolls.

RG 48 Records of the Office of the Secretary of the Interior

Territorial Papers

M430 Interior Department Territorial Papers: Alaska, 1869–1911. 17 rolls. DP.

M429 Interior Department Territorial Papers: Arizona, 1868–1913. 8 rolls. DP.

M431 Interior Department Territorial Papers: Colorado, 1861–1888. 1 roll. DP.

M310 Interior Department Territorial Papers: Dakota, 1863–1889. 3 rolls. DP.

M827 Interior Department Territorial Papers: Hawaii, 1898–1907. 4 rolls. DP.

M191 Interior Department Territorial Papers: Idaho, 1864–1890. 3 rolls. DP.

M192 Interior Department Territorial Papers: Montana, 1867–1889. 2 rolls. DP.

M364 Interior Department Territorial Papers: New Mexico, 1851–1914. 15 rolls. DP.

M828 Interior Department Territorial Papers: Oklahoma, 1889–1912. 5 rolls. DP.

M428 Interior Department Territorial Papers: Utah, 1850–1902. 6 rolls. DP.

M189 Interior Department Territorial Papers: Washington, 1854–1902. 4 rolls. DP.

M204 Interior Department Territorial Papers: Wyoming, 1870–1890. 6 rolls. DP.

Appointment Papers

M1245 Interior Department Appointment Papers: Alaska, 1871–1907. 6 rolls. DP.

M576 Interior Department Appointment Papers: Territory of Arizona, 1857–1907. 22 rolls. DP.

M732 Interior Department Appointment Papers: California, 1849–1907. 29 rolls. DP.

M808 Interior Department Appointment Papers: Territory of Colorado, 1857–1907. 13 rolls. DP.

M1119 Interior Department Appointment Papers: Florida, 1849–1907. 6 rolls. DP.

M693 Interior Department Appointment Papers: Idaho, 1862–1907. 17 rolls. DP.

M849 Interior Department Appointment Papers: Mississippi, 1849–1907. 4 rolls. DP.

M1058 Interior Department Appointment Papers: Missouri, 1849–1907. 9 rolls. DP.

M1033 Interior Department Appointment Papers: Nevada, 1860–1907. 3 rolls. DP.

M750 Interior Department Appointment Papers: Territory of New Mexico, 1850–1907. 18 rolls. DP.

M1022 Interior Department Appointment Papers: New York, 1849–1906. 5 rolls. DP.

M950 Interior Department Appointment Papers: North Carolina, 1849–1892. 1 roll. DP.

M814 Interior Department Appointment Papers: Territory of Oregon, 1849–1907. 10 rolls. DP.

M831 Interior Department Appointment Papers: Territory of Wisconsin, 1849–1907. 9 rolls. DP.

M830 Interior Department Appointment Papers: Wyoming, 1869–1907. 6 rolls. DP.

Other Records

M62 Records of the Office of the Secretary of the Interior Relating to Yellowstone National Park, 1872–1886. 6 rolls. DP.

M95 Records of the Office of the Secretary of the Interior Relating to Wagon Roads, 1857–1887. 16 rolls. DP.

M126 Correspondence of the Office of Explorations and Surveys Concerning Isaac Stevens' Survey of a Northern Route for the Pacific Railroad, 1853–1861. 1 roll.

M160 Records of the Office of the Secretary of the Interior Relating to the Suppression of the African Slave Trade and Negro Colonization, 1854–1872. 10 rolls. DP.

M606 Letters Sent by the Indian Division of the Office of the Secretary of the Interior, 1849–1903. 127 rolls. DP. *See also* Records of the Bureau of Indian Affairs

M620 Letters Sent by the Lands and Railroads Division of the Office of the Secretary of the Interior, 1849–1904. 310 rolls. DP.

M824 Letters Received by the Patents and Miscellaneous Division of the Office of the Secretary of the Interior Relating to Cuba, the Philippine Islands, and Puerto Rico, 1898–1907. 2 rolls. DP.

M825 Selected Classes of Letters Received by the Indian Division of the Office of the Secretary of the Interior, 1849–1880. 32 rolls. DP. *See also* Records of the Bureau of Indian Affairs

T529 Final Rolls of Citizens and Freedmen of the Five Civilized Tribes in Indian Territory (as Approved by the Secretary of the Interior on or Before Mar. 4, 1907, With Supplements Dated Sept. 25, 1914). 3 rolls.

RG 49 Records of the Bureau of Land Management

M8 Journal and Report of James L. Cathcart and James Hutton, Agents Appointed by the Secretary of the Navy to Survey Timber Resources Between the Mermentau and Mobile Rivers, 1818–1819. 1 roll. DP.

M25 Miscellaneous Letters Sent by the General Land Office, 1796–1889. 228 rolls. DP.

M27 Letters Sent by the General Land Office to the Surveyor General, 1796–1901. 31 rolls. DP.

M68 List of North Carolina Land Grants in Tennessee, 1778–1791. 1 roll. DP.

M145 Abstracts of Oregon Donation Land Claims, 1852–1903. 6 rolls. DP.

M203 Abstracts of Washington Donation Land Claims, 1855–1902. 1 roll. DP.

M477 Letters Sent by the Surveyor General of the Territory Northwest of the Ohio River, 1797–1854. 10 rolls. DP.

M478 Letters Received by the Secretary of the Treasury and the Commissioner of the General Land Office From the Surveyor General of the Territory Northwest of the River Ohio, 1797–1849. 10 rolls. DP.

M479 Letters Received by the Surveyor General of the Territory Northwest of the River Ohio, 1797–1856. 43 rolls. DP.

M815 Oregon and Washington Donation Land Files, 1851–1903. 108 rolls. DP.

M848 War of 1812 Military Bounty Land Warrants, 1815–1858. 14 rolls. DP.

M829 U.S. Revolutionary War Bounty Land Warrants Used in the U.S. Military District of Ohio and Related Papers (Acts of 1788, 1803, and 1806). 16 rolls. DP.

M1110 Correspondence of the Surveyors General of Utah, 1874–1916. 86 rolls. DP.

M1288 Correspondence Received by the Surveyors General of New Mexico, 1854–1907. 11 rolls.

M1323 Letters and Surveying Contracts Received by the General Land Office from the Surveyor General for Illinois, Missouri, and Arkansas, 1813–1832. 2 rolls.

M1325 Letters and Surveying Contracts Received by the General Land Office from the Surveyor General for Alabama, 1817–1832. 1 roll.

M1329 Letters Received by the Secretary of the Treasury and the General Land Office from the Surveyor General for Mississippi, 1803–1831. 4 rolls.

M1382 Bound Records of the General Land Office Relating to Private Land Claims in Louisiana, 1767–1892. 8 rolls. DP.

M1385 Unbound Records of the General Land Office Relating to Private Land Claims in Louisiana, 1805–1896. 2 rolls. DP.

M1620 Federal Land Records for Idaho, 1860–1934. 23 rolls.

M1621 Federal Land Records for Oregon. 93 rolls.

M1622 Federal Land Records for Washington, 1860–1910. 72 rolls.

M1627 Records of the Bureau of Land Management, Surveyor General of Arizona, 1891–1950. 2 rolls.

M1628 Records of the Bureau of Land Management, Phoenix General Land Office, 1873–1942. 15 rolls.

M1629 Records of the Bureau of Land Management, Prescott General Land Office, 1871–1908. 16 rolls.

M1630 Records of the Bureau of Land Management, Los Angeles District Land Office, 1859–1936. 60 rolls.

*T910 Records Relating to California Private Land Claims Dockets. 118 rolls.

T1008 Register of Army Land Warrants Issued Under the Act of 1788, for Service in the Revolutionary War: Military District of Ohio. 1 roll.

T1169 Records of the General Land Office Forest Lieu Selection Docket Registers. 6 rolls.

T1234 Township Plats of Selected States. 62 rolls.

T1240 Field Notes From Selected General Land Office Township Surveys. 280 rolls.

RG 51 Records of the Office of Management and Budget

*M2020 World War II Historical Studies Made by the Bureau of the Budget, 1943-1946. 1 roll.

RG 53 Records of the Bureau of the Public Debt

T654 Records of the Bureau of the Public Debt: Connecticut Loan Office Records Relating to the Loan of 1790. 10 rolls.

T784 Records of the Bureau of the Public Debt: Delaware Loan Office Records Relating to the Loan of 1790. 1 roll.

M1008 Records of the Delaware and Maryland Continental Loan Office, 1777-1790. 1 roll. DP.

T694 Records of the Bureau of the Public Debt: Georgia Loan Office Records Relating to the Loan of 1790. 2 rolls.

T788 Records of the Bureau of the Public Debt: Georgia Loan Office Records Relating to Various Loans, 1804-1818. 1 roll.

T697 Records of the Bureau of the Public Debt: Maryland Loan Office Records Relating to the Loan of 1790. 9 rolls.

T957 Records of the Bureau of the Public Debt: Maryland Loan Office Records Relating to Various Loans of 1798 and 1800. 1 roll.

T783 Records of the Bureau of the Public Debt: Massachusetts Loan Office Records Relating to the Loan of 1790. 2 rolls.

M925 Records of the Massachusetts Continental Loan Office, 1777-1791. 4 rolls. DP.

T652 Records of the Bureau of the Public Debt: New Hampshire Loan Office Records Relating to the Loan of 1790. 6 rolls.

M1005 Records of the Connecticut, New Hampshire, and Rhode Island Continental Loan Offices, 1777-1789. 2 rolls. DP.

T698 Records of the Bureau of the Public Debt: New Jersey Loan Office Records Relating to the Loan of 1790. 2 rolls.

M1006 Records of the New Jersey and New York Continental Loan Offices, 1777-1790. 2 rolls. DP.

T695 Records of the Bureau of the Public Debt: North Carolina Loan Office Records Relating to the Loan of 1790. 4 rolls.

T631 Records of the Bureau of the Public Debt: Pennsylvania Loan Office Records Relating to the Loan of 1790. 8 rolls.

M1007 Records of the Pennsylvania Continental Loan Office, 1776-1788. 3 rolls. DP.

T653 Records of the Bureau of the Public Debt: Rhode Island Loan Office Records Relating to the Loan of 1790. 13 rolls.

T719 Records of the Bureau of the Public Debt: South Carolina Loan Office Records Relating to the Loan of 1790. 3 rolls.

T696 Records of the Bureau of the Public Debt: Virginia Loan Office Records Relating to the Loan of 1790. 12 rolls.

M521 Card Index to "Old Loan" Ledgers of the Bureau of the Public Debt, 1790-1836. 15 rolls. DP. 16mm.

T786 Records of the Bureau of the Public Debt: Central Treasury Records Relating to the Loan of 1790. 1 roll.

T787 Records of the Bureau of the Public Debt: Old Loans Records Relating to Selected Loans of the Period 1795-1807. 6 rolls.

RG 54 Records of the Bureau of Plant Industry, Soils, and Agricultural Engineering

M840 Expedition Reports of the Office of Foreign Seed and Plant Introduction of the Department of Agriculture, 1900-1938. 38 rolls. DP.

RG 55 Records of the Government of the Virgin Islands

T39 Customs Journals of the Danish Government of the Virgin Islands. 22 rolls.

T952 Records Relating to the Danish West Indies, 1672-1860, Received From the Danish National Archives. 19 rolls.

RG 56 General Records of the Department of the Treasury

M87 Records of the Commissioners of Claims (Southern Claims Commission), 1871-1880. 14 rolls. DP.

M174 Letters Received by the Secretary of the Treasury From Collectors of Customs ("G," "H," "I" Series), 1833-1869. 226 rolls. DP.

M175 Letters Sent by the Secretary of the Treasury to Collectors of Customs at All Ports, 1789-1847, and at Small Ports, 1847-1878 ("G" Series). 43 rolls. DP.

T1257 Letters Sent by the Secretary of the Treasury to the Collectors of Customs at Baltimore, Boston, New Orleans, and Philadelphia ("I" Series), 1847-1878. 19 rolls.

T1258 Letters Sent by the Secretary of the Treasury to the Collectors of Customs at New York, ("H" Series), 1847-1878. 30 rolls.

M176 Letters Sent by the Secretary of the Treasury to Collectors of Customs at Pacific Ports ("J" Series), 1850-1878. 10 rolls. DP.

M178 Correspondence of the Secretary of the Treasury With Collectors of Customs, 1789-1833. 39 rolls. DP.

M188 Letters Received by the Secretary of the Treasury From Collectors of Customs at Port Townsend, Washington, Relating to Nominations for Office, 1865-1910. 14 rolls. DP.

M415 Letters Sent to the President by the Secretary of the Treasury ("A" Series), 1833-1878. 1 roll.

M502 Registers of Letters Relating to Claims Received in the Office of the Secretary of the Treasury, 1864-1887. 2 rolls. DP.

M503 Letters Relating to Claims Received in the Office of the Secretary of the Treasury, 1864–1887. 91 rolls. DP.

M513 Letters Sent by the Secretary of the Treasury Relating to Restricted Commercial Intercourse ("BE" Series), 1861–1887. 8 rolls. DP.

T712 Treasury Department Papers Relating to the Louisiana Purchase. 1 roll.

M726 Letters Received by the Secretary of the Treasury Relating to Public Lands ("N" Series), 1831–1849. 23 rolls. DP.

M733 Letters Sent by the Secretary of the Treasury Relating to Public Lands ("N" Series), 1801–1878. 4 rolls. DP.

M735 Circular Letters of the Secretary of the Treasury ("T" Series), 1789–1878. 5 rolls. DP.

M736 Letters Received by the Secretary of the Treasury Relating to the Subtreasury System ("U" Series), 1846–1860. 23 rolls. DP.

M737 Letters Sent by the Secretary of the Treasury Relating to the Subtreasury System ("U" Series), 1840–1878. 7 rolls. DP.

M738 Telegrams Sent by the Secretary of the Treasury ("XA" Series), 1850–1874. 3 rolls. DP.

M741 Miscellaneous Letters Sent by the Secretary of the Treasury, 1870–1887, and by the Assistant Secretary, 1876–1893. 4 rolls. DP.

M749 Correspondence of the Secretary of the Treasury Relating to the Administration of Trust Funds for the Chickasaw and Other Tribes ("S" Series), 1834–1872. 1 roll. DP.

*T1256 Estimates and Statements of the Office of the Register of the Department of the Treasury, 1789–1858. 1 roll.

RG 57 Records of the U.S. Geological Survey

M152 Letters Sent by the U.S. Geological Survey, 1879–1895. 29 rolls. DP.

M156 Letters Received by John Wesley Powell, Director of the Geographical and Geological Survey of the Rocky Mountain Region, 1869–1879. 10 rolls. DP.

M157 Registers of Letters Received by the U.S. Geological Survey, 1879–1901. 16 rolls. DP.

M590 Letters Received by the U.S. Geological Survey, 1879–1901. 118 rolls. DP.

M622 Records of the Geological Exploration of the Fortieth Parallel ("King Survey"), 1867–1881. 3 rolls. DP.

M623 Records of the Geological and Geographical Survey of the Territories ("Hayden Survey"), 1867–1879. 21 rolls. DP.

T282 Geological Survey and Marine Corps Surveys and Maps of the Dominican Republic, 1919–1923. 6 rolls.

RG 58 Records of the Internal Revenue Service

Internal Revenue Assessment Lists

M754 Internal Revenue Assessment Lists for Alabama, 1865–1866. 6 rolls. DP.

M755 Internal Revenue Assessment Lists for Arkansas, 1865–1866. 2 rolls. DP.

T1208 Internal Revenue Assessment Lists for Arkansas, 1867–1874. 4 rolls.

M756 Internal Revenue Assessment Lists for California, 1862–1866. 33 rolls. DP.

M757 Internal Revenue Assessment Lists for the Territory of Colorado, 1862–1866. 3 rolls. DP.

M758 Internal Revenue Assessment Lists for Connecticut, 1862–1866. 23 rolls. DP.

M759 Internal Revenue Assessment Lists for Delaware, 1862–1866. 8 rolls. DP.

M760 Internal Revenue Assessment Lists for the District of Columbia, 1862–1866. 8 rolls. DP.

M761 Internal Revenue Assessment Lists for Florida, 1865–1866. 1 roll. DP.

M762 Internal Revenue Assessment Lists for Georgia, 1865–1866. 8 rolls. DP.

M763 Internal Revenue Assessment Lists for the Territory of Idaho, 1865–1866. 1 roll. DP.

T1209 Internal Revenue Assessment Lists for the Territory of Idaho, 1867–1874. 1 roll.

M764 Internal Revenue Assessment Lists for Illinois, 1862–1866. 63 rolls. DP.

M765 Internal Revenue Assessment Lists for Indiana, 1862–1866. 42 rolls. DP.

M766 Internal Revenue Assessment Lists for Iowa, 1862–1866. 16 rolls. DP.

M767 Internal Revenue Assessment Lists for Kansas, 1862–1866. 3 rolls. DP.

M768 Internal Revenue Assessment Lists for Kentucky, 1862–1866. 24 rolls. DP.

M769 Internal Revenue Assessment Lists for Louisiana, 1863–1866. 10 rolls. DP.

M770 Internal Revenue Assessment Lists for Maine, 1862–1866. 15 rolls. DP.

M771 Internal Revenue Assessment Lists for Maryland, 1862–1866. 21 rolls. DP.

M773 Internal Revenue Assessment Lists for Michigan, 1862–1866. 15 rolls. DP.

M774 Internal Revenue Assessment Lists for Minnesota, 1862–1866. 3 rolls. DP.

M775 Internal Revenue Assessment Lists for Mississippi, 1865–1866. 3 rolls. DP.

M776 Internal Revenue Assessment Lists for Missouri, 1862–1865. 22 rolls. DP.

M777 Internal Revenue Assessment Lists for Montana, 1864–1872. 1 roll. DP.

M779 Internal Revenue Assessment Lists for Nevada, 1863–1866. 2 rolls. DP.

M780 Internal Revenue Assessment Lists for New Hampshire, 1862–1866. 10 rolls. DP.

M782 Internal Revenue Assessment Lists for the Territory of New Mexico, 1862–1870, 1872–1874. 1 roll. DP.

M603 Internal Revenue Assessment Lists for New York and New Jersey, 1862–1866. 218 rolls.

M784 Internal Revenue Assessment Lists for North Carolina, 1864–1866. 2 rolls. DP.

M1631 Internal Revenue Assessment Lists, Oregon District, 1867–1873. 2 rolls.

M787 Internal Revenue Assessment Lists for Pennsylvania, 1862–1866. 107 rolls. DP.

M788 Internal Revenue Assessment Lists for Rhode Island, 1862–1866. 10 rolls. DP.

M789 Internal Revenue Assessment Lists for South Carolina, 1864–1866. 2 rolls. DP.

M791 Internal Revenue Assessment Lists for Texas, 1865–1866. 2 rolls. DP.

M792 Internal Revenue Assessment Lists for Vermont, 1862–1866. 7 rolls. DP.

M793 Internal Revenue Assessment Lists for Virginia, 1862–1866. 6 rolls. DP.

M795 Internal Revenue Assessment Lists for West Virginia, 1862–1866. 4 rolls. DP.

Other Records

M372 U.S. Direct Tax of 1798: Tax Lists for the State of Pennsylvania. 24 rolls. DP.

M414 Letters Sent by the Commissioner of the Revenue and the Revenue Office, 1792–1807. 3 rolls. DP.

M667 Corporation Assessment Lists, 1909–1915. 82 rolls. DP.

RG 59 General Records of the Department of State

Diplomatic and Consular Instructions

M61 Foreign Letters of the Continental Congress and the Department of State, 1785–1790. 1 roll. DP.

M28 Diplomatic and Consular Instructions of the Department of State, 1791–1801. 5 rolls. DP.

M77 Diplomatic Instructions of the Department of State, 1801–1906. 175 rolls. DP.

M78 Consular Instructions of the Department of State, 1801–1834. 7 rolls.

Diplomatic Despatches

M69 Despatches From U.S. Ministers to Argentina, 1817–1906. 40 rolls. DP.

T157 Despatches From U.S. Ministers to Austria, 1838–1906. 51 rolls.

M193 Despatches From U.S. Ministers to Belgium, 1832–1906. 37 rolls.

T51 Despatches From U.S. Ministers to Bolivia, 1848–1906. 22 rolls.

M121 Despatches From U.S. Ministers to Brazil, 1809–1906. 74 rolls. DP.

M219 Despatches From U.S. Ministers to Central America, 1824–1906. 93 rolls.

M10 Despatches From U.S. Ministers to Chile, 1823–1906. 52 rolls.

M92 Despatches From U.S. Ministers to China, 1843–1906. 131 rolls. DP.

T33 Despatches From U.S. Ministers to Colombia, 1820–1906. 64 rolls.

T158 Despatches From U.S. Ministers to Cuba, 1902–1906. 18 rolls.

M41 Despatches From U.S. Ministers to Denmark, 1811–1906. 28 rolls.

M93 Despatches From U.S. Ministers to the Dominican Republic, 1883–1906. 15 rolls.

T50 Despatches From U.S. Ministers to Ecuador, 1848–1906. 19 rolls.

M34 Despatches From U.S. Ministers to France, 1789–1906. 128 rolls.

M44 Despatches From U.S. Ministers to the German States and Germany, 1799–1801, 1835–1906. 107 rolls. DP.

M30 Despatches From U.S. Ministers to Great Britain, 1791–1906. 200 rolls. DP.

T159 Despatches From U.S. Ministers to Greece, 1868–1906. 18 rolls.

M82 Despatches From U.S. Ministers to Haiti, 1862–1906. 47 rolls.

T30 Despatches From U.S. Ministers to Hawaii, 1843–1900. 34 rolls.

M90 Despatches From U.S. Ministers to the Italian States, 1832–1906. 44 rolls.

M133 Despatches From U.S. Ministers to Japan, 1855–1906. 82 rolls. DP.

M134 Despatches From U.S. Ministers to Korea, 1883–1905. 22 rolls. DP.

M170 Despatches From U.S. Ministers to Liberia, 1863–1906. 14 rolls.

M97 Despatches From U.S. Ministers to Mexico, 1823–1906. 179 rolls. DP.

T525 Despatches From U.S. Ministers to Montenegro, March 12, 1905–June 14, 1906. 1 roll.

T725 Despatches From U.S. Ministers to Morocco, 1905–1906. 1 roll.

M42 Despatches From U.S. Ministers to The Netherlands, 1794–1906. 46 rolls.

T726 Despatches From U.S. Ministers to Panama, 1903–1906. 5 rolls.

M128 Despatches From U.S. Ministers to Paraguay and Uruguay, 1858–1906. 19 rolls.

M223 Despatches From U.S. Ministers to Persia, 1883–1906. 11 rolls. DP.

T52 Despatches From U.S. Ministers to Peru, 1826–1906. 66 rolls.

M43 Despatches From U.S. Ministers to Portugal, 1790–1906. 41 rolls.

T727 Despatches From U.S. Ministers to Rumania, 1880–1906. 5 rolls.

M35 Despatches From U.S. Ministers to Russia, 1808–1906. 66 rolls.

T630 Despatches From U.S. Ministers to Serbia, July 5, 1900–July 31, 1906. 1 roll.

M172 Despatches From U.S. Ministers to Siam, 1882–1906. 9 rolls. DP.

M31 Despatches From U.S. Ministers to Spain, 1792–1906. 134 rolls. DP.

M45 Despatches From U.S. Ministers to Sweden and Norway, 1813–1906. 28 rolls.

T98 Despatches From U.S. Ministers to Switzerland, 1853–1906. 35 rolls.

T728 Despatches From U.S. Ministers to Texas, 1836–1845. 2 rolls.

M46 Despatches From U.S. Ministers to Turkey, 1818–1906. 77 rolls.

M79 Despatches From U.S. Ministers to Venezuela, 1835–1906. 60 rolls.

Consular Despatches

T502 Despatches From U.S. Consuls in Aarau, Switzerland, 1898–1902. 1 roll.

M143 Despatches From U.S. Consuls in Acapulco, Mexico, 1823–1906. 8 rolls. DP.

T503 Despatches From U.S. Consuls in Aden, Aden, 1880–1906. 3 rolls.

M285 Despatches From U.S. Consuls in Aguascalientes, Mexico, 1901–1906. 1 roll. DP.

T356 Despatches From U.S. Consuls in Aix-la-Chapelle, Germany, 1849–1906. 11 rolls.

T188 Despatches From U.S. Consuls in Aleppo, Syria, 1835–1840. 1 roll.

T504 Despatches From U.S. Consuls in Alexandretta, Turkey, 1896-1906. 1 roll.

T45 Despatches From U.S. Consuls in Alexandria, Egypt, 1835-1873. 7 rolls.

M23 Despatches From U.S. Consuls in Algiers, Algeria, 1785-1906. 19 rolls.

T357 Despatches From U.S. Consuls in Alicante, Spain, 1788-1905. 3 rolls.

T358 Despatches From U.S. Consuls in Altona, Germany, 1838-1869. 5 rolls.

T589 Despatches From U.S. Consuls in Amapala, Honduras, 1873-1886. *See also* Tegucigalpa, Honduras, 1871-1894 (Rolls 1-4). 1 roll.

T590 Despatches From U.S. Consuls in Amherstburg, Canada, 1882-1906. 2 rolls.

T111 Despatches From U.S. Consuls in Amoor River, Russia, 1856-1874. 2 rolls.

M100 Despatches From U.S. Consuls in Amoy, China, 1844-1906. 15 rolls.

M446 Despatches From U.S. Consuls in Amsterdam, The Netherlands, 1790-1906. 7 rolls. DP.

T359 Despatches From U.S. Consuls in Ancona, Italy, 1840-1874. 2 rolls.

T592 Despatches From U.S. Consuls in Annaberg, Germany, 1882-1906. 3 rolls.

T327 Despatches From U.S. Consuls in Antigua, Leeward Islands, British West Indies, 1794-1906. 9 rolls.

T505 Despatches From U.S. Consuls in Antofagasta, Chile, 1893-1906. 1 roll.

M447 Despatches From U.S. Consuls in Antung, Manchuria, China, 1904-1906. 1 roll. DP.

T181 Despatches From U.S. Consuls in Antwerp, Belgium, 1802-1906. 14 rolls.

T27 Despatches From U.S. Consuls in Apia, Samoa, 1843-1906. 27 rolls.

M481 Despatches From U.S. Consuls in Archangel, Russia, 1833-1861. 1 roll. DP.

T328 Despatches From U.S. Consuls in Arica, Chile, 1849-1906. 2 rolls.

T329 Despatches From U.S. Consuls in Asuncion, Paraguay, 1844-1906. 6 rolls.

T362 Despatches From U.S. Consuls in Athens, Greece, 1837-1906. 8 rolls.

T361 Despatches From U.S. Consuls in Augsburg, Germany, 1846-1873. *See also* Munich, Germany. 1 roll.

T330 Despatches From U.S. Consuls in Aux Cayes, Haiti, 1797-1874. 4 rolls.

T509 Despatches From U.S. Consuls in Baghdad, Iraq, 1888-1906. 2 rolls.

T331 Despatches From U.S. Consuls in Bahia, Brazil, 1850-1906. *See also* Sao Salvador, Brazil, for earlier despatches. 8 rolls.

T510 Despatches From U.S. Consuls in Bamberg, Germany, 1892-1906. *See also* Munich, Germany, 1842-1845. 1 roll.

M448 Despatches From U.S. Consuls in Bangkok, Siam, 1856-1906. 6 rolls. DP.

T511 Despatches From U.S. Consuls in Baracoa, Cuba, 1827-1846, 1878-1899. 3 rolls.

T333 Despatches From U.S. Consuls in Barbados, British West Indies, 1823-1906. 17 rolls.

T121 Despatches From U.S. Consuls in Barcelona, Spain, 1797-1906. 15 rolls.

T363 Despatches From U.S. Consuls in Barmen, Germany, 1868-1906. 6 rolls.

T512 Despatches From U.S. Consuls in Barranquilla, Colombia, 1883-1906. *See also* Sabanilla, Colombia, for earlier despatches. 6 rolls.

T364 Despatches From U.S. Consuls in Basle, Switzerland, 1830-1906. 9 rolls.

M449 Despatches From U.S. Consuls in Batavia, Java, Netherlands East Indies, 1818-1906. 6 rolls. DP.

T365 Despatches From U.S. Consuls in Bathurst, Gambia, British Africa, 1857-1889. 2 rolls.

M482 Despatches From U.S. Consuls in Batum, Russia, 1890-1906. 1 roll. DP.

T49 Despatches From U.S. Consuls in Bay of Islands and Auckland, New Zealand, 1839-1906. 13 rolls.

T366 Despatches From U.S. Consuls in Bayonne, France, 1835-1865. 1 roll.

T367 Despatches From U.S. Consuls in Beirut, Lebanon, 1836-1906. 23 rolls.

T368 Despatches From U.S. Consuls in Belfast, Ireland, 1796-1906. 11 rolls.

T513 Despatches From U.S. Consuls in Belgrade, Serbia, 1883-1906. 1 roll.

T334 Despatches From U.S. Consuls in Belize, British Honduras, 1847-1906. 8 rolls.

T514 Despatches From U.S. Consuls in Belleville, Canada, 1878-1906. 2 rolls.

T369 Despatches From U.S. Consuls in Bergen, Norway, 1821-1906. 4 rolls.

T163 Despatches From U.S. Consuls in Berlin, Germany, 1865-1906. 27 rolls.

T262 Despatches From U.S. Consuls in Bermuda, British West Indies, 1818-1906. 11 rolls.

T528 Despatches From U.S. Consuls in Bern, Switzerland, 1882-1906. 3 rolls.

T183 Despatches From U.S. Consuls in Bilbao, Spain, 1791-1875. 1 roll.

T247 Despatches From U.S. Consuls in Birmingham, England, 1869-1906. 6 rolls.

T116 Despatches From U.S. Consuls in Bogota, Colombia, 1851-1906. 4 rolls.

T47 Despatches From U.S. Consuls in Boma, Congo, 1888-1895. 1 roll.

M168 Despatches From U.S. Consuls in Bombay, India, 1838-1906. 8 rolls. DP.

T164 Despatches From U.S. Consuls in Bordeaux, France, 1783-1906. 13 rolls.

T413 Despatches From U.S. Consuls in Boulogne, France, 1866-1874. 1 roll.

T165 Despatches From U.S. Consuls in Bradford, England, 1865-1906. 8 rolls.

T184 Despatches From U.S. Consuls in Bremen, Germany, 1794-1906. 21 rolls.

T532 Despatches From U.S. Consuls in Breslau, Germany, 1878-1906. 3 rolls.

T370 Despatches From U.S. Consuls in Brindisi, Italy, 1864-1876. 1 roll.

T185 Despatches From U.S. Consuls in Bristol, England, 1792-1906. 16 rolls.

T530 Despatches From U.S. Consuls in Brockville, Canada, 1885-1906. 1 roll.

T110 Despatches From U.S. Consuls in Brunei, Borneo, 1862-1868. 1 roll.

T371 Despatches From U.S. Consuls in Brunswick, Germany, 1858-1906. 6 rolls.

T711 Despatches From U.S. Consuls in Brusa (Brousa), Turkey, 1837–1840. 1 roll.

T166 Despatches From U.S. Consuls in Brussels, Belgium, 1863–1906. 4 rolls.

T285 Despatches From U.S. Consuls in Bucharest, Romania, 1866–1885, 1892–1906. 3 rolls.

T531 Despatches From U.S. Consuls in Budapest, Hungary, 1876–1906. 4 rolls.

M140 Despatches From U.S. Consuls in Buenaventura, Colombia, 1867–1885. 1 roll.

M70 Despatches From U.S. Consuls in Buenos Aires, Argentina, 1811–1906. 25 rolls.

T533 Despatches From U.S. Consuls in Burslem, England, 1905–1906. 1 roll.

T89 Despatches From U.S. Consuls in Butaritari, Gilbert Islands, 1888–1892. 1 roll.

T186 Despatches From U.S. Consuls in Cadiz, Spain, 1791–1904. 20 rolls.

T187 Despatches From U.S. Consuls in Cagliari, Italy, 1802–1825. 1 roll.

T41 Despatches From U.S. Consuls in Cairo, Egypt, 1864–1906. 24 rolls.

T373 Despatches From U.S. Consuls in Calais, France, 1804–1906. 1 roll.

M450 Despatches From U.S. Consuls in Calcutta, India, 1792–1906. 7 rolls. DP.

M155 Despatches From U.S. Consuls in Callao, Peru, 1854–1906. 17 rolls. DP.

M288 Despatches From U.S. Consuls in Camargo, Mexico, 1870–1880. 1 roll. DP.

T535 Despatches From U.S. Consuls in Campbellton, Canada, 1897–1906. 1 roll.

M286 Despatches From U.S. Consuls in Campeche, Mexico, 1820–1880. 1 roll. DP.

T374 Despatches From U.S. Consuls in Candia, Crete, 1836–1841. 1 roll.

T190 Despatches From U.S. Consuls in Canea, Crete, 1832–1874. *See also* Cyprus. 2 rolls.

T537 Despatches From U.S. Consuls in Cannes, France, 1891. 1 roll.

M101 Despatches From U.S. Consuls in Canton, China, 1790–1906. 20 rolls. DP.

M9 Despatches From U.S. Consuls in Cap Haitien, Haiti, 1797–1906. 17 rolls.

T538 Despatches From U.S. Consuls in Cape Gracias a Dios, Nicaragua, 1903–1906. 1 roll.

T191 Despatches From U.S. Consuls in Cape Town, Cape Colony, 1800–1906. 22 rolls.

T599 Despatches From U.S. Consuls in Caracas, Venezuela, 1868–1885. 1 roll.

T583 Despatches From U.S. Consuls in Cardenas, Cuba, 1843–1845, 1879–1898. 5 rolls.

T375 Despatches From U.S. Consuls in Cardiff, Wales, 1861–1906. 6 rolls.

T639 Despatches From U.S. Consuls in Carlisle, England, 1867–1869. 1 roll.

T540 Despatches From U.S. Consuls in Carlsbad, Czechoslovakia, 1902–1906. 1 roll.

T541 Despatches From U.S. Consuls in Carlsruhe, Germany, 1854–1874. *See also* Mannheim, Germany, for later despatches. 3 rolls.

T376 Despatches From U.S. Consuls in Carrara, Italy, 1852–1881. 1 roll.

T192 Despatches From U.S. Consuls in Cartagena, Colombia, 1822–1906. 14 rolls.

T377 Despatches From U.S. Consuls in Cartagena, Spain, 1863–1906. 1 roll.

T543 Despatches From U.S. Consuls in Castellammare di Stabia, Italy, 1878–1906. 3 rolls.

T544 Despatches From U.S. Consuls in Catania, Italy, 1883–1906. 4 rolls.

T378 Despatches From U.S. Consuls in Cayenne, French Guiana, 1801–1897. 1 roll.

T545 Despatches From U.S. Consuls in Ceiba, Honduras, 1902–1906. *See also* Tegucigalpa, Honduras, for earlier despatches. 1 roll.

T379 Despatches From U.S. Consuls in Cette, France, 1802–1840. 1 roll.

T462 Despatches From U.S. Consuls in Charlottetown, Canada, 1857–1906. *See also* Pictou, Canada. 5 rolls.

T546 Despatches From U.S. Consuls in Chatham, Canada, 1879–1906. 3 rolls.

T547 Despatches From U.S. Consuls in Chaudiere Junction, Canada, 1898–1905. 1 roll.

M102 Despatches From U.S. Consuls in Chefoo, China, 1863–1906. 9 rolls. DP.

T380 Despatches From U.S. Consuls in Chemnitz, Germany, 1867–1906. 8 rolls.

M289 Despatches From U.S. Consuls in Chihuahua, Mexico, 1830–1906. 3 rolls. DP.

M103 Despatches From U.S. Consuls in Chinkiang, China, 1864–1902. *See also* Nanking, China, for later despatches. 7 rolls.

T669 Despatches From U.S. Consuls in Chios, Greece, 1862–1871. 1 roll.

T122 Despatches From U.S. Consuls in Christiania, Norway, 1869–1906. 5 rolls.

T235 Despatches From U.S. Consuls in Christiansand, Norway, 1810–1891. 1 roll.

M104 Despatches From U.S. Consuls in Chungking, China, 1896–1906. 1 roll.

T548 Despatches From U.S. Consuls in Cienfuegos, Cuba, 1876–1906. *See also* Trinidad, Cuba, for earlier despatches. 8 rolls.

T335 Despatches From U.S. Consuls in Ciudad Bolivar, Venezuela, 1850–1893. 3 rolls.

M308 Despatches From U.S. Consuls in Ciudad del Carmen, Mexico, 1830–1872. 1 roll. DP.

M184 Despatches From U.S. Consuls in Ciudad Juarez (Paso del Norte), Mexico, 1850–1906. 6 rolls.

T549 Despatches From U.S. Consuls in Clifton, Canada, 1864–1906. 7 rolls.

T550 Despatches From U.S. Consuls in Coaticook, Canada, 1864–1906. 4 rolls.

T381 Despatches From U.S. Consuls in Cobija, Bolivia, 1854–1874. 1 roll.

T551 Despatches From U.S. Consuls in Coburg, Germany, 1898–1906. 2 rolls.

T552 Despatches From U.S. Consuls in Cognac, France, 1883–1898. *See also* La Rochelle, France. 2 rolls.

T553 Despatches From U.S. Consuls in Collingwood, Canada, 1879–1906. 3 rolls.

T555 Despatches From U.S. Consuls in Cologne, Germany, 1876-1906. 5 rolls.

M451 Despatches From U.S. Consuls in Colombo, Ceylon, 1850-1906. 4 rolls. DP.

T193 Despatches From U.S. Consuls in Colon, Panama, 1852-1906. 19 rolls.

T556 Despatches From U.S. Consuls in Colonia, Uruguay, 1870-1906. 1 roll.

T194 Despatches From U.S. Consuls in Constantinople, Turkey, 1820-1906. 24 rolls.

T195 Despatches From U.S. Consuls in Copenhagen, Denmark, 1792-1906. 11 rolls.

T332 Despatches From U.S. Consuls in Coquimbo, Chile, 1850-1898. *See also* Valparaiso, Chile, for later despatches. 1 roll.

T557 Despatches From U.S. Consuls in Cordoba, Argentina, 1870-1906. 1 roll.

T196 Despatches From U.S. Consuls in Cork, Ireland, 1800-1906. 12 rolls.

T558 Despatches From U.S. Consuls in Cornwall, Canada, 1901-1906. *See also* Morrisburg, Canada, for earlier despatches. 2 rolls.

T450 Despatches From U.S. Consuls in Corunna, Spain, 1867-1906. 2 rolls.

T559 Despatches From U.S. Consuls in Crefeld, Germany, 1878-1906. 5 rolls.

T197 Despatches From U.S. Consuls in Curacao, Netherlands West Indies, 1793-1906. 13 rolls.

T463 Despatches From U.S. Consuls in Cyprus, 1835-1878. 2 rolls.

T560 Despatches From U.S. Consuls in Dawson City, Canada, 1898-1906. 4 rolls.

T382 Despatches From U.S. Consuls in Denia, Spain, 1852-1898. 2 rolls.

T383 Despatches From U.S. Consuls in Dresden, Germany, 1837-1906. 6 rolls.

T199 Despatches From U.S. Consuls in Dublin, Ireland, 1790-1906. 11 rolls.

T200 Despatches From U.S. Consuls in Dundee, Scotland, 1834-1906. 8 rolls.

T561 Despatches From U.S. Consuls in Dunfermline, Scotland, 1877-1906. 3 rolls.

M290 Despatches From U.S. Consuls in Durango, Mexico, 1886-1906. 1 roll. DP.

T562 Despatches From U.S. Consuls in Dusseldorf, Germany, 1881-1906. 3 rolls.

T602 Despatches From U.S. Consuls in Edinburgh, Scotland, 1893-1906. *See also* Leith, Scotland, for earlier despatches. 1 roll.

T565 Despatches From U.S. Consuls in Eibenstock, Germany, 1902-1906. 1 roll.

T566 Despatches From U.S. Consuls in Elberfeld, Lubeck, and Rostock, Germany, 1804-1849, 1883-1889. 1 roll.

T201 Despatches From U.S. Consuls in Elsinore, Denmark, 1792-1874. 6 rolls.

M291 Despatches From U.S. Consuls in Ensenada, Mexico, 1888-1906. 1 roll. DP.

T563 Despatches From U.S. Consuls in Erfurt, Germany, 1892-1894. 1 roll.

T568 Despatches From U.S. Consuls in Erzerum, Turkey, 1895-1904. 2 rolls.

T202 Despatches From U.S. Consuls in Falmouth, British West Indies, 1790-1905. 12 rolls.

T203 Despatches From U.S. Consuls in Fayal, Azores, Portugal, 1795-1897. *See also* St. Michael Island, Azores. 11 rolls.

T204 Despatches From U.S. Consuls in Florence, Italy, 1824-1906. 10 rolls.

M105 Despatches From U.S. Consuls in Foochow, China, 1849-1906. 10 rolls. DP.

T465 Despatches From U.S. Consuls in Fort Erie, Canada, 1865-1906. 3 rolls.

M161 Despatches From U.S. Consuls in Frankfort on the Main, Germany, 1829-1906. 30 rolls.

T569 Despatches From U.S. Consuls in Freiburg, Germany, 1892-1906. 2 rolls.

T205 Despatches From U.S. Consuls in Funchal, Madeira, Portugal, 1793-1906. 9 rolls.

T689 Despatches From U.S. Consuls in Furth, Germany, 1890-1898. *See also* Solingen, Germany, for later despatches. 1 roll.

T466 Despatches From U.S. Consuls in Gaboon, 1856-1888. 1 roll.

T384 Despatches From U.S. Consuls in Galatz, Romania, 1858-1869. *See also* Bucharest, Romania. 1 roll.

T151 Despatches From U.S. Consuls in Galveston, Texas, 1832-1846. *See also* Texas. 2 rolls.

T570 Despatches From U.S. Consuls in Galway, Ireland, 1834-1863. 1 roll.

T571 Despatches From U.S. Consuls in Garrucha, Spain, 1877-1897. 1 roll.

T467 Despatches From U.S. Consuls in Gaspe Basin, Canada, 1856-1906. 6 rolls.

T385 Despatches From U.S. Consuls in Geestemunde, Germany, 1867-1882. *See also* Hanover, Germany. 1 roll.

T387 Despatches From U.S. Consuls in Geneva, Switzerland, 1855-1906. 6 rolls.

T64 Despatches From U.S. Consuls in Genoa, Italy, 1799-1906. 13 rolls.

T336 Despatches From U.S. Consuls in Georgetown, Demerara, British Guiana, 1827-1906. 23 rolls.

T388 Despatches From U.S. Consuls in Ghent, Belgium, 1860-1906. 6 rolls.

T206 Despatches From U.S. Consuls in Gibraltar, Spain, 1791-1906. 17 rolls.

T207 Despatches From U.S. Consuls in Glasgow, Scotland, 1801-1906. 12 rolls.

T572 Despatches From U.S. Consuls in Glauchau, Germany, 1891-1906. 2 rolls.

T539 Despatches From U.S. Consuls in Gloucester, England, 1879-1886. 1 roll.

T468 Despatches From U.S. Consuls in Goderich, Canada, 1865-1906. 4 rolls.

T573 Despatches From U.S. Consuls in Goree Dakar, French Africa, 1883-1906. 2 rolls.

T276 Despatches From U.S. Consuls in Gothenburg, Sweden, 1800-1906. 4 rolls.

M171 Despatches From U.S. Consuls in Grand Bassa, Liberia, 1868-1882. 1 roll.

T574 Despatches From U.S. Consuls in Grenoble, France, 1893-1906. 1 roll.

T575 Despatches From U.S. Consuls in Grenville, Canada, 1904-1906. 1 roll.

T208 Despatches From U.S. Consuls in Guadeloupe, French West Indies, 1802-1906. 8 rolls.

M1306 Despatches From U.S. Consuls in Guam, 1854–1856. 1 roll.

T337 Despatches From U.S. Consuls in Guatemala City, Guatemala, 1824–1906. 15 rolls.

T209 Despatches From U.S. Consuls in Guayaquil, Ecuador, 1826–1906. 13 rolls.

M284 Despatches From U.S. Consuls in Guaymas, Mexico, 1832–1896. 5 rolls. DP.

T578 Despatches From U.S. Consuls in Guelph, Canada, 1883–1906. 2 rolls.

M292 Despatches From U.S. Consuls in Guerrero, Mexico, 1871–1888. 1 roll. DP.

M452 Despatches From U.S. Consuls in Hakodate, Japan, 1856–1878. *See also* Kanagawa, Japan. 1 roll. DP.

T469 Despatches From U.S. Consuls in Halifax, Canada, 1833–1906. 18 rolls.

T211 Despatches From U.S. Consuls in Hamburg, Germany, 1790–1906. 35 rolls.

T470 Despatches From U.S. Consuls in Hamilton, Canada, 1867–1906. *See also* Montreal, Canada. 8 rolls.

M106 Despatches From U.S. Consuls in Hangchow, China, 1904–1906. 1 roll.

M107 Despatches From U.S. Consuls in Hankow, China, 1861–1906. 8 rolls. DP.

T372 Despatches From U.S. Consuls in Hanover, Germany, 1854–1867, 1893–1906. 2 rolls.

T579 Despatches From U.S. Consuls in Harput, Turkey, 1895–1906. 1 roll.

M899 Despatches From U.S. Consuls in Havana, Cuba, 1783–1906. 133 rolls.

T212 Despatches From U.S. Consuls in Havre, France, 1789–1906. 21 rolls.

M483 Despatches From U.S. Consuls in Helsingfors, Finland, 1851–1906. 1 roll. DP.

M293 Despatches From U.S. Consuls in Hermosillo, Mexico, 1905–1906. 1 roll. DP.

T213 Despatches From U.S. Consuls in Hesse-Cassel, Germany, 1835–1869. 3 rolls.

T390 Despatches From U.S. Consuls in Hesse-Darmstadt, Germany, 1854–1871. *See also* Mayence, Germany, for later despatches. 4 rolls.

T391 Despatches From U.S. Consuls in Hesse-Homburg, Germany, 1854–1866. 1 roll.

T133 Despatches From U.S. Consuls in Hilo, Hawaii, 1853–1872. *See also* Honolulu, Hawaii, for earlier despatches. 4 rolls.

T127 Despatches From U.S. Consuls in Hobart, Australia, 1842–1906. *See also* Sydney, Australia. 4 rolls.

M108 Despatches From U.S. Consuls in Hong Kong, 1844–1906. 21 rolls. DP.

M144 Despatches From U.S. Consuls in Honolulu, Hawaii, 1820–1903. 22 rolls. DP.

T591 Despatches From U.S. Consuls in Horgen, Switzerland, 1882–1898. 3 rolls.

T593 Despatches From U.S. Consuls in Huddersfield, England, 1890–1906. 1 roll.

T594 Despatches From U.S. Consuls in Hull, United Kingdom, 1879–1906. *See also* Leeds-Upon-Hull, England, for earlier despatches. 4 rolls.

T109 Despatches From U.S. Consuls in Iloilo, Philippine Islands, 1878–1886. *See also* Manila, Philippine Islands, for later despatches. 1 roll.

T595 Despatches From U.S. Consuls in Iquique, Chile, 1877–1906. 5 rolls.

M294 Despatches From U.S. Consuls in Jalapa Enriquez, Mexico, 1905–1906. 1 roll. DP.

T596 Despatches From U.S. Consuls in Jerez de la Frontera, Spain, 1903–1906. 1 roll.

M453 Despatches From U.S. Consuls in Jerusalem, Palestine, 1856–1906. 5 rolls. DP.

M135 Despatches From U.S. Consuls in Kanagawa, Japan, 1861–1897. *See also* Yokohama, Japan, for later despatches. 22 rolls.

T597 Despatches From U.S. Consuls in Kehl, Germany, 1882–1906. 5 rolls.

T472 Despatches From U.S. Consuls in Kingston, Canada, 1864–1906. 5 rolls.

T31 Despatches From U.S. Consuls in Kingston, Jamaica, British West Indies, 1796–1906. 40 rolls.

T598 Despatches From U.S. Consuls in Konigsberg, East Prussia, Germany, 1879–1881. 1 roll.

M84 Despatches From U.S. Consuls in La Guaira, Venezuela, 1810–1906. 23 rolls.

T101 Despatches From U.S. Consuls in Lahaina, Hawaii, 1850–1871. *See also* Honolulu, Hawaii. 3 rolls.

T393 Despatches From U.S. Consuls in Lambayeque, Peru, 1860–1888. 3 rolls.

T338 Despatches From U.S. Consuls in La Paz, Bolivia, 1869–1901. 2 rolls.

M282 Despatches From U.S. Consuls in La Paz, Mexico, 1855–1906. 5 rolls. DP.

T394 Despatches From U.S. Consuls in La Rochelle, France, 1794–1906. *See also* Cognac, France. 8 rolls.

T25 Despatches From U.S. Consuls in Lauthala, Fiji Islands, 1844–1890. *See* Levuka, Fiji Islands, for later despatches. 7 rolls.

T395 Despatches From U.S. Consuls in La Union, El Salvador, 1854–1887. 1 roll.

T474 Despatches From U.S. Consuls in Leeds-Upon-Hull, England, 1797–1906. 14 rolls.

T214 Despatches From U.S. Consuls in Leghorn, Italy, 1793–1906. 10 rolls.

T215 Despatches From U.S. Consuls in Leipzig, Germany, 1826–1906. 12 rolls.

T396 Despatches From U.S. Consuls in Leith, Scotland, 1798–1893. *See also* Edinburgh, Scotland, for later despatches. 8 rolls.

T108 Despatches From U.S. Consuls in Levuka and Suva, Fiji Islands, 1891–1906. *See also* Lauthala, Fiji Islands, for earlier despatches. 1 roll.

T664 Despatches From U.S. Consuls in Liberec, Czechoslovakia, 1886–1906. 3 rolls.

T397 Despatches From U.S. Consuls in Liege, Belgium, 1863–1906. 6 rolls.

M154 Despatches From U.S. Consuls in Lima, Peru, 1823–1854. *See also* Callao, Peru, for later despatches. 6 rolls. DP.

T601 Despatches From U.S. Consuls in Limoges, France, 1887–1906. 4 rolls.

T603 Despatches From U.S. Consuls in Lindsay, Canada, 1891–1892. 1 roll.

T180 Despatches From U.S. Consuls in Lisbon, Portugal, 1791-1906. *See also* Fayal, Azores, and Oporto, Portugal. 11 rolls.

M141 Despatches From U.S. Consuls in Liverpool, England, 1790-1906. 55 rolls.

T168 Despatches From U.S. Consuls in London, England, 1790-1906. 64 rolls.

T604 Despatches From U.S. Consuls in London, Canada, 1885-1906. 2 rolls.

T216 Despatches From U.S. Consuls in Londonderry, Ireland, 1835-1876. 3 rolls.

T171 Despatches From U.S. Consuls in Lourenco Marques, Mozambique, Portuguese Africa, 1854-1906. 6 rolls.

T605 Despatches From U.S. Consuls in Lucerne, Switzerland, 1902-1906. 1 roll.

T585 Despatches From U.S. Consuls in Ludwigshafen, Germany, 1858-1874. *See also* Carlsruhe, Germany, for earlier despatches. 1 roll.

T607 Despatches From U.S. Consuls in Luxembourg, Luxembourg, 1893-1896. 1 roll.

T169 Despatches From U.S. Consuls in Lyon, France, 1829-1906. 14 rolls.

M109 Despatches From U.S. Consuls in Macao, China, 1849-1869. *See also* Canton, China. 2 rolls. DP.

T632 Despatches From U.S. Consuls in Madrid, Spain, 1882-1884, 1891-1906. 2 rolls.

T633 Despatches From U.S. Consuls in Magdeburg, Germany, 1890-1906. 2 rolls.

M454 Despatches From U.S. Consuls in Mahe, Seychelles Islands, Indian Ocean, 1868-1888. 1 roll. DP.

T217 Despatches From U.S. Consuls in Malaga, Spain, 1793-1906. 17 rolls.

Malagasy Republic. *See* Tamatave, Madagascar.

T218 Despatches From U.S. Consuls in Malta, 1801-1906. 13 rolls.

T634 Despatches From U.S. Consuls in Managua, Nicaragua, 1884-1906. 5 rolls.

T219 Despatches From U.S. Consuls in Manchester, England, 1847-1906. 7 rolls.

M455 Despatches From U.S. Consuls in Manila, Philippine Islands, 1817-1899. 6 rolls. DP.

T582 Despatches From U.S. Consuls in Mannheim, Germany, 1874-1906. *See also* Carlsruhe, Germany, for earlier despatches. 7 rolls.

T613 Despatches From U.S. Consuls in Manzanillo, Cuba, 1844-1846. 1 roll.

M295 Despatches From U.S. Consuls in Manzanillo, Mexico, 1855-1906. 2 rolls. DP.

T62 Despatches From U.S. Consuls in Maracaibo, Venezuela, 1824-1906. 20 rolls.

T398 Despatches From U.S. Consuls in Maranham (Maranhao), Brazil, 1817-1876. See also Para, Brazil. 3 rolls.

T220 Despatches From U.S. Consuls in Marseilles, France, 1790-1906. 20 rolls.

M281 Despatches From U.S. Consuls in Matamoras, Mexico, 1826-1906. *See also* Texas. 12 rolls. DP.

T339 Despatches From U.S. Consuls in Matanzas, Cuba, 1820-1899. 17 rolls.

T635 Despatches From U.S. Consuls in Mayence, Germany, 1871-1906. *See also* Hesse-Darmstadt, Germany, for earlier despatches. 7 rolls.

M159 Despatches From U.S. Consuls in Mazatlan, Mexico, 1826-1906. 7 rolls. DP.

T341 Despatches From U.S. Consuls in Medellin, Colombia, 1859-1902. 1 roll.

T102 Despatches From U.S. Consuls in Melbourne, Australia, 1852-1906. 16 rolls.

M287 Despatches From U.S. Consuls in Merida, 1843-1897, and Progreso, Mexico, 1897-1906. *See also* Santa Fe, New Mexico. 4 rolls. DP.

T399 Despatches From U.S. Consuls in Messina, Italy, 1822-1906. 7 rolls.

M296 Despatches From U.S. Consuls in Mexico City, Mexico, 1822-1906. 15 rolls. DP.

M297 Despatches From U.S. Consuls in Mier, Mexico, 1870-1878. 1 roll. DP.

T170 Despatches From U.S. Consuls in Milan, Italy, 1874-1906. 4 rolls.

M298 Despatches From U.S. Consuls in Minatitlan, Mexico, 1853-1881. 2 rolls. DP.

T636 Despatches From U.S. Consuls in Moncton, Canada, 1885-1905. 2 rolls.

M169 Despatches From U.S. Consuls in Monrovia, Liberia, 1852-1906. *See also* Despatches From U.S. Ministers to Liberia. 7 rolls. DP.

M138 Despatches From U.S. Consuls in Monterey, Upper California, 1834-1848. 1 roll.

M165 Despatches From U.S. Consuls in Monterrey, Mexico, 1849-1906. 7 rolls. DP.

M71 Despatches From U.S. Consuls in Montevideo, Uruguay, 1821-1906. 15 rolls.

T222 Despatches From U.S. Consuls in Montreal, Canada, 1850-1906. 22 rolls.

T637 Despatches From U.S. Consuls in Morrisburg, Canada, 1882-1901. *See also* Cornwall, Canada, for later despatches. 1 roll.

M456 Despatches From U.S. Consuls in Moscow, Russia, 1857-1906. 2 rolls. DP.

M457 Despatches From U.S. Consuls in Mukden, Manchuria, China, 1904-1906. 1 roll. DP.

T261 Despatches From U.S. Consuls in Munich, Germany, 1833-1906. 13 rolls.

T638 Despatches From U.S. Consuls in Muscat, Oman, 1880-1906. *See also* Zanzibar, British Africa. 2 rolls.

M131 Despatches From U.S. Consuls in Nagasaki, Japan, 1860-1906. 7 rolls.

M110 Despatches From U.S. Consuls in Nanking, China, 1902-1906. *See also* Chinkiang, China, for earlier despatches. 1 roll.

T223 Despatches From U.S. Consuls in Nantes, France, 1790-1906. 8 rolls.

T224 Despatches From U.S. Consuls in Naples, Italy, 1796-1906. 12 rolls.

T415 Despatches From U.S. Consuls in Napoleon-Vendee, France, 1800-1870. 1 roll.

T473 Despatches From U.S. Consuls in Duchy of Nassau, Germany, 1854-1869. 1 roll.

T475 Despatches From U.S. Consuls in Nassau, British West Indies, 1821–1906. 24 rolls.

T92 Despatches From U.S. Consuls in Newcastle, Australia, 1887–1906. 6 rolls.

T416 Despatches From U.S. Consuls in Newcastle upon Tyne, England, 1854–1906. 10 rolls.

M115 Despatches From U.S. Consuls in Newchwang, Manchuria, China, 1865–1906. 7 rolls. DP.

T225 Despatches From U.S. Consuls in New Orleans, Louisiana, 1798–1807. 1 roll.

T417 Despatches From U.S. Consuls in Nice, France, 1819–1906. 7 rolls.

M111 Despatches From U.S. Consuls in Ningpo, China, 1853–1896. 7 rolls.

M283 Despatches From U.S. Consuls in Nogales, Mexico, 1889–1906. 4 rolls. DP.

T641 Despatches From U.S. Consuls in Nottingham, England, 1877–1906. 3 rolls.

T91 Despatches From U.S. Consuls in Noumea, New Caledonia, 1887–1905. 2 rolls.

M458 Despatches From U.S. Consuls in Novorossisk, Russia, 1883–1884. 1 roll. DP.

T418 Despatches From U.S. Consuls in Nuernberg, Germany, 1846–1906. 9 rolls.

T588 Despatches From U.S. Consuls in Nuevitas, Cuba, 1842–1847, 1892–1898. 1 roll.

M280 Despatches From U.S. Consuls in Nuevo Laredo, Mexico, 1871–1906. 4 rolls. DP.

M328 Despatches From U.S. Consuls in Oaxaca, Mexico, 1869–1878. 1 roll. DP.

M459 Despatches From U.S. Consuls in Odessa, Russia, 1831–1906. 7 rolls. DP.

T419 Despatches From U.S. Consuls in Oldenburg, Germany, 1856–1869. 2 rolls.

T477 Despatches From U.S. Consuls in Omoa, Trujillo, and Roatan, Honduras, 1831–1893. *See also* Utila, Honduras, for later despatches. 6 rolls.

T342 Despatches From U.S. Consuls in Oporto, Portugal, 1821–1877. 5 rolls.

T642 Despatches From U.S. Consuls in Orillia, Canada, 1893–1906. 1 roll.

M460 Despatches From U.S. Consuls in Osaka and Hiogo (Kobe), Japan, 1868–1906. 6 rolls. DP.

T542 Despatches From U.S. Consuls in Otranto, Italy, 1861–1867. 1 roll.

T643 Despatches From U.S. Consuls in Ottawa, Canada, 1877–1906. 12 rolls.

M461 Despatches From U.S. Consuls in Padang, Sumatra, Netherlands East Indies, 1853–1898. *See* Batavia, Java, Netherlands East Indies for later despatches. 1 roll. DP.

T600 Despatches From U.S. Consuls in Paita, Peru, 1833–1874. 3 rolls.

T420 Despatches From U.S. Consuls in Palermo, Italy, 1803–1906. 11 rolls.

T647 Despatches From U.S. Consuls in Palmerston, Canada, 1892–1900. 1 roll.

M139 Despatches From U.S. Consuls in Panama City, Panama, 1823–1906. 27 rolls.

T478 Despatches From U.S. Consuls in Para, Brazil, 1831–1906. *See also* Maranham, Brazil. 9 rolls.

T226 Despatches From U.S. Consuls in Paramaribo, Brazil, 1799–1897. 8 rolls.

T1 Despatches From U.S. Consuls in Paris, France, 1790–1906. 32 rolls.

T648 Despatches From U.S. Consuls in Patras, Greece, 1874–1906. 4 rolls.

T344 Despatches From U.S. Consuls in Pernambuco, Brazil, 1817–1906. 17 rolls.

T649 Despatches From U.S. Consuls in Peterborough, Canada, 1905–1906. 1 roll.

T104 Despatches From U.S. Consuls in Petropavlovsk, Russia, 1875–1878. 1 roll.

T479 Despatches From U.S. Consuls in Pictou, Canada, 1837–1897. *See also* Sydney, Canada, for later despatches. 6 rolls.

M299 Despatches From U.S. Consuls in Piedras Negras, Mexico, 1868–1906. 5 rolls. DP.

T534 Despatches From U.S. Consuls in Piraeus, Greece, 1864–1874. 3 rolls.

T536 Despatches From U.S. Consuls in Plauen, Germany, 1887–1906. 3 rolls.

T228 Despatches From U.S. Consuls in Plymouth, England, 1793–1906. 7 rolls.

T90 Despatches From U.S. Consuls in Ponape, Caroline Islands, 1890–1892. 1 roll.

T421 Despatches From U.S. Consuls in Porsgrunn, Norway, 1861–1869. 1 roll.

T650 Despatches From U.S. Consuls in Port Antonio, British West Indies, 1895–1906. 1 roll.

T346 Despatches From U.S. Consuls in Port-au-Prince, Haiti, 1835–1906. 10 rolls.

T651 Despatches From U.S. Consuls in Port Hope, Canada, 1882–1906. 2 rolls.

T656 Despatches From U.S. Consuls in Port Limon, Costa Rica, 1902–1906. 1 roll.

M462 Despatches From U.S. Consuls in Port Louis, Mauritius, Mascarene Islands, 1794–1805, 1817–1906. 8 rolls. DP.

T422 Despatches From U.S. Consuls in Port Mahon, Spain, 1803–1876. 4 rolls.

T567 Despatches From U.S. Consuls in Porto Principe and Xibara, Cuba, 1828–1843. 1 roll.

T657 Despatches From U.S. Consuls in Port Rowan, Canada, 1882–1906. 1 roll.

T658 Despatches From U.S. Consuls in Port Said, Egypt, 1870–1876. 1 roll.

T659 Despatches From U.S. Consuls in Port Stanley, Canada, and St. Thomas, Canada, 1878–1906. 4 rolls.

T480 Despatches From U.S. Consuls in Port Stanley, Falkland Islands, 1851–1906. 4 rolls.

T663 Despatches From U.S. Consuls in Prague, Czechoslovakia, 1869–1906. 4 rolls.

T481 Despatches From U.S. Consuls in Prescott, Canada, 1864–1906. 5 rolls.

T660 Despatches From U.S. Consuls in Pretoria, The Transvaal, 1898–1906. 3 rolls.

T229 Despatches From U.S. Consuls in Puerto Cabello, Venezuela, 1823–1906. 12 rolls.

T661 Despatches From U.S. Consuls in Puerto Cortes, Honduras, 1902–1906. *See also* Tegucigalpa, Honduras, for earlier despatches. 2 rolls.

T662 Despatches From U.S. Consuls in Puerto Plata, Dominican Republic, 1875-1906. 3 rolls.

M76 Despatches From U.S. Consular Representatives in Puerto Rico, 1821-1899. 31 rolls.

T482 Despatches From U.S. Consuls in Quebec, Canada, 1861-1906. *See also* Montreal, Canada. 7 rolls.

T23 Letters Received by the Department of State From the Agent for Red River Affairs, 1867-1870. *See also* Winnipeg, Canada, for related despatches. 1 roll.

M484 Despatches From U.S. Consuls in Reval, Estonia, 1859-1870. 1 roll. DP.

T424 Despatches From U.S. Consuls in Rheims, France, 1867-1906. 3 rolls.

M485 Despatches From U.S. Consuls in Riga, Latvia, 1811-1872, 1890-1906. *See also* St. Petersburg, Russia. 1 roll. DP.

T666 Despatches From U.S. Consuls in Rimouski, Canada, 1897-1906. 1 roll.

T172 Despatches From U.S. Consuls in Rio de Janeiro, Brazil, 1811-1906. 33 rolls.

T145 Despatches From U.S. Consuls in Rio Grande do Sul, Brazil, 1829-1897. 7 rolls.

T425 Despatches From U.S. Consuls in Rio Macha, Colombia, 1835-1883. 1 roll.

T231 Despatches From U.S. Consuls in Rome, Italy, 1801-1906. 20 rolls.

T343 Despatches From U.S. Consuls in Rosario, Argentina, 1858-1906. 3 rolls.

T232 Despatches From U.S. Consuls in Rotterdam, The Netherlands, 1802-1906. 13 rolls.

T667 Despatches From U.S. Consuls in Roubaix, France, 1890-1906. 2 rolls.

T668 Despatches From U.S. Consuls in Rouen, France, 1790, 1878-1906. 4 rolls.

T426 Despatches From U.S. Consuls in Sabanilla, Colombia, 1856-1884. *See also* Barranquilla, Colombia, for earlier despatches. 5 rolls.

T678 Despatches From U.S. Consuls in Sagua la Grande, Cuba, 1878-1900. 6 rolls.

T103 Despatches From U.S. Consuls in Saigon, Vietnam, 1889-1906. 1 roll.

M72 Despatches From U.S. Consuls in St. Bartholomew, French West Indies, 1799-1899. 3 rolls.

T234 Despatches From U.S. Consuls in St. Christopher, West Indies Federation, 1800-1906. 3 rolls.

T233 Despatches From U.S. Consuls in St. Croix, Virgin Islands, 1791-1876. *See also* St. Thomas, Virgin Islands. 8 rolls.

M463 Despatches From U.S. Consuls in St. Denis, Reunion Island, Mascarene Islands, Indian Ocean, 1880-1892. 1 roll. DP.

T672 Despatches From U.S. Consuls in St. Etienne, France, 1877-1906. 3 rolls.

T236 Despatches From U.S. Consuls in St. Eustatius, Netherlands West Indies, 1793-1838. 1 roll.

T673 Despatches From U.S. Consuls in St. Gall, Switzerland, 1878-1906. 6 rolls.

T173 Despatches From U.S. Consuls in St. George, British West Indies, 1878-1906. *See also* Bermuda, British West Indies. 1 roll.

T428 Despatches From U.S. Consuls in St. Helena, British West Africa, 1831-1906. 20 rolls.

T674 Despatches From U.S. Consuls in St. Hyacinthe, Canada, 1882-1906. 2 rolls.

T485 Despatches From U.S. Consuls in St. John, New Brunswick, Canada, 1835-1906. 10 rolls.

T129 Despatches From U.S. Consuls in St. John's, Newfoundland, Canada, 1852-1906. *See also* Pictou, Canada. 9 rolls.

T484 Despatches From U.S. Consuls in St. Johns, Quebec, Canada, 1864-1906. 3 rolls.

T486 Despatches From U.S. Consuls in St. Marc, Haiti, 1861-1891. 1 roll.

T429 Despatches From U.S. Consuls in St. Martin, Netherlands, West Indies. 3 rolls.

T675 Despatches From U.S. Consuls in St. Michael Island, Azores, 1897-1906. *See also* Fayal, Azores. 1 roll.

T430 Despatches From U.S. Consuls in St. Paul de Loanda, Portuguese Africa, 1854-1893. *See also* Valencia, Spain. 5 rolls.

M81 Despatches From U.S. Consuls in St. Petersburg, Russia, 1803-1906. 18 rolls. DP.

T431 Despatches From U.S. Consuls in St. Pierre, Martinique, French West Indies, 1790-1906. 11 rolls.

T487 Despatches From U.S. Consuls in St. Pierre and Miquelon, 1850-1906. 4 rolls.

T676 Despatches From U.S. Consuls in St. Stephen, Canada, 1882-1906. 2 rolls.

T350 Despatches From U.S. Consuls in St. Thomas, Virgin Islands, 1804-1906. 17 rolls.

T564 Despatches From U.S. Consuls in St. Ubes, Portugal, 1835-1842. 1 roll.

T414 Despatches From U.S. Consuls in Salonica, Greece, 1832-1840. 1 roll.

M300 Despatches From U.S. Consuls in Saltillo, Mexico, 1876-1906. 1 roll. DP.

T670 Despatches From U.S. Consuls in Samana, Dominican Republic, 1873-1905. 2 rolls.

T554 Despatches From U.S. Consuls in San Andres, Colombia, 1870-1878. 1 roll.

M301 Despatches From U.S. Consuls in San Blas, Mexico, 1837-1892. 1 roll. DP.

M442 Despatches From U.S. Consuls in San Dimas, Mexico, 1871-1873. 1 roll. DP.

T35 Despatches From U.S. Consuls in San Jose, Costa Rica, 1852-1906. 7 rolls.

T348 Despatches From U.S. Consuls in San Juan del Norte, Nicaragua, 1851-1906. 21 rolls.

T584 Despatches From U.S. Consuls in San Juan de los Remedios, Cuba, 1844-1846, 1879-1898. 2 rolls.

T152 Despatches From U.S. Consuls in San Juan del Sur, Nicaragua, 1847-1881. 4 rolls.

M302 Despatches From U.S. Consuls in San Luis Potosi, Mexico, 1869-1886. 1 roll. DP.

T237 Despatches From U.S. Consuls in San Salvador, El Salvador, 1868-1906. 10 rolls.

T483 Despatches From U.S. Consuls in Santa Catarina, Brazil, 1831-1874. 2 rolls.

M199 Despatches From U.S. Consuls in Santa Fe, New Mexico, 1830-1846. *See also* Merida, Mexico. 1 roll. DP.

T427 Despatches From U.S. Consuls in Santa Marta, Colombia, 1823-1883. 2 rolls.

T433 Despatches From U.S. Consuls in Santander, Spain, 1862-1892. 1 roll.

T434 Despatches From U.S. Consuls in Santiago, Cape Verde Islands, 1818-1898. 7 rolls.

T55 Despatches From U.S. Consuls in Santiago de Cuba, Cuba, 1799-1906. 17 rolls.

T56 Despatches From U.S. Consuls in Santo Domingo, Dominican Republic, 1837-1906. 19 rolls.

T351 Despatches From U.S. Consuls in Santos, Brazil, 1831-1906. 6 rolls.

T432 Despatches From U.S. Consuls in Sao Salvador, Brazil, 1808-1849. *See also* Bahia, Brazil, for later despatches. 4 rolls.

T488 Despatches From U.S. Consuls in Sarnia, Canada, 1864-1906. 4 rolls.

T679 Despatches From U.S. Consuls in Sault Ste. Marie, Canada, 1891-1906. 1 roll.

T435 Despatches From U.S. Consuls in Schwerin, Germany, 1862-1869. 1 roll.

M167 Despatches From U.S. Consuls in Seoul, Korea, 1886-1906. 2 rolls. DP.

T436 Despatches From U.S. Consuls in Seville, Spain, 1859-1906. 2 rolls.

M112 Despatches From U.S. Consuls in Shanghai, China, 1847-1906. 53 rolls. DP.

T248 Despatches From U.S. Consuls in Sheffield, England, 1864-1906. 12 rolls.

T680 Despatches From U.S. Consuls in Sherbrooke, Canada, 1879-1906. 3 rolls.

T438 Despatches From U.S. Consuls in Sierra Leone, British Africa, 1858-1906. 5 rolls.

M464 Despatches From U.S. Consuls in Singapore, Straits Settlements, 1833-1906. 16 rolls. DP.

T681 Despatches From U.S. Consuls in Sivas, Turkey, 1886-1906. 2 rolls.

T238 Despatches From U.S. Consuls in Smyrna, Turkey, 1802-1906. 15 rolls.

T682 Despatches From U.S. Consuls in Sofia, Bulgaria, 1901-1904. 1 roll.

T683 Despatches From U.S. Consuls in Solingen, Germany, 1898-1905. *See also* Furth, Germany, for earlier despatches. 2 rolls.

T439 Despatches From U.S. Consuls in Sonneberg, Germany, 1851-1898. 7 rolls.

T440 Despatches From U.S. Consuls in Sonsonate, El Şalvador, 1868-1887. T440. 1 roll.

T684 Despatches From U.S. Consuls in Sorel, Canada, 1882-1898. 1 roll.

T239 Despatches From U.S. Consuls in Southampton, England, 1790-1906. 10 rolls.

T441 Despatches From U.S. Consuls in Spezia, Italy, 1856-1869. 3 rolls.

T685 Despatches From U.S. Consuls in Stanbridge Station, Canada, 1878-1906. 2 rolls.

T686 Despatches From U.S. Consuls in Stavanger, Norway, 1905-1906. 1 roll.

T59 Despatches From U.S. Consuls in Stettin, Germany, 1830-1906. 10 rolls.

T230 Despatches From U.S. Consuls in Stockholm, Sweden, 1810-1906. 9 rolls.

T442 Despatches From U.S. Consuls in Strasbourg, France, 1866-1872. 1 roll.

T687 Despatches From U.S. Consuls in Stratford, Canada, 1887-1906. 2 rolls.

T443 Despatches From U.S. Consuls in Stuttgart, Germany, 1830-1906. *See also* Carlsruhe, Germany. 8 rolls.

T688 Despatches From U.S. Consuls in Swansea, Wales, 1892-1906. 1 roll.

M113 Despatches From U.S. Consuls in Swatow, China, 1860-1881. *See also* Canton, China. 4 rolls.

M173 Despatches From U.S. Consuls in Sydney, Australia, 1836-1906. *See also* Hobart, Australia. 18 rolls. DP.

T490 Despatches From U.S. Consuls in Sydney, Canada, 1838-1906. *See also* Pictou, Canada. 2 rolls.

M303 Despatches From U.S. Consuls in Tabasco, Mexico, 1832-1874. 2 rolls. DP.

M465 Despatches From U.S. Consuls in Tahiti, Society Islands, French Oceania, 1836-1906. 5 rolls. DP.

T115 Despatches From U.S. Consuls in Talcahuano, Chile, 1836-1895. *See also* Valparaiso, Chile, for later despatches. 5 rolls.

T60 Despatches From U.S. Consuls in Tamatave, Madagascar, 1853-1906. 11 rolls.

M304 Despatches From U.S. Consuls in Tampico, Mexico, 1824-1906. 8 rolls. DP.

M117 Despatches From U.S. Consuls in Tamsui, Formosa, 1898-1906. 1 roll.

T61 Despatches From U.S. Consuls in Tangier, Morocco, 1797-1906. 27 rolls.

T444 Despatches From U.S. Consuls in Taranto, Italy, 1861-1876. 1 roll.

T352 Despatches From U.S. Consuls in Tegucigalpa, Honduras, 1860-1906. *See also* Ceiba, Honduras, for later despatches. 8 rolls.

T305 Despatches From U.S. Consuls in Teheran, Iran, 1883-1906. 2 rolls.

M305 Despatches From U.S. Consuls in Tehuantepec, Mexico, 1850-1867. 1 roll. DP.

T690 Despatches From U.S. Consuls in Teneriffe, Canary Islands, 1795-1906. 10 rolls.

T156 Despatches From U.S. Consuls in Tetuan, Morocco, 1877-1888. 1 roll.

T153 Despatches From U.S. Consuls in Texas, 1825-1844. *See also* Galveston, Texas. 1 roll.

T691 Despatches From U.S. Consuls in Three Rivers, Canada, 1881-1906. 3 rolls.

M114 Despatches From U.S. Consuls in Tientsin, China, 1868-1906. 8 rolls. DP.

T491 Despatches From U.S. Consuls in Toronto, Canada, 1864-1906. *See also* Montreal, Canada. 9 rolls.

T700 Despatches From U.S. Consuls in Trebizond, Turkey, 1904-1906. *See also* Constantinople, Turkey. 1 roll.

T242 Despatches From U.S. Consuls in Trieste, Italy, 1800-1906. 13 rolls.

T699 Despatches From U.S. Consuls in Trinidad, Cuba, 1824-1876. *See also* Cienfuegos, Cuba, for later despatches. 9 rolls.

T148 Despatches From U.S. Consuls in Trinidad, West Indies Federation, 1824–1906. 11 rolls.

M466 Despatches From U.S. Consuls in Tripoli, Libya, 1796–1885. 7 rolls. DP.

T353 Despatches From U.S. Consuls in Tumbes, Peru, 1852–1874. 2 rolls.

T303 Despatches From U.S. Consuls in Tunis, Tunisia, 1797–1906. 12 rolls.

T445 Despatches From U.S. Consuls in Tunstall, England, 1869–1905. 3 rolls.

T174 Despatches From U.S. Consuls in Turin, Italy, 1877–1906. 2 rolls.

T446 Despatches From U.S. Consuls in Turks Island, British West Indies, 1818–1906. 18 rolls.

M306 Despatches From U.S. Consuls in Tuxpan, Mexico, 1879–1906. 2 rolls. DP.

T701 Despatches From U.S. Consuls in Utila, Honduras, 1894–1906. *See also* Omoa, Honduras, for earlier despatches. 2 rolls.

T447 Despatches From U.S. Consuls in Valencia, Spain, 1816–1906. *See also* Barcelona, Spain. 4 rolls.

M146 Despatches From U.S. Consuls in Valparaiso, Chile, 1812–1906. *See also* Coquimbo, Chile, and Talcahuano, Chile, for earlier despatches. 14 rolls. DP.

T114 Despatches From U.S. Consuls in Vancouver, Canada, 1890–1906. 5 rolls.

M153 Despatches From U.S. Consuls in Venice, Italy, 1830–1906. 7 rolls.

M183 Despatches From U.S. Consuls in Veracruz, Mexico, 1822–1906. 18 rolls. DP.

T130 Despatches From U.S. Consuls in Victoria, Canada, 1862–1906. 16 rolls.

T243 Despatches From U.S. Consuls in Vienna, Austria, 1830–1906. *See also* Dresden, Germany. 20 rolls.

T449 Despatches From U.S. Consuls in Vigo, Spain, 1852–1862. *See also* Corunna, Spain, for later despatches. 1 roll.

M486 Despatches From U.S. Consuls in Vladivostok, Russia, 1898–1906. 1 roll. DP.

T702 Despatches From U.S. Consuls in Wallaceburg, Canada, 1888–1905. 1 roll.

M467 Despatches From U.S. Consuls in Warsaw, Poland, 1871–1906. 3 rolls. DP.

T704 Despatches From U.S. Consuls in Waubaushene, Canada, 1890–1893. 1 roll.

T705 Despatches From U.S. Consuls in Weimar, Germany, 1893–1906. 1 roll.

T706 Despatches From U.S. Consuls in Windsor, Nova Scotia, Canada, 1872–1906. 3 rolls.

T492 Despatches From U.S. Consuls in Windsor, Ontario, Canada, 1864–1906. 4 rolls.

T24 Despatches From U.S. Consuls in Winnipeg, Canada, 1869–1906. *See also* Red River, Canada, for earlier despatches. 10 rolls.

T707 Despatches From U.S. Consuls in Woodstock, Canada, 1882–1906. 1 roll.

T708 Despatches From U.S. Consuls in Yarmouth, Canada, 1886–1906. 3 rolls.

M136 Despatches From U.S. Consuls in Yokohama, Japan, 1897–1906. 5 rolls.

M307 Despatches From U.S. Consuls in Zacatecas, Mexico, 1860–1884. *See also* Mexico City, Mexico. 1 roll. DP.

T451 Despatches From U.S. Consuls in Zante, Greece, 1853–1862. 3 rolls.

M468 Despatches From U.S. Consuls in Zanzibar, British Africa, 1836–1906. 5 rolls. DP.

T709 Despatches From U.S. Consuls in Zittau, Germany, 1897–1906. 1 roll.

T452 Despatches From U.S. Consuls in Zurich, Switzerland, 1852–1906. 8 rolls.

Notes From Foreign Legations

M47 Notes From the Argentine Legation in the United States to the Department of State, 1811–1906. 14 rolls.

M48 Notes From the Austrian Legation in the United States to the Department of State, 1820–1906. 15 rolls.

M194 Notes From the Belgian Legation in the United States to the Department of State, 1832–1906. 12 rolls.

T795 Notes From the Bolivian Legation in the United States to the Department of State, 1837–1906. 1 roll.

M49 Notes From the Brazilian Legation in the United States to the Department of State, 1824–1906. 8 rolls. DP.

M50 Notes From the British Legation in the United States to the Department of State, 1791–1906. 145 rolls.

T34 Notes From Central American Legations in the United States to the Department of State, 1823–1906. 10 rolls.

M73 Notes From the Chilean Legation in the United States to the Department of State, 1811–1906. 6 rolls.

M98 Notes From the Chinese Legation in the United States to the Department of State, 1868–1906. 6 rolls. DP.

M51 Notes From the Colombian Legation in the United States to the Department of State, 1810–1906. 11 rolls.

T799 Notes From the Costa Rican Legation in the United States to the Department of State, 1878–1906. 2 rolls.

T800 Notes From the Cuban Legation in the United States to the Department of State, 1844–1906. 2 rolls.

M52 Notes From the Danish Legation in the United States to the Department of State, 1801–1906. 9 rolls.

T801 Notes From the Legation of the Dominican Republic in the United States to the Department of State, 1844–1906. 3 rolls.

T810 Notes From the Ecuadorean Legation in the United States to the Department of State, 1839–1906. 2 rolls.

T798 Notes From the Legation of El Salvador in the United States to the Department of State, 1879–1906. 2 rolls.

M53 Notes From the French Legation in the United States to the Department of State, 1789–1906. 32 rolls. DP.

M58 Notes From the Legations of the German States and Germany in the United States to the Department of State, 1817–1906. 35 rolls.

T808 Notes From the Greek Legation in the United States to the Department of State, 1823–1892. 1 roll.

T803 Notes From the Haitian Legation in the United States to the Department of State, 1861-1906. 6 rolls.

T160 Notes From the Hawaiian Legation in the United States to the Department of State, 1841-1899. 4 rolls.

T796 Notes From the Honduran Legation in the United States to the Department of State, 1878-1906. 1 roll.

M202 Notes From the Italian Legation in the United States to the Department of State, 1861-1906. 18 rolls. DP.

M163 Notes From the Japanese Legation in the United States to the Department of State, 1858-1906. 9 rolls. DP.

M166 Notes From the Korean Legation in the United States to the Department of State, 1883-1906. 1 roll.

T807 Notes From the Liberian Legation in the United States to the Department of State, 1862-1898. 1 roll.

T814 Notes From the Luxembourg Legation in the United States to the Department of State, 1876-1903. 1 roll.

T806 Notes From the Madagascan Legation in the United States to the Department of State, 1883-1894. 1 roll.

M54 Notes From the Mexican Legation in the United States to the Department of State, 1821-1906. 39 rolls. DP.

T953 Notes From Miscellaneous Foreign States to the Department of State, 1817-1906. 4 rolls.

T614 Notes From the Montenegrin Legation in the United States to the Department of State, 1896-1905. 1 roll.

M56 Notes From the Netherlands Legation in the United States to the Department of State, 1784-1906. 13 rolls. DP.

T797 Notes From the Nicaraguan Legation in the United States to the Department of State, 1862-1906. 4 rolls.

T811 Notes From the Norwegian Legation in the United States to the Department of State, 1905-1906. 1 roll.

T812 Notes From the Panamanian Legation in the United States to the Department of State, 1903-1906. 1 roll.

M350 Notes From the Paraguayan Legation in the United States to the Department of State, 1853-1906. 1 roll.

M511 Notes From the Persian Legation in the United States to the Department of State, 1887-1906. 1 roll.

T802 Notes From the Peruvian Legation in the United States to the Department of State, 1827-1906. 6 rolls.

M57 Notes From the Portuguese Legation in the United States to the Department of State, 1796-1906. 8 rolls.

M39 Notes From the Russian Legation in the United States to the Department of State, 1809-1906. 12 rolls. DP.

T805 Notes From the Samoan Legation in the United States to the Department of State, 1856-1894. 1 roll.

M201 Notes From the Sardinian Legation in the United States to the Department of State, 1838-1861. 1 roll.

M512 Notes From the Siamese Legation in the United States to the Department of State, 1876-1906. 1 roll. DP.

M55 Notes From the Kingdom of the Two Sicilies Legation in the United States to the Department of State, 1826-1860. 2 rolls.

M59 Notes From the Spanish Legation in the United States to the Department of State, 1790-1906. 31 rolls. DP.

M60 Notes From the Swedish Legation in the United States to the Department of State, 1813-1906. 9 rolls.

T813 Notes From the Swiss Legation in the United States to the Department of State, 1882-1906. 6 rolls.

T809 Notes From the Texan Legation in the United States to the Department of State, 1836-1845. 1 roll.

M67 Notes From the Tunisian Legation in the United States to the Department of State, 1805-1806. 1 roll.

T815 Notes From the Turkish Legation in the United States to the Department of State, 1867-1906. 8 rolls.

T804 Notes From the Uruguayan Legation in the United States to the Department of State, 1834-1906. 1 roll.

T93 Notes From the Venezuelan Legation in the United States to the Department of State, 1835-1906. 8 rolls.

Notes To and From Foreign Legations and Consulates

M38 Notes From the Department of State to Foreign Ministers and Consuls in the United States, 1793-1834. 5 rolls.

M99 Notes to Foreign Legations in the United States From the Department of State, 1834-1906. 99 rolls.

M663 Notes to Foreign Consuls in the United States From the Department of State, 1853-1906. 4 rolls.

M664 Notes From Foreign Consuls in the United States to the Department of State, 1789-1906. 11 rolls.

Decimal File, 1910–1963

M600 Manual for Classification of Correspondence, Department of State (4th ed., 1938). 1 roll.

M973 Purport Lists for the Department of State Decimal File, 1910-1944. 654 rolls. DP.

M1275 Records of the Department of State, Records Codification Manual, Central Decimal File, 1950-1963. 1 roll.

M1219 Records of the Department of State Relating to Internal Affairs of Afghanistan, 1930-1944. 7 rolls.

M1211 Records of the Department of State Relating to the Internal Affairs of Albania, 1910-1944. 16 rolls.

M1276 Records of the Department of State Relating to Political Relations Between the United States and Other American States (Monroe Doctrine), 1910-1949. 30 rolls.

M514 Records of the Department of State Relating to Internal Affairs of Argentina, 1910-1929. 44 rolls. DP.

M1230 Records of the Department of State Relating to Internal Affairs of Argentina, 1930-1939. 32 rolls.

M1322 Records of the Department of State Relating to Internal Affairs of Argentina, 1940-1944. 40 rolls.

M515 Records of the Department of State Relating to Political Relations Between the United States and Argentina, 1910-1929. 1 roll. DP.

M516 Records of the Department of State Relating to Political Relations Between Argentina and Other States, 1910-1929. 1 roll. DP.

T1192 Records of the Department of State Relating to Internal Affairs of Armenia, 1910-1929. 8 rolls.

T1193 Records of the Department of State Relating to Political Relations Between Armenia and Other States, 1910-1929. 2 rolls.

M722 Records of the Department of State Relating to Internal Affairs of Asia, 1910-1929. 28 rolls. DP.

M723 Records of the Department of State Relating to Political Relations Between the United States and Asia, 1920-1929. 1 roll. DP.

M724 Records of the Department of State Relating to Political Relations Between Asia and Other States, 1910-1929. 1 roll. DP.

M695 Records of the Department of State Relating to Internal Affairs of Austria-Hungary and Austria, 1910-1929. 69 rolls. DP.

M696 Records of the Department of State Relating to Political Relations Between the United States and Austria-Hungary and Austria, 1910-1929. 4 rolls. DP.

M697 Records of the Department of State Relating to Political Relations Between Austria-Hungary and Austria and Other States, 1910-1929. 3 rolls. DP.

M708 Records of the Department of State Relating to Internal Affairs of Austria-Hungary and Hungary, 1912-1929. 38 rolls. DP.

M709 Records of the Department of State Relating to Political Relations Between the United States and Austria-Hungary and Hungary, 1921-1929. 1 roll. DP.

M710 Records of the Department of State Relating to Political Relations Between Austria-Hungary and Hungary and Other States, 1920-1929. 2 rolls. DP.

M1209 Records of the Department of State Relating to Internal Affairs of Austria, 1930-1944. 32 rolls.

T1190 Records of the Department of State Relating to Internal Affairs of Australia, 1910-1944. 36 rolls.

T1191 Records of the Department of State Relating to Political Relations Between the United States and Australia, 1910-1944. 1 roll.

M1447 Records of the Department of State Relating to Internal Affairs of the Balkan States, 1910-1939. 5 rolls.

M1220 Records of the Department of State Relating to Internal Affairs of the Balkan States, 1940-1944. 1 roll.

M1185 Records of the Department of State Relating to Internal Affairs of the Baltic States, 1910-1944. 8 rolls.

M675 Records of the Department of State Relating to Internal Affairs of Belgium, 1910-1929. 78 rolls. DP.

M676 Records of the Department of State Relating to Political Relations Between the United States and Belgium, 1910-1929. 1 roll. DP.

M677 Records of the Department of State Relating to Political Relations Between Belgium and Other States, 1910-1929. 4 rolls. DP.

M644 Records of the Department of State Relating to Internal Affairs of Bolivia, 1910-1929. 33 rolls. DP.

M646 Records of the Department of State Relating to Political Relations Between Bolivia and Other States, 1910-1929. 18 rolls. DP.

M519 Records of the Department of State Relating to Internal Affairs of Brazil, 1910-1929. 54 rolls. DP.

M1472 Records of the Department of State Relating to Internal Affairs of Brazil, 1930-1939. 48 rolls.

M1515 Records of the Department of State Relating to Internal Affairs of Brazil, 1940-1944. 84 rolls.

M1492 Records of the Department of State Relating to Internal Affairs of Brazil, 1945-1949. 48 rolls. DP.

M1487 Records of the Department of State Relating to Internal Political and National Defense Affairs of Brazil, 1950-1954. 14 rolls. DP.

M1489 Records of the Department of State Relating to Internal Economic, Industrial, and Social Affairs of Brazil, 1950-1954. 34 rolls. DP.

M525 Records of the Department of State Relating to Political Relations Between the United States and Brazil, 1910-1929. 1 roll. DP.

M526 Records of the Department of State Relating to Political Relations Between Brazil and Other States, 1910-1929. 2 rolls. DP.

M1511 Records of the Department of State Relating to Internal Political and National Defense Affairs of Brazil, 1955-59. 8 rolls.

M583 Records of the Department of State Relating to Internal Affairs of British Africa, 1910-1929. 33 rolls. DP.

M584 Records of the Department of State Relating to Political Relations Between the United States and British Africa, 1910-1929. 1 roll.

M585 Records of the Department of State Relating to Political Relations Between British Africa and Other States, 1910-1929. 1 roll.

M712 Records of the Department of State Relating to Internal Affairs of British Asia, 1910-1929. 21 rolls. DP.

M713 Records of the Department of State Relating to Political Relations Between British Asia and Other States, Including the United States, 1910-1929. 1 roll. DP.

M1207 Records of the Department of State Relating to Internal Affairs of Bulgaria, 1910-1944. 21 rolls.

M1435 Records of the Department of State Relating to Internal Affairs of Canada, 1910-1929. 54 rolls.

M672 Records of the Department of State Relating to Internal Affairs of Central America, 1910-1929. 16 rolls. DP.

M1330 Records of the Department of State Relating to Internal Affairs of Central America, 1930-1949. 6 rolls.

M673 Records of the Department of State Relating to Political Relations Between the United States and Central America, 1911-1929. 1 roll. DP.

M674 Records of the Department of State Relating to Political Relations Between Central America and Other States, 1910–1929. 2 rolls. DP.

M487 Records of the Department of State Relating to Internal Affairs of Chile, 1910–1929. 40 rolls. DP.

M489 Records of the Department of State Relating to Political Relations Between the United States and Chile, 1910–1929. 1 roll. DP.

M490 Records of the Department of State Relating to Political Relations Between Chile and Other States, 1910–1929. 2 rolls. DP.

M329 Records of the Department of State Relating to Internal Affairs of China, 1910–1929. 227 rolls. DP.

M339 Records of the Department of State Relating to Political Relations Between the United States and China, 1910–1929. 2 rolls. DP.

M976 Records of the Department of State Relating to Political Relations Between China and Japan, 1930–1944. 96 rolls. DP.

M341 Records of the Department of State Relating to Political Relations Between China and Other States, 1910–1929. 34 rolls. DP.

*C0012 Records of the Office of Chinese Affairs, 1945–1955. 41 rolls.

M1294 Records of the Department of State Relating to Internal Affairs of Colombia, 1910–1929. 45 rolls.

M669 Records of the Department of State Relating to Internal Affairs of Costa Rica, 1910–1929. 40 rolls. DP.

M670 Records of the Department of State Relating to Political Relations Between the United States and Costa Rica, 1910–1929. 1 roll. DP.

M671 Records of the Department of State Relating to Political Relations Between Costa Rica and Other States, 1910–1929. 10 rolls. DP.

M488 Records of the Department of State Relating to Internal Affairs of Cuba, 1910–1929. 99 rolls. DP.

M509 Records of the Department of State Relating to Political Relations Between the United States and Cuba, 1910–1929. 2 rolls. DP.

M510 Records of the Department of State Relating to Political Relations Between Cuba and Other States, 1910–1929. 1 roll. DP.

M1218 Records of the Department of State Relating to Internal Affairs of Czechoslovakia, 1910–1944. 32 rolls.

*C0037 Records of the Department of State Relating to the Internal Affairs of Czechoslovakia, 1955–59 (Decimal Files 749, 849, and 949). 8 rolls.

M1378 Records of the Department of State Relating to Internal Affairs of the Free City of Danzig, 1910–1929. 11 rolls.

M1452 Records of the Department of State Relating to Internal Affairs of Denmark, 1910–1939. 38 rolls.

M626 Records of the Department of State Relating to Internal Affairs of the Dominican Republic, 1910–1929. 79 rolls.

M1272 Records of the Department of State Relating to Internal Affairs of the Dominican Republic, 1930–1939. 37 rolls.

M1277 Records of the Department of State Relating to Internal Affairs of the Dominican Republic, 1940–1944. 20 rolls.

T1243 Records of the Department of State Relating to Political Relations of Eastern Europe, 1930–1939. 46 rolls.

T1244 Records of the Department of State Relating to Political Relations of Eastern Europe, 1940–1944. 5 rolls.

*C0033 Records of the Department of State Relating to the Internal Affairs of East Germany, 1955–59 (Decimal Files 762B and 862B). 10 rolls.

M1468 Records of the Department of State Relating to Internal Affairs of Ecuador, 1910–1929. 27 rolls.

M571 Records of the Department of State Relating to Internal Affairs of Egypt, 1910–1929. 31 rolls. DP.

T1251 Records of the Department of State Relating to Internal Affairs of Egypt, 1930–1939. 22 rolls.

M572 Records of the Department of State Relating to Political Relations Between the United States and Egypt, 1910–1929. 1 roll. DP.

M573 Records of the Department of State Relating to Political Relations Between Egypt and Other States, 1910–1929. 1 roll. DP.

*C0027 Records of the Department of State Relating to Internal Affairs of Egypt, 1955–59 (Decimal Files 774, 874, and 974). 30 rolls.

*C0028 Records of the Department of State Relating to the Foreign Affairs of Egypt, 1955–59 (Decimal Files 674 and 611). 7 rolls.

M658 Records of the Department of State Relating to Internal Affairs of El Salvador, 1910–1929. 22 rolls. DP.

M659 Records of the Department of State Relating to Political Relations Between the United States and El Salvador, 1910–1929. 1 roll. DP.

M660 Records of the Department of State Relating to Political Relations Between El Salvador and Other States, 1910–1929. 1 roll. DP.

M1170 Records of the Department of State Relating to Internal Affairs of Estonia, 1910–1944. 23 rolls.

M411 Records of the Department of State Relating to Internal Affairs of Ethiopia, 1910–1929. 4 rolls. DP.

M412 Records of the Department of State Relating to Political Relations Between the United States and Ethiopia, 1910–1929. 1 roll. DP.

*C0045 Department of State Central Files Relating to the Far East, 1945–49 (Decimal File Numbers 890, 790, and 711). 21 rolls.

*C0046 Department of State Central Files Relating to the Far East, 1950–54 (Decimal File Numbers 790, 890, 990, 690, and 611). 26 rolls.

*C0047 Department of State Central Files Relating to the Far East, 1955–59 (Decimal File Numbers 790, 890, 990, 690, and 611). 30 rolls.

T1184 Records of the Department of State Relating to Internal Affairs of Finland, 1910–1944. 32 rolls.

T1185 Records of the Department of State Relating to Political Relations Between the United States and Finland, 1910–1944. 2 rolls.

T1186 Records of the Department of State Relating to Political Relations Between Finland and Other States, 1910–1944. 8 rolls.

M560 Records of the Department of State Relating to Internal Affairs of France, 1910–1929. 162 rolls. DP.

M1442 Records of the Department of State Relating to Internal Affairs of France, 1930–1939. 89 rolls.

M568 Records of the Department of State Relating to Political Relations Between the United States and France, 1910–1929. 5 rolls. DP.

M569 Records of the Department of State Relating to Political Relations Between France and Other States, 1910–1929. 7 rolls. DP.

M336 Records of the Department of State Relating to Internal Affairs of Germany, 1910–1929. 182 rolls. DP.

M355 Records of the Department of State Relating to Political Relations Between the United States and Germany, 1910–1929. 4 rolls. DP.

T1253 Records of the Department of State Relating to Political Relations Between the United States and Germany, 1930–1939. 2 rolls.

M354 Records of the Department of State Relating to Political Relations Between Germany and Other States, 1910–1929. 4 rolls. DP.

*C0040 Records of the Department of State Relating to the Internal and Foreign Affairs of Germany, 1950–54 (Decimal Files 762, 862, 962, 662, 611, and 711). 45 rolls.

*C0041 Records of the Department of State Relating to the Internal and Foreign Affairs of Germany, 1955–59 (Decimal Files 762, 862, 962, 611, and 662). 37 rolls.

M580 Records of the Department of State Relating to Internal Affairs of Great Britain, 1910–1929. 249 rolls. DP.

M1455 Records of the Department of State Relating to Internal Affairs of Great Britain, 1930–1939. 78 rolls.

M581 Records of the Department of State Relating to Political Relations Between the United States and Great Britain, 1910–1929. 15 rolls. DP.

T1252 Records of the Department of State Relating to Political Relations Between the United States and Great Britain, 1930–1939. 6 rolls.

M582 Records of the Department of State Relating to Political Relations Between Great Britain and Other States, 1910–1929. 13 rolls. DP.

M443 Records of the Department of State Relating to Internal Affairs of Greece, 1910–1929. 45 rolls. DP.

M1179 Records of the Department of State Relating to Internal Affairs of Greece, 1930–1939. 16 rolls.

M475 Records of the Department of State Relating to Political Relations Between the United States and Greece, 1910–1929. 3 rolls.

M476 Records of the Department of State Relating to Political Relations Between Greece and Other States, 1910–1929. 6 rolls. DP.

M655 Records of the Department of State Relating to Internal Affairs of Guatemala, 1910–1929. 40 rolls. DP.

M1280 Records of the Department of State Relating to Internal Affairs of Guatemala, 1930–1944. 22 rolls.

M1527 Records of the Department of State Relating to Internal Affairs of Guatemala, 1945–1949. 12 rolls.

M656 Records of the Department of State Relating to Political Relations Between the United States and Guatemala, 1910–1929. 1 roll. DP.

M657 Records of the Department of State Relating to Political Relations Between Guatemala and Other States, 1910–1929. 27 rolls. DP.

M610 Records of the Department of State Relating to Internal Affairs of Haiti, 1910–1929. 94 rolls. DP.

M1246 Records of the Department of State Relating to Internal Affairs of Haiti, 1930–1939. 36 rolls.

M611 Records of the Department of State Relating to Political Relations Between the United States and Haiti, 1910–1929. 2 rolls.

M612 Records of the Department of State Relating to Political Relations Between Haiti and Other States, 1910–1929. 4 rolls.

M647 Records of the Department of State Relating to Internal Affairs of Honduras, 1910–1929. 49 rolls. DP.

M648 Records of the Department of State Relating to Political Relations Between the United States and Honduras, 1910–1929. 1 roll. DP.

M1206 Records of the Department of State Relating to Internal Affairs of Hungary, 1930–1944. 17 rolls.

*C0026 Records of the Department of State Relating to the Internal Affairs of Hungary, 1955–59 (Decimal File 764, 864, and 964). 25 rolls.

M335 Records of the Department of State Relating to Internal Affairs of India and Burma, 1910–1929. 26 rolls. DP.

M343 Records of the Department of State Relating to Political Relations Between the United States and India and Burma, 1910–1929. 1 roll.

M344 Records of the Department of State Relating to Political Relations Between India and Burma and Other States, 1910–1929. 1 roll.

M1202 Records of the Department of State Relating to Internal Affairs of Iran, 1930–1939. 24 rolls.

T1180 Records of the Department of State Relating to Internal Affairs of Iraq, 1930–1944. 18 rolls.

M1231 Records of the Department of State Relating to Internal Affairs of the Republic of Ireland and Northern Ireland. 17 rolls.

M527 Records of the Department of State Relating to Internal Affairs of Italy, 1910–1929. 60 rolls. DP.

M1423 Records of the Department of State Relating to Internal Affairs of Italy, 1930–1939. 33 rolls.

M529 Records of the Department of State Relating to Political Relations Between the United States and Italy, 1910–1929. 3 rolls. DP.

M530 Records of the Department of State Relating to Political Relations Between Italy and Other States, 1910–1929. 8 rolls. DP.

*C0003 Records of the Department of State Relating to Internal Political and National Defense Affairs of Italy, 1950–1954. (Decimal File 765) 17 rolls.

*C0004 Records of the Department of State Relating to Internal Economic, Industrial, and Social Affairs of Italy, Including Records Relating to Communications, Transportation, and Science, 1950-54 (Decimal Files 865 and 965). 35 rolls.

*C0007 Records of the Department of State Relating to the Foreign Affairs of Italy, Including International Political Relations, Bilateral Treaties, And U.S. Italian Relations, 1950–1954. (Decimal Files 611.0-5 and 665). 5 rolls.

*C0008 Confidential U.S. State Department Central Files Relating to the Internal Affairs and Foreign Affairs of Indochina, 1955–1959 (Decimal Files 651, 751, 851, 951, and 611). 54 rolls.

M422 Records of the Department of State Relating to Internal Affairs of Japan, 1910–1929. 43 rolls. DP.

M423 Records of the Department of State Relating to Political Relations Between the United States and Japan, 1910–1929. 9 rolls. DP.

M424 Records of the Department of State Relating to Political Relations Between Japan and Other States, 1910–1929. 1 roll. DP.

*C0009 Records of the Department of State Relating to the Internal Affairs of Japan, 1955–1959 (Decimal File 794 and 894). 48 rolls.

*C0010 Records of the Department of State Relating to the Political Relations of Japan, 1955–1959 (Decimal File 694). 3 rolls.

*C0011 Records of the Department of State Relating to U.S. Political Relations with Japan, 1955–1959 (Decimal File 611). 8 rolls.

*C0043 Department of State Special Files Relating to Japan, 1947–56 (Lot File Numbers 54-D-423, 57-D-149, 58-D-118, and 58-D-637). 37 rolls.

*C0050 Records of the Department of State Relating to the Internal and Foreign Affairs of Jordan, 1955–59 (Decimal File Numbers 785, 885, 985, and 611). 10 rolls.

M426 Records of the Department of State Relating to Internal Affairs of Korea, 1910–1929. 9 rolls. DP.

*C0018 Records of the Department of State Relating to U.S. Political Relations with Korea, 1955–1959 (Decimal File 611). 3 rolls.

*C0019 Records of the Department of State Relating to the Internal Affairs of Korea, 1955–1959 (Decimal File 795, 895, 995). 22 rolls.

*C0038 Records of the Department of State Relating to Political Relations Between Korea and Other States, 1955–59 (Decimal Files 695A and 695B) 1 roll.

*C0042 Department of State Special Files Relating to Korea, 1950–57 (Lot File Numbers 55-D-128, 58-D-643, and 59-D-407). 11 rolls.

M1177 Records of the Department of State Relating to Internal Affairs of Latvia, 1910–1944. 19 rolls.

T1178 Records of the Department of State Relating to Internal Affairs of Lebanon, 1930–1944. 5 rolls.

*C0051 Records of the Department of State Relating to the Internal and Foreign Affairs of Lebanon, 1955–59 (Decimal File Numbers 783A, 883A, 983A, and 611). 16 rolls.

M613 Records of the Department of State Relating to Internal Affairs of Liberia, 1910–1929. 34 rolls. DP.

M614 Records of the Department of State Relating to Political Relations Between Liberia and Other States, Including the United States, 1919–1929. 1 roll. DP.

M1178 Records of the Department of State Relating to Internal Affairs of Lithuania, 1910–1944. 22 rolls.

M274 Records of the Department of State Relating to Internal Affairs of Mexico, 1910–1929. 243 rolls. DP.

M1370 Records of the Department of State Relating to Internal Affairs of Mexico, 1930–1939. 165 rolls.

M314 Records of the Department of State Relating to Political Relations Between the United States and Mexico, 1910–1929. 29 rolls. DP.

M315 Records of the Department of State Relating to Political Relations Between Mexico and Other States, 1910–1929. 2 rolls. DP.

M349 Records of the Department of State Relating to Internal Affairs of Montenegro and to Political Relations Between the United States and Montenegro, 1910–1929. 2 rolls.

M577 Records of the Department of State Relating to Internal Affairs of Morocco, 1910–1929. 26 rolls. DP.

M578 Records of the Department of State Relating to Political Relations Between the United States and Morocco, 1910–1929. 1 roll. DP.

M579 Records of the Department of State Relating to Political Relations Between Morocco and Other States, 1910–1929. 1 roll. DP.

M682 Records of the Department of State Relating to Internal Affairs of The Netherlands, 1910–1929. 54 rolls. DP.

M683 Records of the Department of State Relating to Political Relations Between the United States and The Netherlands, 1910–1929. 6 rolls. DP.

M684 Records of the Department of State Relating to Political Relations Between The Netherlands and Other States, 1910–1929. 1 roll. DP.

M632 Records of the Department of State Relating to Internal Affairs of Nicaragua, 1910–1929. 106 rolls. DP.

M1273 Records of the Department of State Relating to Internal Affairs of Nicaragua, 1930–1944. 53 rolls.

M633 Records of the Department of State Relating to Political Relations Between the United States and Nicaragua, 1910–1929. 2 rolls.

M634 Records of the Department of State Relating to Political Relations Between Nicaragua and Other States, 1910–1929. 3 rolls.

*C0044 Department of State Special Files Relating to Northeast Asia, 1943–56 (Lot File Numbers 54-D-278, 58-D-529, 58-D-184, 58-D-208, 59-D-476, and 60-D-330). 24 rolls.

M1406 Records of the Department of State Relating to Internal Affairs of Norway, 1910–1939. 22 rolls.

M1448 Records of the Department of State Relating to Internal Affairs of Pakistan, 1945–1949. 6 rolls.

M1037 Records of the Department of State Relating to Internal Affairs of Palestine, 1930–1944. 26 rolls. DP.

M1390 Records of the Department of State Relating to Internal Affairs of Palestine, 1945–1949. 27 rolls.

*C0048 Records of the Department of State Relating to the Foreign Affairs of Palestine-Israel, 1955–59 (Decimal File Numbers 684, 684A, and 611) 17 rolls.

*C0049 Records of the Department of State Relating to Internal Affairs of Palestine-Israel, 1955–59 (Decimal File Numbers 784, 784A, 884, 884A, and 984A). 19 rolls.

M607 Records of the Department of State Relating to Internal Affairs of Panama, 1910–1929. 58 rolls. DP.

M608 Records of the Department of State Relating to Political Relations Between the United States and Panama, 1910–1929. 14 rolls.

M609 Records of the Department of State Relating to Political Relations Between Panama and Other States, 1910–1929. 3 rolls. DP.

*C0029 Records of the Department of State Relating to the Internal Affairs of Panama, 1930–39 (Decimal File 819). 24 rolls.

*C0030 Records of the Department of State Relating to the Foreign Affairs of Panama, 1930–39 (Decimal Files 719 and 711). 11 rolls.

*C0031 Records of the Department of State Relating to the Internal and Foreign Affairs of Panama, 1940–44 (Decimal Files 819, 719, and 711). 26 rolls.

*C0032 Records of the Department of State Relating to the Internal and Foreign Affairs of Panama, 1945–49 (Decimal Files 819, 719, and 711). 22 rolls.

M561 Records of the Department of State Relating to Internal Affairs of the Papal States (Holy See), 1910–1929. 1 roll.

M562 Records of the Department of State Relating to Political Relations Between the United States and the Papal States (Holy See), 1910–1929. 1 roll.

M563 Records of the Department of State Relating to Political Relations Between the Papal States (Holy See) and Other States, 1910–1929. 1 roll.

M1470 Records of the Department of State Relating to Internal Affairs of Paraguay, 1910–1939. 22 rolls.

M715 Records of the Department of State Relating to Internal Affairs of Persia, 1910–1929. 37 rolls. DP.

M716 Records of the Department of State Relating to Political Relations Between the United States and Persia, 1921–1929. 1 roll. DP.

M717 Records of the Department of State Relating to Political Relations Between Persia and Other States, 1921–1929. 1 roll. DP.

M746 Records of the Department of State Relating to Internal Affairs of Peru, 1910–1929. 30 rolls. DP.

M748 Records of the Department of State Relating to Political Relations Between Peru and Other States, 1910–1929. 52 rolls. DP.

M1197 Records of the Department of State Relating to Internal Affairs of Poland, 1916–1944. 75 rolls.

*C0035 Records of the Department of State Relating to the Internal Affairs of Poland, 1955–59 (Decimal Files 748, 848, and 948). 16 rolls.

M705 Records of the Department of State Relating to Internal Affairs of Portugal, 1910–1929. 34 rolls. DP.

M1198 Records of the Department of State Relating to Internal Affairs of Romania, 1910–1944. 44 rolls.

*C0039 Records of the Department of State Relating to the Internal Affairs of Romania, 1955–59 (Decimal Files 766, 866, and 966). 7 rolls.

M316 Records of the Department of State Relating to Internal Affairs of Russia and the Soviet Union, 1910–1929. 177 rolls. DP.

T1249 Records of the Department of State Relating to Internal Affairs of the Soviet Union, 1930–1939. 75 rolls.

T1250 Records of the Department of State Relating to Internal Affairs of the Soviet Union, 1940–1944. 34 rolls.

M333 Records of the Department of State Relating to Political Relations Between the United States and Russia and the Soviet Union, 1910–1929. 7 rolls. DP.

T1241 Records of the Department of State Relating to Political Relations Between the United States and the Soviet Union, 1930–1939. 3 rolls.

T1242 Records of the Department of State Relating to Political Relations Between the United States and the Soviet Union, 1940–1944. 1 roll.

M340 Records of the Department of State Relating to Political Relations Between Russia and the Soviet Union and Other States, 1910–1929. 20 rolls. DP.

T1247 Records of the Department of State Relating to Political Relations Between the Soviet Union and Other States, 1930–1939. 14 rolls.

T1248 Records of the Department of State Relating to Political Relations Between the Soviet Union and Other States, 1940–1944. 4 rolls.

T1179 Records of the Department of State Relating to Internal Affairs of Saudi Arabia, 1930–1944. 8 rolls.

*C0052 Records of the Department of State Relating to the Internal and Foreign Affairs of Saudi Arabia, 1955–59 (Decimal File Numbers 786A, 886A, 986A, and 611). 11 rolls.

M357 Records of the Department of State Relating to Internal Affairs of Serbia and to Political Relations Between the United States and Serbia, 1910–1929. 3 rolls.

M729 Records of the Department of State Relating to Internal Affairs of Siam, 1910–1929. 18 rolls. DP.

M730 Records of the Department of State Relating to Political Relations Between the United States and Siam, 1910–1929. 1 roll. DP.

M731 Records of the Department of State Relating to Political Relations Between Siam and Other States, 1910–1929. 1 roll. DP.

*C0014 (Formerly) Confidential Department of State Special Files Relating to Southeast Asia, 1944–1958 (Lot Files 54-D-190, 55-D-480, 55-D-481, 55-D-266, 59-D-630, 63-D-3, 58-D-782, 58-D-782, 58-D-726, 58-D-257). 39 rolls.

*C0015 (Formerly) Confidential U.S. State Department Central Files Relating to the Foreign Affairs of the Soviet Union, 1955–1959 (Decimal File 611). 15 rolls.

*C0016 (Formerly) Confidential U.S. State Department Central Files Relating to the Internal Affairs of the Soviet Union, 1955–1959 (Decimal Files 761, 861, and 961). 46 rolls.

M1369 Records of the Department of State Relating to Internal Affairs of Spain, 1910–1929. 38 rolls.

M1424 Records of the Department of State Relating to Internal Affairs of Sweden, 1910–1939. 44 rolls.

M1457 Records of the Department of State Relating to Internal Affairs of Switzerland, 1910–1939. 27 rolls.

T1177 Records of the Department of State Relating to Internal Affairs of Syria, 1930–1944. 11 rolls.

T1181 Records of the Department of State Relating to Internal Affairs of Trans-Jordan, 1930–1944. 1 roll.

M353 Records of the Department of State Relating to Internal Affairs of Turkey, 1910–1929. 88 rolls. DP.

M1224 Records of the Department of State Relating to Internal Affairs of Turkey, 1930–1944. 36 rolls.

M1292 Records of the Department of State Relating to Internal Affairs of Turkey, 1945–1949. 20 rolls.

M365 Records of the Department of State Relating to Political Relations Between the United States and Turkey, 1910–1929. 8 rolls. DP.

M1223 Records of the Department of State Relating to Political Relations Between the United States and Turkey, 1930–1944. 2 rolls.

M363 Records of the Department of State Relating to Political Relations Between Turkey and Other States, 1910–1929. 29 rolls. DP.

T1245 Records of the Department of State Relating to Political Relations of Turkey, Greece, and the Balkan States, 1930–1939. 11 rolls.

T1246 Records of the Department of State Relating to Political Relations of Turkey, Greece, and the Balkan States, 1940–1944. 2 rolls.

M366 Records of the Department of State Relating to Internal Affairs of Venezuela, 1910–1929. 32 rolls. DP.

M368 Records of the Department of State Relating to Political Relations Between the United States and Venezuela, 1910–1929. 1 roll. DP.

M369 Records of the Department of State Relating to Political Relations Between Venezuela and Other States, 1910–1929. 2 rolls.

M358 Records of the Department of State Relating to Internal Affairs of Yugoslavia, 1910–1929. 27 rolls. DP.

M1203 Records of the Department of State Relating to Internal Affairs of Yugoslavia, 1930–1944. 28 rolls.

M362 Records of the Department of State Relating to Political Relations Between the United States and Yugoslavia, 1910–1929. 1 roll. DP.

M361 Records of the Department of State Relating to Political Relations Between Yugoslavia and Other States, 1910–1929. 9 rolls. DP.

*C0034 Records of the Department of State Relating to the Internal Affairs of Yugoslavia, 1955–59 (Decimal Files 768, 868, and 968). 18 rolls.

State Department Territorial Papers

M342 State Department Territorial Papers, Arizona, 1864–1872. 1 roll. DP.

M3 State Department Territorial Papers, Colorado, 1859–1874. 1 roll. DP.

M309 State Department Territorial Papers, Dakota, 1861–1873. 1 roll. DP.

M116 State Department Territorial Papers, Florida, 1777–1824. 11 rolls.

M445 State Department Territorial Papers, Idaho, 1863–1872. 1 roll. DP.

M218 State Department Territorial Papers, Kansas, 1854–1861. 2 rolls. DP.

M1134 State Department Territorial Papers, Missouri, 1812–1820. 1 roll.

M356 State Department Territorial Papers, Montana, 1864–1872. 2 rolls. DP.

M228 State Department Territorial Papers, Nebraska, 1854–1867. 1 roll. DP.

M13 State Department Territorial Papers, Nevada, 1861–1864. 2 rolls.

T17 State Department Territorial Papers, New Mexico, 1851–1872. 4 rolls.

M419 State Department Territorial Papers, Oregon, 1848–1858. 1 roll.

T260 State Department Territorial Papers, Orleans, 1764–1813. 13 rolls.

M470 State Department Territorial Papers, Territory Northwest of the River Ohio, 1787–1801. 1 roll. DP.

M471 State Department Territorial Papers, Territory Southwest of the River Ohio, 1790–1795. 1 roll. DP.

M12 State Department Territorial Papers, Utah, 1853–1873. 2 rolls. DP.

M26 State Department Territorial Papers, Washington, 1854–1872. 2 rolls. DP.

M85 State Department Territorial Papers, Wyoming, 1868–1873. 1 roll.

Letters of Application and Recommendation

M406 Letters of Application and Recommendation During the Administration of John Adams, 1797–1801. 3 rolls. DP.

M418 Letters of Application and Recommendation During the Administration of Thomas Jefferson, 1801–1809. 12 rolls. DP.

M438 Letters of Application and Recommendation During the Administration of James Madison, 1809–1817. 8 rolls. DP.

M439 Letters of Application and Recommendation During the Administration of James Monroe, 1817–1825. 19 rolls. DP.

M531 Letters of Application and Recommendation During the Administration of John Quincy Adams, 1825–1829. 8 rolls. DP.

M639 Letters of Application and Recommendation During the Administration of Andrew Jackson, 1829–1837. 27 rolls. DP.

M687 Letters of Application and Recommendation During the Administrations of Martin Van Buren, William Henry Harrison, and John Tyler, 1837–1845. 35 rolls. DP.

M873 Letters of Application and Recommendation During the Administrations of James Polk, Zachary Taylor, and Millard Fillmore, 1845–1853. 98 rolls. DP.

M967 Letters of Application and Recommendation During the Administrations of Franklin Pierce and James Buchanan, 1853–1861. 50 rolls. DP.

M650 Letters of Application and Recommendation During the Administrations of Abraham Lincoln and Andrew Johnson, 1861–1869. 53 rolls. DP.

M968 Letters of Application and Recommendation During the Administration of Ulysses S. Grant, 1869–1877. 69 rolls. DP.

Other General Records of the Department of State

M17 Registers of Correspondence of the Department of State, 1870–1906. 71 rolls.

M36 Records of Negotiations Connected With the Treaty of Ghent, 1813–1815. 2 rolls.

M37 Despatches From Special Agents of the Department of State, 1794–1906. 22 rolls. DP.

M40 Domestic Letters of the Department of State, 1784–1906. 171 rolls.

M83 Journal of the Voyage of the U.S.S. *Nonsuch* up the Orinoco, July 11–August 24, 1819. 1 roll.

M86 Journal of Charles Mason, Kept During the Survey of the Mason and Dixon Line, 1763–1768. 1 roll. DP.

M179 Miscellaneous Letters of the Department of State, 1789–1906. 1,310 rolls. DP.

M238 Consular Trade Reports, 1943–1950. 681 rolls. 16mm.

M367 Records of the Department of State Relating to World War I and Its Termination, 1914–1929. 518 rolls. DP.

M570 Copybooks of George Washington's Correspondence With Secretaries of State, 1789–1796. 1 roll. DP.

M586 List of U.S. Diplomatic Officers, 1789–1939. 3 rolls. DP.

M587 List of U.S. Consular Officers, 1789–1939. 21 rolls. DP.

M588 "War of 1812 Papers" of the Department of State, 1789–1815. 7 rolls. DP.

M679 Records of the Department of State Special Interrogation Mission to Germany, 1945–1946. 3 rolls.

M743 Personal and Confidential Letters From Secretary of State Lansing to President Wilson, 1915–1918. 1 roll. DP.

M800 Reports of Clerks and Bureau Officers of the Department of State, 1790–1911. 8 rolls. DP.

M862 Numerical and Minor Files of the Department of State, 1906–1910. 1,241 rolls. DP.

M974 Records of the Department of State Relating to Guano Islands, 1852–1912. 7 rolls. DP.

M982 Records of the Department of State Relating to World War II, 1939–1945. 252 rolls. DP.

M1135 Marshall/Lovett Memorandums to President Truman, 1947–1948. 3 rolls. DP.

M1171 Policy Planning Staff Numbered Papers, 1–63; 1947–1949. 71 cards (microfiche).

M1175 Palestine Reference Files of Dean Rusk and Robert McClintock, 1947–1949. 12 rolls. DP.

M1221 Intelligence Reports, 1941–1961.* Approximately 9,000 cards (microfiche). *These records continue to be filmed. Contact the Military Reference Branch (NWCTM) for information.

M1244 Records of the Office of European Affairs, 1934–1947. 18 rolls. DP.

M1284 Records of the Department of State Relating to the Problems of Relief and Refugees in Europe Arising from World War II and Its Aftermath, 1938–1949. 70 rolls. DP.

M1371 Registers and Indexes for Passport Applications, 1810–1906. 13 rolls. DP.

M1372 Passport Applications, 1795–1905. 694 rolls.

*M1490 Passport Applications, January 2, 1906–March 31, 1923. 2740 rolls.

M1751 Records of the Polish Ministry of Foreign Affairs, 1918–1940. 56 rolls.

*M1834 Emergency Passport Application (Passports Issued Abroad), 1877–1907. 56 rolls.

*M1848 Index to Passport Applications, 1850–52, 1869–80, 1881, 1906–23. 61 rolls.

*M2025 Registers of Applications for the Release of Impressed Seamen, 1793–1802, and Related Indexes. 2 rolls.

*M2032 Passenger Lists of European Immigrants Arriving at Vera Cruz, Mexico, 1921–1923, and Related Correspondence, 1921–1931. 1 roll.

T119 Minutes of Treaty Conferences Between the United States and Japanese Representatives, and Treaty Drafts, 1872. 1 roll.

T286 Correspondence Relating to the Filibustering Expedition Against the Spanish Government of Mexico, 1811–1816. 1 roll.

*T326 Letters From and Opinions of Attorneys General, 1791–1811. 1 roll.

T461 Records of the Department of State Relating to Property Claims of U.S. Citizens Against Poland, 1930–1944. 8 rolls.

T493 Miscellaneous Documents Relating to Reciprocity Negotiations of the Department of State, 1848–1854, 1884–1885, 1891–1892. 1 roll.

T495 Papers Relating to the Cession of Alaska, 1856–1867; Enclosures 2 and 3 to Despatch 2115, Dated Dec. 2, 1936, From the U.S. Embassy in the Soviet Union. 1 roll.

T640 Records of the Department of State Relating to U.S. Claims Against Russia, 1910–1929. 8 rolls.

T645 Acceptances and Orders for Commissions in the Records of the Department of State, 1789–1828. 2 rolls.

T730 Resignations and Declinations Among the Records of the Department of State, 1789-1827. 1 roll.

T841 Correspondence of Secretary of State Bryan With President Wilson, 1913-1915. 4 rolls.

T903 Daybook of the Department of State for Miscellaneous and Contingent Expenses, Feb. 1, 1798-Nov. 3, 1820. 1 roll.

T904 Cashbook of the Department of State, 1785-1795. 1 roll.

T908 Despatches Received by the Department of State From the U.S. Commission to Central and South America, July 14, 1884-December 26, 1885. 1 roll.

T967 Copies of Presidential Pardons and Remissions, 1794-1893. 7 rolls.

T1024 *The Alaska Treaty*, by David Hunter Miller, Department of State. 1 roll.

T1171 Codebooks of the Department of State, 1867-1876. 1 roll.

T1197 Minutes of Meetings of the Interdivisional Area Committee on the Far East, 1943-1946. 1 roll.

T1212 Records of Special Agents for Securing the Florida Archives, 1819-1835. 6 rolls.

T1221 State Department Documents of the Interdivisional Country and Area Committee, 1943-1946. 6 rolls.

T1222 State Department Documents of the Post War Programs Committee, 1944. 4 rolls.

RG 60 General Records of the Department of Justice

M699 Letters Sent by the Department of Justice: General and Miscellaneous, 1818-1904. 81 rolls. DP.

M700 Letters Sent by the Department of Justice Concerning Judiciary Expenses, 1849-1884. 24 rolls. DP.

M701 Letters Sent by the Department of Justice: Instructions to U.S. Attorneys and Marshals, 1867-1904. 212 rolls. DP.

M702 Letters Sent by the Department of Justice to Executive Officers and Members of Congress, 1871-1904. 91 rolls. DP.

M703 Letters Sent by the Department of Justice to Judges and Clerks, 1874-1904. 34 rolls. DP.

M1356 Letters Received by the Department of Justice from the State of Alabama, 1871-1884. 7 rolls. DP.

M1418 Letters Received by the Department of Justice from the State of Arkansas, 1871-1884. 5 rolls. DP.

M1535 Letters Received by the Department of Justice from the Territory of Dakota, 1871-1884. 3 rolls. DP.

M1327 Letters Received by the Department of Justice from the State of Florida, 1871-1884. 2 rolls. DP.

M996 Letters Received by the Department of Justice from the State of Georgia, 1871-1884. 5 rolls. DP.

M1362 Letters Received by the Department of Justice from the State of Kentucky, 1871-1884. 2 rolls. DP.

M940 Letters Received by the Department of Justice from the State of Louisiana, 1871-1884. 6 rolls. DP.

M1352 Letters Received by the Department of Justice from the State of Maryland, 1871-1884. 2 rolls. DP.

M970 Letters Received by the Department of Justice from Mississippi, 1871-1884. 4 rolls. DP.

M1345 Letters Received by the Department of Justice from the State of North Carolina, 1871-1884. 3 rolls. DP.

M947 Letters Received by the Department of Justice from South Carolina, 1871-1884. 9 rolls. DP.

M1471 Letters Received by the Department of Justice from the State of Tennessee, 1871-1884. 4 rolls. DP.

M1449 Letters Received by the Department of Justice from the State of Texas, 1871-1884. 7 rolls.

M1250 Letters Received by the Department of Justice from the State of Virginia, 1871-1884. 4 rolls. DP.

M681 Records Relating to the Appointment of Federal Judges, Attorneys, and Marshals for the Territory and State of Idaho, 1861-1899. 9 rolls. DP.

M224 Records Relating to the Appointment of Federal Judges, Attorneys, and Marshals for Oregon, 1853-1903. 3 rolls. DP.

M680 Records Relating to the Appointment of Federal Judges, Attorneys, and Marshals for the Territory and State of Utah, 1853-1901. 14 rolls. DP.

M198 Records Relating to the Appointment of Federal Judges and U.S. Marshals for the Territory and State of Washington, 1853-1902. 17 rolls. DP.

M1491 "The Pumpkin Papers": Microfilm Evidence Used in *United States* v. *Alger Hiss*, 1948-1951. 1 roll.

*M2010 Correspondence Relating to the Enforcement of the "Passenger Acts," 1852-1857. 1 roll.

*M2012 Appellate Case File No. 2161, *United States* v. *The Amistad*, 40 U.S. 518 (15 Peters 518), Decided March 9, 1841, and Related Lower Court and Department of Justice Records. 1 roll. DP.

*M2015 Select Letters and Related Documents from the Files of the Department of Justice Concerning Judge Isaac C. Parker, 1875-1896. 1 roll. DP.

*M2023 Appellate Case File No. 13879, *Thomas Cunningham, Sheriff of the Country of San Joaquin, California V. David Neagle,* and Related Department of Justice Records. 2 rolls

*M2028 Records Relating to U.S. Marshal Crawley P. Dake, the Earp Brothers, and the Lawlessness and "Cowboy Depredations" in Arizona Territory, 1881-1885. 1 roll.

T412 Opinions of the Attorney General, 1817-1832. 3 rolls.

T577 Index to Names of U.S. Marshals, 1789-1960. 1 roll. 16mm.

RG 61 Records of the War Industries Board

M1073 Minutes of War Industries Board Meetings, 1917-1918. 2 rolls. DP.

RG 62 Records of the Council of National Defense

M1069 Minutes of the Meetings of the Council of National Defense, 1916-1921; the Advisory Commission of the Council of National Defense, 1916-1918; the Interdepartmental Advisory Committee, 1917; the Joint Weekly Conference, 1917-1918; and the Interdepartmental Defense Board, 1919-1920. 1 roll.

M1074 Minutes of Meetings of the Committee on Women's Defense Work, May 2, 1917-Feb. 12, 1919, and Weekly and Monthly Reports of the Committee on Women's Defense Work, May 12, 1917-Oct. 15, 1918. 1 roll.

RG 63 Records of the Committee on Public Information

*M2038 Records of the Division of Work With the Foreign Born, Committee on Public Information, 1918. 1 roll.

RG 64 Records of the National Archives and Records Administration

M190 *Federal Register*, 1936-1983. 432 rolls. DP.

M248 Publications of the National Archives, 1935-1968. 24 rolls. DP.

M604 *National Archives Procedures: A General Services Administration Handbook* (1960). 1 roll.

M839 Weekly Compilations of Presidential Documents, 1965-1969. 5 rolls.

M1137 *Finding Aids to National Archives Photographs Relating to the Third German Reich*. 73 cards (microfiche).

T94 Guide to Records of the Italian Armed Forces. 1 roll.

T733 Guide to German Records Microfilmed at Alexandria. 9 rolls.

T820 National Archives Disposal Registers. 3 rolls.

T1167 *The Archives of the U.S. Government: A Documentary History, 1774-1934*, Compiled by Percy Scott Flippin. 5 rolls.

T1183 *Guide to Captured German Documents"* (Maxwell Air Force Base, Alabama, Dec. 1952) and *Supplement* (National Archives, Washington, DC, 1959). 1 roll.

T1195 *Prologue: The Journal of the National Archives, 1969-1978.* 2 rolls.

RG 65 Records of the Federal Bureau of Investigation

M1085 Investigative Case Files of the Bureau of Investigation, 1908-1922. 955 rolls. DP.

M1531 Index to Federal Bureau of Investigation Class 61—Treason or Misprision of Treason, 1921-1931. 15 rolls. DP.

RG 66 Records of the Commission of Fine Arts

M1148 Photographs of the Commission of Fine Arts, 1901-1950. 9 rolls.

RG 69 Records of the Work Projects Administration

M1366 Records of the Federal Writers' Project, Work Projects Administration, Relating to Louisiana, 1935-1943. 3 rolls. DP.

M1367 Selected Documents from the Louisiana Section of the Work Projects Administration General Correspondence File ("State Series"), 1935-1943. 30 rolls. DP.

T935 Index to Reference Cards for Work Projects Administration Project Files, 1935-1937. 79 rolls. 16mm.

T936 Index to Reference Cards for Work Projects Administration Project Files, 1938. 15 rolls. 16mm.

T937 Index to Reference Cards for Work Projects Administration Project Files, 1939-1942. 19 rolls. 16mm.

RG 71 Records of the Bureau of Yards and Docks

M1099 Annual Reports of the Department of the Navy, 1822-1866. 8 rolls. DP.

T1023 Plans of Buildings and Machinery Erected in the Navy Yard, Boston, 1830-1840. 1 roll.

RG 75 Records of the Bureau of Indian Affairs

M4 Letter Book of the Creek Trading House, 1795-1816. 1 roll. DP.

M15 Letters Sent by the Secretary of War Relating to Indian Affairs, 1800-1824. 6 rolls.

M16 Letters Sent by the Superintendent of Indian Trade, 1807-1823. 6 rolls. DP.

M18 Register of Letters Received by the Office of Indian Affairs, 1824-1880. 126 rolls. DP.

M21 Letters Sent by the Office of Indian Affairs, 1824-1881. 166 rolls. DP.

M74 Letters of Tench Coxe, Commissioner of the Revenue, Relating to the Procurement of Military, Naval, and Indian Supplies, 1794-1796. 1 roll. DP.

M142 Letter Book of the Arkansas Trading House, 1805-1810. 1 roll. DP.

M208 Records of the Cherokee Indian Agency in Tennessee, 1801-1835. 14 rolls. DP.

M234 Letters Received by the Office of Indian Affairs, 1824-1881. 962 rolls. DP.

M271 Letters Received by the Office of the Secretary of War Relating to Indian Affairs, 1800-1823. 4 rolls.

M348 Report Books of the Office of Indian Affairs, 1838-1885. 53 rolls. DP.

M574 Special Files of the Office of Indian Affairs, 1807-1904. 85 rolls. DP.

M595 Indian Census Rolls, 1884-1940. 692 rolls. DP.

M685 Records Relating to Enrollment of Eastern Cherokee by Guion Miller, 1908-1910. 12 rolls. DP.

M740 Records Relating to Investigations of the Fort Philip Kearney (or Fetterman) Massacre, 1866-1867. 1 roll. DP.

M941 Miscellaneous Letters Sent by the Pueblo Indian Agency, 1874-1891. 10 rolls. DP.

M1011 Superintendent's Annual Narrative and Statistical Reports from Field Jurisdictions of the Bureau of Indian Affairs, 1907-1938. 174 rolls. DP.

M1059 Selected Letters Received by the Office of Indian Affairs Relating to the Cherokee of North Carolina, 1851-1905. 7 rolls. DP.

M1121 Procedural Issuances of the Bureau of Indian Affairs: Orders and Circulars, 1854-1960. 17 rolls.

M1186 Enrollment Cards for the Five Civilized Tribes, 1898-1914. 93 rolls. DP.

M1229 Miscellaneous Letters Sent by the Agent at the Pine Ridge Indian Agency, 1876-1914. 76 rolls. DP.

M1282 Letters Sent to the Office of Indian Affairs by the Pine Ridge Agency, 1875-1914. 52 rolls. DP.

M1301 Applications for Enrollment of the Commission to the Five Civilized Tribes, 1898-1914. 468 rolls.

M1304 Records Created by Bureau of Indian Affairs Field Agencies Having Jurisdiction Over the Pueblo Records, 1874-1900. 32 rolls. DP.

M1314 Index to Letters Received by the Commission to the Five Civilized Tribes, 1897-1913. 23 rolls.

M1333 Records of the Alaska Division of the Bureau of Indian Affairs Concerning Metlakatla, 1887-1933. 14 rolls.

M1334 Records of the Creek Factory of the Office of Indian Trade of the Bureau of Indian Affairs, 1795-1821. 13 rolls.

M1343 Applications for Enrollment and Allotment of Washington Indians, 1911-1919. 6 rolls.

M1344 Records Concerning Applications for Adoption by the Quinaielt Indians, 1910-1919. 5 rolls.

M1350 Selected Records of the Bureau of Indian Affairs Relating to the Enrollment of Indians on the Flathead Reservation, 1903-1908. 3 rolls.

M1473 Bureau of Indian Affairs Records Created by the Santa Fe Indian School, 1890-1918. 38 rolls.

M1650 Applications from the Bureau of Indian Affairs, Muskogee Area Office, Relating to Enrollment in the Five Civilized Tribes Under the Act of 1896. 54 rolls. DP.

*M1831 Miscellaneous Indian Removal Muster Rolls, 1832-1846. 1 roll.

*M1833 Revisions to the Wallace Rolls of Cherokee Freedmen and Delaware And Shawnee Cherokees, ca.1890-96. 1 roll.

*M1853 Indians of California Census Rolls Authorized Under the Act of May 18, 1928 (45 Stat.602) as Amended, Approved May 16-17, 1933. 1 roll. DP.

*M1854 Statistical Records and Reports of the Alaska Division of the Bureau of Indian Affairs, 1912-1941. 12 rolls. DP.

*M1971 Letters Sent by the Office of Education, Alaska Division, Records of the Bureau of Indian Affairs, 1877-1908. 32 rolls. DP.

*M2039 Correspondence, Field Notes, and the Census Roll of All Persons and Their Descendants Who Were on the Roll of the Ottawa and the Chippewa Tribes of Michigan in 1870, and Living on March 4, 1907 (Durant Roll). 4 rolls. DP.

*M2043 Indexes to General Correspondence of the Office of Education, Alaska Division, Bureau of Indian Affairs, 1910-1930. 2 rolls.

T58 Letters Received by the Superintendent of Indian Trade, 1806-1824. 1 roll.

T275 Census of Creek Indians Taken by Parsons and Abbott in 1832. 1 roll.

T494 Documents Relating to the Negotiation of Ratified and Unratified Treaties With Various Indian Tribes, 1801-1869. 10 rolls.

T496 Census Roll of the Cherokee Indians East of the Mississippi and Index to the Roll, 1835. 1 roll.

T500 Records of the Choctaw Trading House, 1803-1824. 6 rolls.

T985 "Old Settler" Cherokee Census Roll, 1895, and Index to Payment Roll, 1896. 2 rolls.

T1029 Letterbook of the Natchitoches-Sulphur Fork Factory, 1809-1821. 1 roll.

*P2186 Registers of Letters Received, 1881-1907. 147 rolls.

*P2187 Indexes of Letters Received, 1881-1907. 35 rolls.

Records of the Superintendencies of Indian Affairs

M734 Records of the Arizona Superintendency of Indian Affairs, 1863-1873. 8 rolls. DP.

M856 Records of the Central Superintendency of Indian Affairs, 1813-1878. 108 rolls. DP.

M1016 Records of the Dakota Superintendency of Indian Affairs, 1861-1870, 1877-1878, and the Wyoming Superintendency, 1870. 13 rolls. DP.

M832 Records of the Idaho Superintendency of Indian Affairs, 1863-1870. 3 rolls. DP.

M1 Records of the Michigan Superintendency of Indian Affairs, 1814-1851. 71 rolls. DP.

M842 Records of the Minnesota Superintendency of Indian Affairs, 1849-1856. 9 rolls. DP.

M833 Records of the Montana Superintendency of Indian Affairs, 1867-1873. 3 rolls. DP.

M837 Records of the Nevada Superintendency of Indian Affairs, 1869-1870. 1 roll. DP.

T21 Records of the New Mexico Superintendency of Indian Affairs, 1849-1880. 30 rolls.

M1166 Records of the Northern Superintendency of Indian Affairs, 1851-1876. 35 rolls. DP.

M2 Records of the Oregon Superintendency of Indian Affairs, 1848-1873. 29 rolls. DP.

M640 Records of the Southern Superintendency of Indian Affairs, 1832-1870. 22 rolls. DP.

M834 Records of the Utah Superintendency of Indian Affairs, 1853-1870. 2 rolls. DP.

M5 Records of the Washington Superintendency of Indian Affairs, 1853-1874. 26 rolls. DP.

M951 Records of the Wisconsin Superintendency of Indian Affairs, 1836–1848, and the Green Bay Subagency, 1850. 4 rolls. DP.

RG 76 Records of Boundary and Claims Commissions and Arbitrations

T606 Records Relating to the First Northwest Boundary Survey Commission, 1853–1869. 4 rolls.

T1187 Records Relating to Claims Against Brazil Under the Convention of 1849. 19 rolls.

T716 Records of and Relating to the C.S.S. *Florida*, 1862–1864. 4 rolls.

RG 77 Records of the Office of the Chief of Engineers

M65 Letters Sent by the Office of the Chief of Engineers Relating to Internal Improvements, 1824–1830. 3 rolls. DP.

M66 Letters Sent by the Topographical Bureau of the War Department and by Successor Divisions in the Office of the Chief of Engineers, 1829–1870. 37 rolls. DP.

M417 Buell Collection of Historical Documents Relating to the Corps of Engineers, 1801–1819. 3 rolls. DP.

M505 Registers of Letters Received by the Topographical Bureau of the War Department, 1824–1866. 4 rolls. DP.

M506 Letters Received by the Topographical Bureau of the War Department, 1824–1865. 86 rolls. DP.

M1108 Harrison-Bundy Files Relating to the Development of the Atomic Bomb, 1942–1946. 9 rolls. DP.

M1109 Correspondence ("Top Secret") of the Manhattan Engineer District, 1942–1946. 5 rolls. DP.

M1113 Letters Sent by the Chief of Engineers, 1812–1869. 8 rolls.

M1702 Name and Subject Index to Field Survey Records, 1793–1916. 1 roll.

M1703 General Information Index to Names and Subjects ("The De Grange Index"), 1789–1889. 7 rolls.

*M2063 Selected Military Service Records Relating to Robert E. Lee. 1 roll.

RG 78 Records of the U.S. Naval Observatory

T54 Correspondence of the U.S. Naval Astronomical Expedition to the Southern Hemisphere, 1846–1861. 1 roll.

RG 80 General Records of the Department of the Navy, 1798–1947

M181 Annual Reports of the Governors of Guam, 1901–1941. 3 rolls. DP.

M971 Annual Reports of Fleets and Task Forces of the U.S. Navy, 1920–1941. 15 rolls. DP.

M1052 General and Special Indexes to the General Correspondence of the Office of the Secretary of the Navy, July 1897–Aug. 1926. 119 rolls. DP.

M1067 Name and Subject Index to the General Correspondence of the Office of the Secretary of the Navy, 1930–1942. 187 rolls. DP.

M1092 Indexes and Subject Cards to the "Secret and Confidential" Correspondence of the Office of the Secretary of the Navy, Mar. 1917–July 1919. 11 rolls. DP.

M1140 Secret and Confidential Correspondence of the Office of the Chief of Naval Operations and the Office of the Secretary of the Navy, 1919–1927. 117 rolls. DP.

M1141 Indexes and Register to the Correspondence of the Office of the Chief of Naval Operations and the Office of the Secretary of the Navy, 1919–1927. 9 rolls. DP.

M1493 Proceedings of the General Board of the U.S. Navy, 1900–1950. 28 rolls. DP.

RG 81 Records of the U.S. International Trade Commission

A1150 U.S. Imports for Consumption, 1930–1938. 41 rolls.

RG 82 Records of the Federal Reserve System

M591 Minutes of the Federal Open Market Committee, 1936–1974, and of Its Executive Committee, 1936–1955. 43 rolls. DP.

RG 84 Records of the Foreign Service Posts of the Department of State

Selected Records of U.S. Legations

M20 Selected Records of the U.S. Legation in Chile, 1893–1905. 14 rolls.

T898 Selected Records of the U.S. Legation in China, 1849–1931. 20 rolls.

M14 Selected Records of the U.S. Legation in France, 1836–1842. 10 rolls.

T400 Selected Records of the U.S. Legation in Japan, 1855–1912. 94 rolls.

T693 Selected Records of the U.S. Legation in Paraguay, 1861–1907. 5 rolls.

T724 Selected Records of the U.S. Legation in Peru, 1826–1912. 88 rolls.

Selected Records of U.S. Consular Posts

T403 Selected Records of the U.S. Consulate in Bangkok, Siam, 1856–1912. 14 rolls.

T307 Selected Records of the U.S. Consulate in Bombay, India, 1894–1912. 7 rolls.

T781 Selected Records of the U.S. Consulate at Callao-Lima, Peru, 1825–1912. 73 rolls.

T402 Selected Records of the U.S. Consulate in Kunming, China, 1922–1928. 19 rolls.

T308 Selected Records of the U.S. Consulate in Madras, India, 1908–1912. 8 rolls.

*M1945 General Records of the American Embassy in Warsaw, 1945–1947. 24 rolls.

M1520 Bound Volumes of the General Records of the U.S. Consulate at Yokohama, Japan, 1936–1939. 22 rolls. DP.

RG 85 Records of the Immigration and Naturalization Service

Passenger Lists, Crew Lists, and Indexes

See also Records of the U.S. Customs (RG 36)

INDEXES TO PASSENGER, SHIP, AND CREW LISTS

T517 Index to Passenger Lists of Vessels Arriving at Ports in Alabama, Florida, Georgia, and South Carolina, 1890-1924. 26 rolls.

T520 Index (Soundex) to Passenger Lists of Vessels Arriving at Baltimore, Maryland, 1897-July 1952. 42 rolls. 16mm.

T790 Book Indexes, Boston Passenger Lists, 1899-1940. 107 rolls.

T521 Index to Passenger Lists of Vessels Arriving at Boston, Massachusetts, Jan. 1, 1902-June 30, 1906. 11 rolls. 16mm.

T617 Index to Passenger Lists of Vessels Arriving at Boston, Massachusetts, July 1, 1906-Dec. 31, 1920. 11 rolls. 16mm.

*M1514 Indexes of Vessels Arriving at Brownsville, Texas, 1935-1955; Houston, Texas, 1948-1954; and at Port Arthur and Beaumont, Texas, and Lake Charles, Louisiana, 1908-1954. 1 roll.

M1357 Index to Passenger Lists of Vessels Arriving at Galveston, Texas, 1896-Sept. 1906. 3 rolls. 16mm.

M1358 Index to Passenger Lists of Vessels Arriving at Galveston, Texas, Oct. 1906-1951. 7 rolls. 16mm.

T523 Index to Passengers Arriving at Gulfport, Mississippi, Aug. 27, 1904-Aug. 28, 1954, and at Pascagoula, Mississippi, July 15, 1903-May 21, 1935. 1 roll. 16mm.

T522 Index to Passengers Arriving at New Bedford, Massachusetts, July 1, 1902-Nov. 18, 1954. 2 rolls. 16mm.

T618 Index to Passenger Lists of Vessels Arriving at New Orleans, Louisiana, 1900-1952. 22 rolls. 16mm.

T519 Index to Passenger Lists of Vessels Arriving at New York, New York, June 16, 1897-June 30, 1902. 115 rolls. 16mm.

T612 Book Indexes, New York Passenger Lists, 1906-1942. 807 rolls.

T621 Index (Soundex) to Passenger Lists of Vessels Arriving at New York, New York, July 1, 1902-Dec. 31, 1943. 744 rolls.

M1417 Index (Soundex) to Passengers Arriving in New York, New York, 1944-1948. 94 rolls.

T526 Index (Soundex) Cards, Ship Arrivals at Philadelphia, Pennsylvania, Jan. 1, 1883-June 28, 1948. 60 rolls. 16mm.

T791 Book Indexes, Philadelphia Passenger Lists, 1906-1926. 23 rolls.

T793 Book Indexes, Portland, Maine, Passenger Lists, 1907-1930. 12 rolls.

T524 Index to Passengers Arriving at Portland, Maine, Jan. 29, 1893-Nov. 22, 1954. 1 roll. 16mm.

T792 Book Indexes, Providence Passenger Lists, 1911-1934. 15 rolls.

T518 Index to Passengers Arriving at Providence, Rhode Island, June 18, 1911-Oct. 5, 1954. 2 rolls.

M1461 Soundex Index to Canadian Border Entries through the St. Albans, Vermont, District, 1895-1924. 400 rolls. 16mm.

M1463 Soundex Index to Entries into the St. Albans, Vermont, District through Canadian Pacific and Atlantic Ports, 1924-1952. 98 rolls. 16mm.

*M1761 Index to Passenger Arrivals at San Diego, California, ca. 1904-ca. 1952. 6 rolls.

M1389 Indexes to Passenger Lists of Vessels Arriving at San Francisco, California, 1893-1934. 28 rolls. 16mm.

M1437 Indexes to Vessels Arriving at San Francisco, 1882-1957. 1 roll.

*M1763 Index to Passenger Lists of Vessels Arriving at San Pedro/Wilmington/Los Angeles, California, 1907-1936. 7 rolls.

*M1764 Passenger Lists of Vessels Arriving at San Pedro/Wilmington/Los Angeles, California, June 29, 1907-June 30, 1948. 118 rolls.

IMMIGRATION AND PASSENGER LISTS

*M1481 Alphabetical Card Manifests of Alien Arrivals at Alexandria Bay, Cape Vincent, Champlain, Clayton, Fort Covington, Mooers, Rouses Point, Thousand Island Bridge, and Trout River, New York, July 1929-April 1956. 3 rolls.

*M2030 Statistical and Nonstatistical Manifests, and Related Indexes, of Aliens Arriving at Andrade and Campo (Tecate), California, 1910-1952. 5 rolls. DP.

T844 Passenger Lists of Vessels Arriving at Baltimore, Maryland, 1891-1909. 150 rolls.

T843 Passenger Lists of Vessels Arriving at Boston, Massachusetts, 1891-1943. 454 rolls.

*M1320 Passenger and Crew Lists of Vessels (February 1929-February 1959) and Airplanes (April 1946-February 1959) Arriving at Bridgeport, Groton, Hartford, New Haven, and New London, Connecticut. 13 rolls.

*M1502 Statistical and Nonstatistical Manifests of Alien Arrivals at Brownsville, Texas, February 1905-June 1953, and Related Indexes. 40 rolls. DP.

*M2042 Alphabetical Manifest Cards of Alien Arrivals at Calais, Maine, ca. 1906-1952. 5 rolls.

M1478 Card Manifests (Alphabetical) of Individuals Entering through the Port of Detroit, Michigan, 1906-54. 117 rolls.

M1479 Passenger and Alien Crew Lists of Vessels Arriving at the Port of Detroit, Michigan, 1946-57. 23 rolls.

*M1759 Nonstatistical Manifests and Statistical Index Cards of Aliens Arriving at Douglas, Arizona, July 1908-December 1952. 4 rolls. DP.

*M2016 Alphabetical Index of Alien Arrivals at Eagle, Hyder, Ketchikan, Nome, and Skagway, Alaska, June 1906-August 1946. 1 roll.

*M2018 Lists of Aliens Arriving at Eagle, Alaska, December 1910-October 1938. 1 roll.

*M1754 Nonstatistical Manifests and Statistical Index Cards of Aliens Arriving at Eagle Pass, Texas, June 1905-November 1929. 27 rolls. DP.

*M1755 Permanent and Statistical Manifests of Alien Arrivals at Eagle Pass, Texas, June 1905–June 1953. 30 rolls. DP.

*M2040 Index to Manifests of Permanent and Statistical Arrivals at Eagle Pass, Texas, December 1, 1929–June 1953. 2 rolls. DP.

*M2041 Temporary and Nonstatistical Manifests of Aliens Arriving at Eagle Pass, Texas, July 1928–June 1953. 14 rolls. DP.

*M1756 Applications for Nonresident Alien's Border Crossing Identification Cards Made at El Paso, Texas, ca. July 1945–December 1952. 62 rolls. DP.

*M1757 Manifests of Aliens Granted Temporary Admission at El Paso, Texas, ca. July 1924–1954. 97 rolls. DP.

*M1768 Alphabetical Card Manifests of Alien Arrivals at Fabens, Texas, July 1924–1954. 7 rolls. DP.

*M2064 Alphabetical Manifest Cards of Alien and Citizen Arrivals at Fort Fairfield, Maine, ca. 1909–April 1953. 1 roll.

*M1766 Alphabetical Card Manifests of Alien Arrivals at Fort Hancock, Texas, 1924–1954. 2 rolls.

M1359 Passenger Lists of Vessels Arriving at Galveston, Texas, 1896–1951. 36 rolls.

*M1842 Passenger Lists of Vessels Arriving at Georgetown, South Carolina, 1923–1939, and at Apalachicola, Boynton, Boca Grande, Carrabelle, Fernandina, Fort Pierce, Hobs Sounds, Lake Worth, Mayport, Millville, Port Inglis, Port St. Joe, St. Andrews, and Stuart, Florida, 1904–1942. 1 roll.

*M1321 Passenger Lists of Vessels Arriving at Gloucester, Massachusetts, October 1906–March 1942. 1 roll. DP.

*M1778 Passenger and Crew Lists of Vessels Departing the Trust Territory of the Pacific Islands for Arrival at Guam, 1947–1952, and Related Records. 1 roll.

*M1482 Soundex Card Manifests of Alien and Citizen Arrivals at Hogansburg, Malone, Morristown, Nyando, Ogdensburg, Rooseveltown, and Waddington, New York, July 1929–April 1956. 3 rolls

T940 Passenger Lists of Vessels Arriving at Key West, Florida, 1898–1945. 122 rolls.

*M1771 Alphabetical Manifests of Non-Mexican Aliens Granted Temporary Admission at Laredo, Texas, December 1, 1929–April 8, 1955. 5 rolls.

*M2008 Lists of Aliens Arriving at Laredo, Texas, from July 1903 to June 1907, via the Mexican National Railroad or the Laredo Foot Bridge. 1 roll.

T944 Passenger Lists of Vessels Arriving at New Bedford, Massachusetts, 1902–1942. 8 rolls.

T905 Passenger Lists of Vessels Arriving at New Orleans, Louisiana, 1903–1945. 189 rolls.

T715 Passenger and Crew Lists of Vessels Arriving at New York, New York, 1897–1957. 8,892 rolls.

*M1840 Passenger Lists of Aliens (1927–1939) and Citizens (1933–1939) Arriving in Panama City, Florida. 1 roll. DP.

*M2021 Passenger Lists of Citizens (June 1924–Aug. 1948) and Aliens (March 1946–Nov. 1948) Arriving at Pensacola, Florida, and Passenger Lists of Vessels Departing from Pensacola, Florida (Aug. 1926–March 1948). 1 roll.

T840 Passenger Lists of Vessels Arriving at Philadelphia, Pennsylvania, 1883–1945. 181 rolls.

A1151 Passenger Lists of Vessels Arriving at Portland, Maine, Nov. 29, 1893–Mar. 1943. 35 rolls.

M1484 Customs Passenger Lists of Vessels Arriving at Port Townsend and Tacoma, Washington, 1894–1909. 1 roll. DP.

*M1851 Index and Manifests of Alien Arrivals at Progreso/Thayer, Texas, October 1928–May 1955. 6 rolls.

A1188 Passenger Lists of Vessels Arriving at Providence, Rhode Island, 1911–1943. 49 rolls.

*M1770 Indexes and Manifests of Alien Arrivals at Rio Grande City, Texas, November 1908–May 1955. 6 rolls.

*M1503 Index and Manifests of Alien Arrivals at Roma, Texas, March 1928–May 1955. 5 rolls.

M1464 Manifests of Passengers Arriving in the St. Albans, Vermont, District through Canadian Pacific and Atlantic Ports, 1895–1954. 640 rolls.

M1465 Manifests of Passengers Arriving in the St. Albans, Vermont, District through Canadian Pacific Ports, 1929–1949. 25 rolls.

*M1959 Passenger Lists of Vessels Arriving at St. Petersburg, Florida, December 1926–March 1941. 1 roll.

*M1973 Statistical Manifests of Alien Arrivals by Airplane at San Antonio, Texas, May 17, 1944–March 1952. 1 roll.

M1414 Lists of Chinese Passenger Arrivals at San Francisco, 1882–1914. 32 rolls.

M1410 Passenger Lists of Vessels Arriving at San Francisco, 1893–1953. 429 rolls.

M1494 Passenger Lists of Vessels Arriving at San Francisco from Honolulu, 1902–1907. 1 roll.

M1412 Customs Passenger Lists of Vessels Arriving at San Francisco, 1903–1918. 13 rolls.

M1438 Passenger Lists of Vessels Arriving at San Francisco from Insular Possessions, 1907–1911. 2 rolls.

M1411 Passenger and Crew Lists of Vessels Arriving at San Francisco, 1954–1957. 19 rolls.

*A3361 Register of Citizen (1943–1947) and Alien (1936–1949) Arrivals by Aircraft at San Francisco, California. 2 rolls.

*M1504 Manifests of Alien Arrivals at San Luis, Arizona, July 24, 1929–December 1952. 2 rolls.

*M1767 Manifests of Alien Arrivals at San Ysidro (Tia Juana), California, April 21, 1908–December 1952. 20 rolls. DP.

*M1850 Index and Manifests of Alien Arrivals at Sasabe/San Fernando, Arizona, 1919–1952. 3 rolls. DP.

T943 Passenger Lists of Vessels Arriving at Savannah, Georgia, 1906–1945. 4 rolls.

M1364 Lists of Chinese Passengers Arriving at Seattle (Port Townsend), Washington, 1882–1916. 10 rolls.

M1383 Passenger and Crew Lists of Vessels Arriving at Seattle, Washington, 1890–1957. 357 rolls.

M1485 Passenger Lists of Vessels Arriving at Seattle from Insular Possessions, 1908–1917. 1 roll.

M1398 Passenger Lists of Vessels Arriving at Seattle, Washington, 1949–1954. 5 rolls.

*M2017 Lists of Aliens Arriving at Skagway (White Pass) Alaska, October 1906–November 1934. 1 roll.

*M1844 Passenger Lists of Vessels Arriving at Tampa, Florida, November 2, 1898-December 31, 1945. 65 rolls.

*M2071 Alphabetical Manifests Cards of Alien Arrivals at Vanceboro, Maine, ca. 1906-December 24, 1952. 13 rolls.

*A3363 Passenger and Crew Lists of Vessels Arriving at Ventura, California, May 1929-December 1956. 1 roll.

*M2032 Passenger Lists of European Immigrants Arriving at Vera Cruz, Mexico, 1921-1923, and Related Correspondence, 1921-1931. 1 roll.

*M1849 Manifests of Alien Arrivals at Yseleta, Texas, 1924-1954. 7 rolls.

*M2024 Indexes and Manifests of Alien Arrivals at Zapata, Texas, August 1923-September 1953. 2 rolls. DP.

CREW LISTS

*M2005 Crew Lists of Vessels Arriving at Ashland, Wisconsin, August 1922-October 1954. 2 rolls. DP.

T938 Crew Lists of Vessels Arriving at Boston, Massachusetts, 1917-1943. 269 rolls.

T941 Crew Lists of Vessels Arriving at Gloucester, Massachusetts, 1918-1943. 13 rolls.

T942 Crew Lists of Vessels Arriving at New Bedford, Massachusetts, 1917-1943. 2 rolls.

T939 Crew Lists of Vessels Arriving at New Orleans, Louisiana, 1910-1945. 311 rolls.

*M2027 Admitted Alien Crew Lists of Vessels Arriving at Pascagoula, Mississippi, July 1903-May 1935. 1 roll.

M1436 Admitted Alien Crew Lists of Vessels Arriving at San Francisco, 1896-1921. 8 rolls.

M1416 Crew Lists of Vessels Arriving at San Francisco, 1905-1954. 174 rolls.

M1399 Crew Lists of Vessels Arriving at Seattle, Washington, 1903-1917. 15 rolls.

OTHER RECORDS

T458 Subject Index to Correspondence and Case Files of the Immigration and Naturalization Service, 1903-1952. 31 rolls.

M1299 Index to New England Naturalization Records, 1791-1906. 117 rolls.

M1144 Case Files of Chinese Immigrants, 1895-1920, from District No. 4 (Philadelphia) of the Immigration and Naturalization Service. 51 rolls. DP.

M1500 Records of the Special Boards of Inquiry, District No. 4 (Philadelphia), Immigration and Naturalization Service, 1893-1909. 18 rolls. DP.

M1387 Minutes of the Boards of Special Inquiry at the San Francisco Immigration Office, 1899-1909. 2 rolls.

M1413 Registers of Chinese Laborers Returning to the U.S. Through the Port of San Francisco, 1882-1888. 12 rolls.

M1439 Lists of U.S. Citizens Arriving at San Francisco, 1930-1949. 50 rolls.

M1476 Lists of Chinese Applying for Admission to the United States Through the Port of San Francisco, 1903-1947. 27 rolls.

M1285 Soundex Index to Naturalization Petitions for the United States District and Circuit Courts, Northern District of Illinois, and Immigration and Naturalization Service District 9, 1840-1950. 179 rolls. DP.

M1365 Certificates of Head Tax Paid by Aliens Arriving at Seattle from Foreign Contiguous Territory, 1917-1924. 10 rolls.

M1462 Alphabetical Index to Canadian Border Entries through Small Ports in Vermont, 1895-1924. 6 rolls.

M1638 Immigration and Naturalization Service Case Files of Chinese Immigrants, Portland, Oregon, 1890-1914. 15 rolls.

*M1852 Record of Persons Held for Boards of Special Inquiry at the San Pedro, California, Immigration Office, November 3, 1930-September 27, 1936. 1 roll.

RG 87 Records of the U.S. Secret Service

T917 Register of Monthly Reports by U.S. Secret Service Agents, Dec. 1864-Feb. 1871. 7 rolls.

T915 Daily Reports of U.S. Secret Service Agents, 1875-1936. 836 rolls.

RG 90 Records of the Public Health Service, 1912–1968

M753 Letters Received by the National Board of Health, 1879-1884, and Related Register, 1879-1882. 59 rolls. DP.

RG 92 Records of the Office of the Quartermaster General

M745 Letters Sent by the Office of the Quartermaster General, Main Series, 1818-1870. 61 rolls. DP.

M918 Register of Confederate Soldiers, Sailors, and Citizens Who Died in Federal Prisons and Military Hospitals in the North, 1861-1865. 1 roll. DP.

M1780 Selected Records of the National Military Cemetery at Fayetteville, Arkansas, 1867-1914. 1 roll.

*M1845 Card Records of Headstones Provided for Deceased Union Civil War Veterans, ca. 1879-ca. 1903. 22 rolls. DP.

M2014 Burial Registers for Military Posts, Camps, and Stations, 1768-1921. 1 roll. DP.

RG 93 War Department Collection of Revolutionary War Records

Indexes to Compiled Service Records

M860 General Index to Compiled Military Service Records of Revolutionary War Soldiers. 58 rolls. DP. 16mm.

M879 Index to Compiled Service Records of American Naval Personnel Who Served During the Revolutionary War. 1 roll. DP.

M920 Index to Compiled Service Records of Revolutionary War Soldiers Who Served With the American Army in Connecticut Military Organizations. 25 rolls. DP.

M1051 Index to Compiled Service Records of Revolutionary War Soldiers Who Served With the American Army in Georgia Military Organizations. 1 roll. DP.

M257 Index to Compiled Service Records of Volunteer Soldiers Who Served During the Revolutionary War in Organizations from the State of North Carolina. 2 rolls. DP. 16mm.

Compiled Service Records

M880 Compiled Service Records of American Naval Personnel and Members of the Departments of the Quartermaster General and the Commissary General of Military Stores Who Served During the Revolutionary War. 4 rolls. DP.

M881 Compiled Service Records of Soldiers Who Served in the American Army During the Revolutionary War. 1,096 rolls. DP.

Other Records

M246 Revolutionary War Rolls, 1775-1783. 138 rolls. DP.

M847 Special Index to Numbered Records in the War Department Collection of Revolutionary War Records, 1775-1783. 39 rolls. DP.

M853 Numbered Record Books Concerning Military Operations and Service, Pay and Settlement of Accounts, and Supplies in the War Department Collection of Revolutionary War Records. 41 rolls. DP.

M859 Miscellaneous Numbered Records (The Manuscript File) in the War Department Collection of Revolutionary War Records, 1775-1790s. 125 rolls. DP.

M913 Personnel Returns of the 6th Massachusetts Battalion, 1779-1780, and Returns and Accounts of Military Stores for the 8th and 9th Massachusetts Regiments, 1779-1782. 1 roll. DP.

M922 Orders, Returns, Morning Reports, and Accounts of British Troops, 1776-1781. 1 roll. DP.

M926 Letters, Returns, Accounts, and Estimates of the Quartermaster General's Department, 1776-1783, in the War Department Collection of Revolutionary War Records. 1 roll. DP.

T42 General Orders Kept by Gen. William Heath, May 23, 1777-Oct. 20, 1778. 1 roll.

RG 94 Records of the Adjutant General's Office, 1780s–1917

Correspondence

M698 Index to General Correspondence of the Adjutant General's Office, 1890-1917. 1,269 rolls. DP.

M725 Indexes to Letters Received by the Office of the Adjutant General (Main Series), 1846, 1861-1889. 9 rolls. DP.

M711 Registers of Letters Received, Office of the Adjutant General (Main Series), 1812-1889. 85 rolls. DP.

M566 Letters Received by the Office of the Adjutant General, 1805-1821. 144 rolls. DP.

M567 Letters Received by the Office of the Adjutant General (Main Series), 1822-1860. 636 rolls. DP.

M619 Letters Received by the Office of the Adjutant General (Main Series), 1861-1870. 828 rolls. DP.

M666 Letters Received by the Office of the Adjutant General (Main Series), 1871-1880. 593 rolls. DP.

M689 Letters Received by the Office of the Adjutant General (Main Series), 1881-1889. 740 rolls. DP.

M565 Letters Sent by the Office of the Adjutant General (Main Series), 1800-1890. 63 rolls. DP.

Indexes to Compiled Service Records

1784–MEXICAN WAR

M694 Index to Compiled Service Records of Volunteer Soldiers Who Served from 1784-1811. 9 rolls. DP. 16mm.

M602 Index to Compiled Service Records of Volunteer Soldiers Who Served During the War of 1812. 234 rolls. DP. 16mm.

M229 Index to Compiled Service Records of Volunteer Soldiers Who Served During the War of 1812 in Organizations from the State of Louisiana. 3 rolls. DP. 16mm.

M250 Index to Compiled Service Records of Volunteer Soldiers Who Served During the War of 1812 in Organizations from the State of North Carolina. 5 rolls. DP. 16mm.

M652 Index to Compiled Service Records of Volunteer Soldiers Who Served During the War of 1812 in Organizations from the State of South Carolina. 7 rolls. DP. 16mm.

M629 Index to Compiled Service Records of Volunteer Soldiers Who Served During Indian Wars and Disturbances, 1815-1858. 42 rolls. DP. 16mm.

M243 Index to Compiled Service Records of Volunteer Soldiers Who Served During the Cherokee Removal in Organizations from the State of Alabama. 1 roll. DP. 16mm.

M907 Index to Compiled Service Records of Volunteer Soldiers Who Served During the Cherokee Disturbances and Removal in Organizations from the State of Georgia. 1 roll. DP. 16mm.

M256 Index to Compiled Service Records of Volunteer Soldiers Who Served During the Cherokee Disturbances and Removal in Organizations from the State of North Carolina. 1 roll. DP. 16mm.

M908 Index to Compiled Service Records of Volunteer Soldiers Who Served During the Cherokee Disturbances and Removal in Organizations from the State of Tennessee and the Field and Staff of the Army of the Cherokee Nation. 2 rolls. DP. 16mm.

M244 Index to Compiled Service Records of Volunteer Soldiers Who Served During the Creek War in Organizations from the State of Alabama. 2 rolls. DP. 16mm.

M245 Index to Compiled Service Records of Volunteer Soldiers Who Served During the Florida War in Organizations from the State of Alabama. 1 roll. DP. 16mm.

M239 Index to Compiled Service Records of Volunteer Soldiers Who Served During the Florida War in Organizations from the State of Louisiana. 1 roll. DP. 16mm.

M241 Index to Compiled Service Records of Volunteer Soldiers Who Served During the War of 1837-1838 in Organizations from the State of Louisiana. 1 roll. DP. 16mm.

M630 Index to Compiled Service Records of Volunteer Soldiers Who Served from the State of Michigan During the Patriot War, 1838-1839. 1 roll. DP. 16mm.

M631 Index to Compiled Service Records of Volunteer Soldiers Who Served from the State of New York During the Patriot War, 1838. 1 roll. DP. 16mm.

M616 Index to Compiled Service Records of Volunteer Soldiers Who Served During the Mexican War. 41 rolls. DP. 16mm.

CIVIL WAR

M1290 Alphabetical Card Name Indexes to the Compiled Service Records of Volunteer Soldiers Who Served in Union Organizations not Raised by States or Territories, Excepting the Veterans Reserve Corps and the U.S. Colored Troops. 36 rolls. DP.

M263 Index to Compiled Service Records of Volunteer Union Soldiers Who Served in Organizations from the State of Alabama. 1 roll. DP. 16mm.

M532 Index to Compiled Service Records of Volunteer Union Soldiers Who Served in Organizations from the Territory of Arizona. 1 roll. DP. 16mm.

M383 Index to Compiled Service Records of Volunteer Union Soldiers Who Served in Organizations from the State of Arkansas. 4 rolls. DP. 16mm.

M533 Index to Compiled Service Records of Volunteer Union Soldiers Who Served in Organizations from the State of California. 7 rolls. DP. 16mm.

M534 Index to Compiled Service Records of Volunteer Union Soldiers Who Served in Organizations from the Territory of Colorado. 3 rolls. DP. 16mm.

M535 Index to Compiled Service Records of Volunteer Union Soldiers Who Served in Organizations from the State of Connecticut. 17 rolls. DP. 16mm.

M536 Index to Compiled Service Records of Volunteer Union Soldiers Who Served in Organizations from the Territory of Dakota. 1 roll. DP. 16mm.

M537 Index to Compiled Service Records of Volunteer Union Soldiers Who Served in Organizations from the State of Delaware. 4 rolls. DP. 16mm.

M538 Index to Compiled Service Records of Volunteer Union Soldiers Who Served in Organizations from the District of Columbia. 3 rolls. DP. 16mm.

M264 Index to Compiled Service Records of Volunteer Union Soldiers Who Served in Organizations from the State of Florida. 1 roll. DP. 16mm.

M385 Index to Compiled Service Records of Volunteer Union Soldiers Who Served in Organizations from the State of Georgia. 1 roll. DP. 16mm.

M539 Index to Compiled Service Records of Volunteer Union Soldiers Who Served in Organizations from the State of Illinois. 101 rolls. DP. 16mm.

M540 Index to Compiled Service Records of Volunteer Union Soldiers Who Served in Organizations from the State of Indiana. 86 rolls. DP. 16mm.

M541 Index to Compiled Service Records of Volunteer Union Soldiers Who Served in Organizations from the State of Iowa. 29 rolls. DP. 16mm.

M542 Index to Compiled Service Records of Volunteer Union Soldiers Who Served in Organizations from the State of Kansas. 10 rolls. DP. 16mm.

M386 Index to Compiled Service Records of Volunteer Union Soldiers Who Served in Organizations from the State of Kentucky. 30 rolls. DP. 16mm.

M387 Index to Compiled Service Records of Volunteer Union Soldiers Who Served in Organizations from the State of Louisiana. 4 rolls. DP. 16mm.

M543 Index to Compiled Service Records of Volunteer Union Soldiers Who Served in Organizations from the State of Maine. 23 rolls. DP. 16mm.

M388 Index to Compiled Service Records of Volunteer Union Soldiers Who Served in Organizations from the State of Maryland. 13 rolls. DP. 16mm.

M544 Index to Compiled Service Records of Volunteer Union Soldiers Who Served in Organizations from the State of Massachusetts. 44 rolls. DP. 16mm.

M545 Index to Compiled Service Records of Volunteer Union Soldiers Who Served in Organizations from the State of Michigan. 48 rolls. DP. 16mm.

M546 Index to Compiled Service Records of Volunteer Union Soldiers Who Served in Organizations from the State of Minnesota. 10 rolls. DP. 16mm.

M389 Index to Compiled Service Records of Volunteer Union Soldiers Who Served in Organizations from the State of Mississippi. 1 roll. DP. 16mm.

M390 Index to Compiled Service Records of Volunteer Union Soldiers Who Served in Organizations from the State of Missouri. 54 rolls. DP. 16mm.

M547 Index to Compiled Service Records of Volunteer Union Soldiers Who Served in Organizations from the Territory of Nebraska. 2 rolls. DP. 16mm.

M548 Index to Compiled Service Records of Volunteer Union Soldiers Who Served in Organizations from the State of Nevada. 1 roll. DP. 16mm.

M549 Index to Compiled Service Records of Volunteer Union Soldiers Who Served in Organizations from the State of New Hampshire. 13 rolls. DP. 16mm.

M550 Index to Compiled Service Records of Volunteer Union Soldiers Who Served in Organizations from the State of New Jersey. 26 rolls. DP. 16mm.

M242 Index to Compiled Service Records of Volunteer Union Soldiers Who Served in Organizations from the Territory of New Mexico. 4 rolls. DP. 16mm.

M551 Index to Compiled Service Records of Volunteer Union Soldiers Who Served in Organizations from the State of New York. 157 rolls. DP. 16mm.

M391 Index to Compiled Service Records of Volunteer Union Soldiers Who Served in Organizations from the State of North Carolina. 2 rolls. DP. 16mm.

M552 Index to Compiled Service Records of Volunteer Union Soldiers Who Served in Organizations from the State of Ohio. 122 rolls. DP. 16mm.

M553 Index to Compiled Service Records of Volunteer Union Soldiers Who Served in Organizations from the State of Oregon. 1 roll. DP. 16mm.

M554 Index to Compiled Service Records of Volunteer Union Soldiers Who Served in Organizations from the State of Pennsylvania. 136 rolls. DP. 16mm.

M555 Index to Compiled Service Records of Volunteer Union Soldiers Who Served in Organizations from the State of Rhode Island. 7 rolls. DP. 16mm.

M392 Index to Compiled Service Records of Volunteer Union Soldiers Who Served in Organizations from the State of Tennessee. 16 rolls. DP. 16mm.

M393 Index to Compiled Service Records of Volunteer Union Soldiers Who Served in Organizations from the State of Texas. 2 rolls. DP. 16mm.

M556 Index to Compiled Service Records of Volunteer Union Soldiers Who Served in Organizations from the Territory of Utah. 1 roll. DP. 16mm.

M557 Index to Compiled Service Records of Volunteer Union Soldiers Who Served in Organizations from the State of Vermont. 14 rolls. DP. 16mm.

M394 Index to Compiled Service Records of Volunteer Union Soldiers Who Served in Organizations from the State of Virginia. 1 roll. DP. 16mm.

M558 Index to Compiled Service Records of Volunteer Union Soldiers Who Served in Organizations from the Territory of Washington. 1 roll. DP. 16mm.

M507 Index to Compiled Service Records of Volunteer Union Soldiers Who Served in Organizations from the State of West Virginia. 13 rolls. DP. 16mm.

M559 Index to Compiled Service Records of Volunteer Union Soldiers Who Served in Organizations from the State of Wisconsin. 33 rolls. DP. 16mm.

M636 Index to Compiled Service Records of Volunteer Union Soldiers Who Served in the Veteran Reserve Corps. 44 rolls. DP. 16mm.

M589 Index to Compiled Service Records of Volunteer Union Soldiers Who Served With U.S. Colored Troops. 98 rolls. DP. 16mm.

WAR WITH SPAIN AND PHILIPPINE INSURRECTION

M871 General Index to Compiled Service Records of Volunteer Soldiers Who Served During the War With Spain. 126 rolls. DP. 16mm.

M240 Index to Compiled Service Records of Volunteer Soldiers Who Served During the War With Spain in Organizations from the State of Louisiana. 1 roll. DP. 16mm.

M413 Index to Compiled Service Records of Volunteer Soldiers Who Served During the War With Spain in Organizations from the State of North Carolina. 2 rolls. DP. 16mm.

M872 Index to Compiled Service Records of Volunteer Soldiers Who Served During the Philippine Insurrection. 24 rolls. DP. 16mm.

Compiled Service Records of Volunteer Soldiers

1784–MEXICAN WAR

M905 Compiled Service Records of Volunteer Soldiers Who Served from 1784 to 1811. 32 rolls. DP. 16mm.

M678 Compiled Service Records of Volunteer Soldiers Who Served During the War of 1812 in Organizations from the Territory of Mississippi. 22 rolls. DP. 16mm.

M1505 Compiled Military Service Records of Michigan and Illinois Volunteers Who Served During the Winnebago Indian Disturbances of 1827. 3 rolls. DP.

M1086 Compiled Service Records of Volunteer Soldiers Who Served in Organizations from the State of Florida During the Florida Indian Wars, 1835-1858. 63 rolls. DP.

M351 Compiled Service Records of Volunteer Soldiers Who Served During the Mexican War in Mormon Organizations. 3 rolls. DP. 16mm.

M863 Compiled Service Records of Volunteer Soldiers Who Served During the Mexican War in Organizations from the State of Mississippi. 9 rolls. DP. 16mm.

M1028 Compiled Service Records of Volunteer Soldiers Who Served During the Mexican War in Organizations from the State of Pennsylvania. 13 rolls. DP.

M638 Compiled Service Records of Volunteer Soldiers Who Served During the Mexican War in Organizations from the State of Tennessee. 15 rolls. DP. 16mm.

M278 Compiled Service Records of Volunteer Soldiers Who Served During the Mexican War in Organizations from the State of Texas. 19 rolls. DP. 16mm.

CIVIL WAR

M276 Compiled Service Records of Volunteer Union Soldiers Who Served in Organizations from the State of Alabama. 10 rolls. DP. 16mm.

M399 Compiled Service Records of Volunteer Union Soldiers Who Served in Organizations from the State of Arkansas. 60 rolls. DP. 16mm.

*M1960 Compiled Military Service Records of Volunteer Union Soldiers Who Served in Organizations from the Territory of Dakota: 1st Battalion Cavalry. 3 rolls. DP.

*M1961 Compiled Military Service Records of Volunteer Union Soldiers Who Served in Organizations from the State of Delaware. 117 rolls.

M400 Compiled Service Records of Volunteer Union Soldiers Who Served in Organizations from the State of Florida. 11 rolls. DP. 16mm.

M403 Compiled Service Records of Volunteer Union Soldiers Who Served in Organizations from the State of Georgia. 1 roll. DP. 16mm.

M397 Compiled Service Records of Volunteer Union Soldiers Who Served in Organizations from the State of Kentucky. 515 rolls. DP. 16mm.

M396 Compiled Service Records of Volunteer Union Soldiers Who Served in Organizations from the State of Louisiana. 50 rolls. DP. 16mm.

M384 Compiled Service Records of Volunteer Union Soldiers Who Served in Organizations from the State of Maryland. 238 rolls. DP. 16mm.

*M1898 Compiled Military Service Records of Volunteer Union Soldiers Who Served With the United States Colored Troops: 54th Massachusetts Infantry Regiment (Colored). 20 rolls. DP.

*M1801 Compiled Military Service Records of Volunteers Who Served with the United States Colored Troops: 55th Massachusetts Infantry (Colored). 16 rolls. DP.

*M1817 Compiled Military Service Records of Volunteer Union Soldiers who Served with the United States Colored Troops: 1st through 5th United States Colored Cavalry, 5th Massachusetts Cavalry (Colored), 6th United States Colored Cavalry. 107 rolls. DP.

M404 Compiled Service Records of Volunteer Union Soldiers Who Served in Organizations from the State of Mississippi. 4 rolls. DP. 16mm.

M405 Compiled Service Records of Volunteer Union Soldiers Who Served in Organizations from the State of Missouri. 854 rolls. DP. 16mm.

M1787 Compiled Service Records of Volunteer Union Soldiers Who Served in Organizations from the Territory of Nebraska. 43 rolls. DP.

*M1789 Compiled Service Records of Volunteer Union Soldiers Who Served in Organizations from the Territory and State of Nevada. 16 rolls. DP.

M427 Compiled Service Records of Volunteer Union Soldiers Who Served in Organizations from the Territory of New Mexico. 46 rolls. DP. 16mm.

M401 Compiled Service Records of Volunteer Union Soldiers Who Served in Organizations from the State of North Carolina. 25 rolls. DP. 16mm.

*M1816 Compiled Service Records of Volunteer Union Soldiers Who Served in Organizations from the State of Oregon. 34 rolls. DP.

*M1819 Compiled Military Service Records of Volunteer Union Who Served With the United States Colored Troops: 1st United States Colored Infantry, 1st South Carolina Volunteers (Colored), Company A, 1st United States Colored Infantry (1 Year). 19 rolls. DP.

M395 Compiled Service Records of Volunteer Union Soldiers Who Served in Organizations from the State of Tennessee. 220 rolls. DP. 16mm.

*M1820 Compiled Military Service Records of Volunteer Union Soldiers Who Served with the United States Colored Troops: Infantry Organization, 2d through 7th, including the 3d Tennessee, the 6th Louisiana, and the 7th Louisiana. 108 rolls.

M402 Compiled Service Records of Volunteer Union Soldiers Who Served in Organizations from the State of Texas. 13 rolls. DP. 16mm.

M692 Compiled Service Records of Volunteer Union Soldiers Who Served in Organizations from the Territory of Utah. 1 roll. DP. 16mm.

M398 Compiled Service Records of Volunteer Union Soldiers Who Served in Organizations from the State of Virginia. 7 rolls. DP. 16mm.

M508 Compiled Service Records of Volunteer Union Soldiers Who Served in Organizations from the State of West Virginia. 261 rolls. DP. 16mm.

*M1818 Compiled Military Service Records of Volunteer Union Soldiers Who Served With the United States Colored Troops: Artillery Organizations. 299 rolls. DP.

M1017 Compiled Service Records of Former Confederate Soldiers Who Served in the 1st Through 6th U.S. Volunteer Infantry Regiments, 1864–1866. 65 rolls. DP.

WAR WITH SPAIN

M1087 Compiled Service Records of Volunteer Soldiers Who Served in the Florida Infantry During the War With Spain. 13 rolls. DP.

OTHER RECORDS

M29 Orders of Gen. Zachary Taylor to the Army of Occupation in the Mexican War, 1845–1847. 3 rolls.

M91 Records Relating to the U.S. Military Academy, 1812–1867. 29 rolls. DP.

M182 Letters Sent by the Governors and the Secretary of State of California, 1847–1848. 1 roll. DP.

M233 Register of Enlistments in the U.S. Army, 1798–1914. 81 rolls.

M594 Compiled Records Showing Service of Military Units in Volunteer Union Organizations. 225 rolls. DP. 16mm.

M654 Gen. James Wilkinson's Order Book, Dec. 31, 1796–Mar. 8, 1808. 3 rolls. DP. 16mm.

M617 Returns from U.S. Military Posts, 1800–1916. 1,550 rolls. DP.

M661 Historical Information Relating to Military Posts and Other Installations, ca. 1700–1900. 8 rolls. DP.

M665 Returns from Regular Army Infantry Regiments, June 1821–Dec. 1916. 300 rolls. DP.

M686 Index to General Correspondence of the Record and Pension Office, 1889–1920. 385 rolls. DP. 16mm.

M688 U.S. Military Academy Cadet Application Papers, 1805–1866. 242 rolls. DP.

M690 Returns from Regular Army Engineer Battalions, Sept. 1846–June 1916. 10 rolls. DP.

M691 Returns from Regular Army Coast Artillery Corps Companies, Feb. 1901–June 1916. 81 rolls. DP.

M719 *History of the Philippine Insurrection Against the United States, 1899–1903*, and Documents Relating to the War Department Project for Publishing the History. 9 rolls. DP.

M727 Returns from Regular Army Artillery Regiments, June 1821–Jan. 1901. 38 rolls. DP.

M728 Returns from Regular Army Field Artillery Batteries and Regiments, Feb. 1901–Dec. 1916. 14 rolls. DP.

M797 Case Files of Investigations by Levi C. Turner and Lafayette C. Baker, 1861–1866. 137 rolls. DP.

M823 Official Battle Lists of the Civil War, 1861–1865. 2 rolls. DP.

M851 Returns of the Corps of Engineers, Apr. 1832–Dec. 1916. 22 rolls. DP.

M852 Returns of the Corps of Topographical Engineers, Nov. 1831–Feb. 1863. 2 rolls. DP.

M858 The Negro in the Military Service of the United States, 1639–1886. 5 rolls. DP.

M904 War Department Collection of Post-Revolutionary War Manuscripts. 4 rolls. DP.

M983 Reports and Correspondence Relating to the Army Investigations of the Battle of Wounded Knee and to the Sioux Campaign of 1890–1891. 2 rolls. DP.

M1003 Case Files of Applications From Former Confederates for Presidential Pardons ("Amnesty Papers"), 1865–1867. 73 rolls. DP.

M1064 Letters Received by the Commission Branch of the Adjutant General's Office, 1863–1870. 527 rolls. DP.

M1094 General Orders and Circulars of the War Department and Headquarters of the Army, 1809–1860. 8 rolls. DP.

M1098 U.S. Army Generals' Reports of Civil War Service, 1864–1887. 8 rolls. DP.

M1125 Name and Subject Index to the Letters Received by the Appointment, Commission, and Personal Branch of the Adjutant General's Office, 1871-1894. 4 rolls. DP.

M1136 Records Relating to the 1811 and 1815 Courts-Martial of Maj. Gen. James Wilkinson. 2 rolls. DP.

*M1395 Letters Received by the Appointment, Commission, and Personal Branch, Adjutant General's Office, 1871-1894. 1693 microfiches.

M1523 Proceedings of U.S. Army Courts-martial and Military Commissions of Union Soldiers Executed by U.S. Military Authorities, 1861-1866. 8 rolls. DP.

M1747 Index to Records Relating to War of 1812 Prisoners of War. 3 rolls.

M1659 Records of the Fifty-fourth Massachusetts Infantry Regiment (Colored), 1863-1865. 7 rolls. DP.

*M1828 Index to Surgeons' Reports in "File A and Bound Manuscripts," of the Adjutant General's Office, 1861-1865. 1 roll.

*M1829 Compiled Military Service Records of Major Uriah Blue's Detachment of Chickasaw Indians in the War of 1812. 1 roll.

*M1830 Compiled Military Service Records of Major McIntosh's Company of Creek Indians in the War of 1812. 1 roll.

*M1832 Returns of Killed and Wounded in Battles or Engagements With Indians, British, and Mexican Troops, 1790-1848, Compiled by Lt. Col. J.H. Eaton (Eaton's Compilation). 1 roll.

*M1836 Register of Flags Captured of Recaptured by Union Troops, 1861-65. 1 roll.

*M2019 Records Relating to War of 1812 Prisoners of War. 1 roll.

*M2035 Selected Military Service and Pension Records Relating to Ulysses S. Grant. 1 roll.

*M2037 Register of Cadet Applicants, 1819-1867. 5 rolls.

*M2047 Engineer Department Letters Received Relating to the United States Military Academy, 1819-1866. 46 rolls.

*M2048 War Department Letters and Telegrams Sent Relating to the United States Military Academy, 1867-1904. 4 rolls.

*M2061 Military Academy Registers, 1867-1894. 3 rolls.

*M2063 Selected Military Service Records Relating to Robert E. Lee. 1 roll.

*T32 Records of the Adjutant General's Office re: Affairs on the Rio Grande and Texas Frontier, 1875-1881. 6 rolls.

T36 Lt. Zebulon Pike's Notebook of Maps, Traverse Tables, and Meteorological Observations, 1805-1807. 1 roll.

T817 Lists of the Adjutant General's Office for Carded Records of Military Organizations: Revolutionary War through Philippine Insurrection ("The Ainsworth List"). 112 rolls.

T1085 Muster Rolls and Payrolls of Militia and Regular Army Organizations in the Battle of Tippecanoe, Nov. 1811. 1 roll.

T1104 *Artillery for the U.S. Land Service With Plates*, by Bvt. Maj. Alfred Mordecai (Washington, 1848-1849). 1 roll.

T1107 Publications of the Office of Military History, U.S. Army, American Forces in Action. 3 rolls.

T1108 Publications of the Office of Military History, U.S. Army, Department of the Army Pamphlets. 7 rolls.

T1109 *Cavalry Tactics, U.S. Army, Assimilated to the Tactics of Infantry and Artillery* (New York, 1874). 1 roll.

T1114 Orders and Special Orders by Maj. Gen. William O. Butler and Maj. Gen. W. J. Worth to the Army in Mexico, 1848. 1 roll.

T1115 Orders Issued by Brig. Gen. Stephen W. Kearney and Brig. Gen. Sterling Price to the Army of the West, 1846-1848. 1 roll.

T1117 *The Ordnance Manual for the Officers of the U.S. Army* (3rd ed., Philadelphia, 1862). 1 roll.

P2282 Correspondence of Military Commands Utilized in The War of The Rebellion: A Compilation of the Official Records of the Union and Confederate Armies, 1861-65. 124 rolls.

RG 95 Records of the Forest Service

M1025 Minutes of the Service Committee of the Forest Service, Mar. 14, 1903-Oct. 16, 1935. 8 rolls. DP.

M1128 Shelf List of Captions for the General Photograph File, U.S. Forest Service. 27 rolls. 16mm.

M1127 General Photographic File of the U.S. Forest Service, 1886-. 121 rolls.

RG 101 Records of the Office of the Comptroller of the Currency

M816 Registers of Signatures of Depositors in Branches of the Freedman's Savings and Trust Company, 1865-1874. 27 rolls. DP.

M817 Indexes to Deposit Ledgers in Branches of the Freedman's Savings and Trust Company, 1865-1874. 5 rolls. DP.

M874 Journal of the Board of Trustees and Minutes of Committees and Inspectors of the Freedman's Savings and Trust Company, 1865-1874. 2 rolls. DP.

RG 102 Records of the Children's Bureau

*C0020 Records of the Children's Bureau, Part One: Child Welfare. 92 rolls.

*C0021 Records of the Children's Bureau, Part Two: Child Legislation. 16 rolls.

*C0022 Records of the Children's Bureau, Part Three: Children's Bureau History. 92 rolls.

*C0023 Records of the Children's Bureau, Part Four: Maternal and Child Health. 68 rolls.

*C0024 Records of the Children's Bureau, Part Five: Merritt Files. 20 rolls.

*C0025 Records of the Children's Bureau, Part Six: Chief's Files. 6 rolls.

RG 103 Records of the Farm Credit Administration

T947 Records of Farmers' Marketing and Purchasing Cooperatives. 38 rolls.

RG 104 Records of the U.S. Mint

M64 Letters Sent by the Director of the U.S. Mint at Philadelphia, 1795–1817. 1 roll. DP.

T587 Bullion Ledgers of the U.S. Mint at Philadelphia, 1794–1802. 1 roll.

T646 Correspondence of the U.S. Mint at Philadelphia With the Branch Mint at Dahlonega, Georgia, 1835–1861. 3 rolls.

RG 105 Records of the Bureau of Refugees, Freedmen, and Abandoned Lands

M742 Selected Series of Records Issued by the Commissioner of the Bureau of Refugees, Freedmen, and Abandoned Lands, 1865–1872. 7 rolls. DP.

M752 Registers and Letters Received by the Commissioner of the Bureau of Refugees, Freedmen, and Abandoned Lands, 1865–1872. 74 rolls. DP.

M803 Records of the Education Division of the Bureau of Refugees, Freedmen, and Abandoned Lands, 1865–1871. 35 rolls. DP.

M809 Records of the Assistant Commissioner for the State of Alabama, Bureau of Refugees, Freedmen, and Abandoned Lands, 1865–1870. 23 rolls. DP.

M810 Records of the Superintendent of Education for the State of Alabama, Bureau of Refugees, Freedmen, and Abandoned Lands, 1865–1870. 8 rolls. DP.

M979 Records of the Assistant Commissioner for the State of Arkansas, Bureau of Refugees, Freedmen, and Abandoned Lands, 1865–1869. 52 rolls. DP.

M980 Records of the Superintendent of Education for the State of Arkansas, Bureau of Refugees, Freedmen, and Abandoned Lands, 1865–1871. 5 rolls. DP.

M1055 Records of the Assistant Commissioner for the District of Columbia, Bureau of Refugees, Freedmen, and Abandoned Lands, 1865–1872. 21 rolls. DP.

M1056 Records of the Superintendent of Education for the District of Columbia, Bureau of Refugees, Freedmen, and Abandoned Lands, 1865–1872. 24 rolls. DP.

M798 Records of the Assistant Commissioner for the State of Georgia, Bureau of Refugees, Freedmen, and Abandoned Lands. 36 rolls. DP.

M799 Records of the Superintendent of Education for the State of Georgia, Bureau of Refugees, Freedmen, and Abandoned Lands, 1865–1870. 28 rolls. DP.

M1027 Records of the Assistant Commissioner for the State of Louisiana, Bureau of Refugees, Freedmen, and Abandoned Lands, 1865–1869. 37 rolls. DP.

M1026 Records of the Superintendent of Education for the State of Louisiana, Bureau of Refugees, Freedmen, and Abandoned Lands, 1864–1869. 12 rolls. DP.

M1483 Records of the New Orleans Field Offices, Bureau of Refugees, Freedmen, and Abandoned Lands, 1865–69. 10 rolls. DP.

M826 Records of the Assistant Commissioner for the State of Mississippi, Bureau of Refugees, Freedmen, and Abandoned Lands, 1865–1869. 50 rolls. DP.

M843 Records of the Assistant Commissioner for the State of North Carolina, Bureau of Refugees, Freedmen, and Abandoned Lands, 1865–1870. 38 rolls. DP.

M844 Records of the Superintendent of Education for the State of North Carolina, Bureau of Refugees, Freedmen, and Abandoned Lands, 1865–1870. 16 rolls. DP.

M869 Records of the Assistant Commissioner for the State of South Carolina, Bureau of Refugees, Freedmen, and Abandoned Lands, 1865–1870. 44 rolls. DP.

M999 Records of the Assistant Commissioner for the State of Tennessee, Bureau of Refugees, Freedmen, and Abandoned Lands, 1865–1869. 34 rolls. DP.

M1000 Records of the Superintendent of Education for the State of Tennessee, Bureau of Refugees, Freedmen, and Abandoned Lands, 1865–1870. 9 rolls. DP.

T142 Selected Records of the Tennessee Field Office of the Bureau of Refugees, Freedmen, and Abandoned Lands, 1865–1872. 73 rolls.

M821 Records of the Assistant Commissioner for the State of Texas, Bureau of Refugees, Freedmen, and Abandoned Lands, 1865–1869. 32 rolls. DP.

M822 Records of the Superintendent of Education for the State of Texas, Bureau of Refugees, Freedmen, and Abandoned Lands, 1865–1870. 18 rolls. DP.

M1048 Records of the Assistant Commissioner for the State of Virginia, Bureau of Refugees, Freedmen, and Abandoned Lands, 1865–1869. 67 rolls. DP.

M1053 Records of the Superintendent of Education for the State of Virginia, Bureau of Refugees, Freedmen, and Abandoned Lands, 1865–1870. 20 rolls. DP.

RG 107 Records of the Office of the Secretary of War

M22 Registers of Letters Received by the Office of the Secretary of War, Main Series, 1800–1870. 134 rolls. DP.

M491 Registers of Letters Received by the Secretary of War, Irregular Series, 1861–1866. 4 rolls. DP.

M493 Registers of Letters Received by the Secretary of War from the President, Executive Departments, and War Department Bureaus, 1862–1870. 12 rolls. DP.

M495 Indexes to Letters Received by the Secretary of War, 1861–1870. 14 rolls. DP.

M420 Indexes to Letters Sent by the Secretary of War Relating to Military Affairs, 1871–1889. 12 rolls. DP.

M564 Index to Telegrams Collected by the Office of the Secretary of War (Unbound), 1860–1870. 20 rolls. DP. 16mm.

M221 Letters Received by the Secretary of War, Main Series, 1801–1870. 317 rolls. DP.

M222 Letters Received by the Secretary of War, Unregistered Series, 1789-1861. 34 rolls. DP.

M492 Letters Received by the Secretary of War, Irregular Series, 1861-1866. 36 rolls. DP.

M494 Letters Received by the Secretary of War from the President, Executive Departments, and War Department Bureaus, 1862-1870. 117 rolls. DP.

M6 Letters Sent by the Secretary of War Relating to Military Affairs, 1800-1889. 110 rolls. DP.

M370 Miscellaneous Letters Sent by the Secretary of War, 1800-1809. 3 rolls. DP.

M127 Letters Sent to the President by the Secretary of War, 1800-1863. 6 rolls. DP.

M421 Letters Sent by the Secretary of War to the President and Executive Departments, 1863-1870. 5 rolls. DP.

M7 Confidential and Unofficial Letters Sent by the Secretary of War, 1814-1847. 2 rolls. DP.

M504 Telegrams Collected by the Office of the Secretary of War (Unbound), 1860-1870. 454 rolls. DP.

M473 Telegrams Collected by the Office of the Secretary of War (Bound), 1861-1882. 282 rolls. DP.

M220 Reports to Congress from the Secretary of War, 1803-1870. 5 rolls. DP.

M444 Orders and Endorsements Sent by the Secretary of War, 1846-1870. 13 rolls. DP.

M1062 Correspondence of the War Department Relating to Indian Affairs, Military Pensions, and Fortifications, 1791-1797. 1 roll. DP.

RG 108 Records of the Headquarters of the Army

M857 Letters Sent by the Headquarters of the Army (Main Series), 1828-1903. 15 rolls. DP.

M1635 Letters Received by the Headquarters of the Army, 1827-1903. 139 rolls. DP.

RG 109 War Department Collection of Confederate Records

Indexes to Compiled Service Records

M253 Consolidated Index to Compiled Service Records of Confederate Soldiers. 535 rolls. DP. 16mm.

M818 Index to Compiled Service Records of Confederate Soldiers Who Served in Organizations Raised Directly by the Confederate Government and of Confederate General and Staff Officers and Nonregimental Enlisted Men. 26 rolls. DP. 16mm.

M374 Index to Compiled Service Records of Confederate Soldiers Who Served in Organizations from the State of Alabama. 49 rolls. DP. 16mm.

M375 Index to Compiled Service Records of Confederate Soldiers Who Served in Organizations from the Territory of Arizona. 1 roll. DP. 16mm.

M376 Index to Compiled Service Records of Confederate Soldiers Who Served in Organizations from the State of Arkansas. 26 rolls. DP. 16mm.

M225 Index to Compiled Service Records of Confederate Soldiers Who Served in Organizations from the State of Florida. 9 rolls. DP. 16mm.

M226 Index to Compiled Service Records of Confederate Soldiers Who Served in Organizations from the State of Georgia. 67 rolls. DP. 16mm.

M377 Index to Compiled Service Records of Confederate Soldiers Who Served in Organizations from the State of Kentucky. 14 rolls. DP. 16mm.

M378 Index to Compiled Service Records of Confederate Soldiers Who Served in Organizations from the State of Louisiana. 31 rolls. DP. 16mm.

M379 Index to Compiled Service Records of Confederate Soldiers Who Served in Organizations from the State of Maryland. 2 rolls. DP. 16mm.

M232 Index to Compiled Service Records of Confederate Soldiers Who Served in Organizations from the State of Mississippi. 45 rolls. DP. 16mm.

M380 Index to Compiled Service Records of Confederate Soldiers Who Served in Organizations from the State of Missouri. 16 rolls. DP. 16mm.

M230 Index to Compiled Service Records of Confederate Soldiers Who Served in Organizations from the State of North Carolina. 43 rolls. DP. 16mm.

M381 Index to Compiled Service Records of Confederate Soldiers Who Served in Organizations from the State of South Carolina. 35 rolls. DP. 16mm.

M231 Index to Compiled Service Records of Confederate Soldiers Who Served in Organizations from the State of Tennessee. 48 rolls. DP. 16mm.

M227 Index to Compiled Service Records of Confederate Soldiers Who Served in Organizations from the State of Texas. 41 rolls. DP. 16mm.

M382 Index to Compiled Service Records of Confederate Soldiers Who Served in Organizations from the State of Virginia. 62 rolls. DP. 16mm.

Compiled Service Records

M258 Compiled Service Records of Confederate Soldiers Who Served in Organizations Raised Directly by the Confederate Government. 123 rolls. DP. 16mm.

M331 Compiled Service Records of Confederate Generals and Staff Officers, and Nonregimental Enlisted Men. 275 rolls. DP. 16mm.

M347 Unfiled Papers and Slips Belonging in Confederate Compiled Service Records. 442 rolls. DP. 16mm.

M311 Compiled Service Records of Confederate Soldiers Who Served in Organizations from the State of Alabama. 508 rolls. DP. 16mm.

M318 Compiled Service Records of Confederate Soldiers Who Served in Organizations from the Territory of Arizona. 1 roll. DP. 16mm.

M317 Compiled Service Records of Confederate Soldiers Who Served in Organizations from the State of Arkansas. 256 rolls. DP. 16mm.

M251 Compiled Service Records of Confederate Soldiers Who Served in Organizations from the State of Florida. 104 rolls. DP. 16mm.

M266 Compiled Service Records of Confederate Soldiers Who Served in Organizations from the State of Georgia. 607 rolls. DP. 16mm.

M319 Compiled Service Records of Confederate Soldiers Who Served in Organizations from the State of Kentucky. 136 rolls. DP. 16mm.

M320 Compiled Service Records of Confederate Soldiers Who Served in Organizations from the State of Louisiana. 414 rolls. DP. 16mm.

M321 Compiled Service Records of Confederate Soldiers Who Served in Organizations from the State of Maryland. 22 rolls. DP. 16mm.

M269 Compiled Service Records of Confederate Soldiers Who Served in Organizations from the State of Mississippi. 427 rolls. DP. 16mm.

M322 Compiled Service Records of Confederate Soldiers Who Served in Organizations from the State of Missouri. 193 rolls. DP. 16mm.

M270 Compiled Service Records of Confederate Soldiers Who Served in Organizations from the State of North Carolina. 580 rolls. DP. 16mm.

M267 Compiled Service Records of Confederate Soldiers Who Served in Organizations from the State of South Carolina. 392 rolls. DP. 16mm.

M268 Compiled Service Records of Confederate Soldiers Who Served in Organizations from the State of Tennessee. 359 rolls. DP. 16mm.

M323 Compiled Service Records of Confederate Soldiers Who Served in Organizations from the State of Texas. 445 rolls. DP. 16mm.

M324 Compiled Service Records of Confederate Soldiers Who Served in Organizations from the State of Virginia. 1,075 rolls. DP. 16mm.

Other Records

M119 Letters Sent by Lt. Col. G. H. Hill, Commander of the Confederate Ordnance Works at Tyler, Texas, 1864–1865. 1 roll. DP.

M260 Records Relating to Confederate Naval and Marine Personnel. 7 rolls. DP. 16mm.

M345 Union Provost Marshal's File of Papers Relating to Individual Civilians. 300 rolls. DP. 16mm.

M346 Confederate Papers Relating to Citizens or Business Firms. 1,158 rolls. DP. 16mm.

M359 Records of the Louisiana State Government, 1850–1888, in the War Department Collection of Confederate Records. 24 rolls. DP.

M409 Index to the Letters Received by the Confederate Secretary of War, 1861–1865. 34 rolls. DP. 16mm.

M410 Index to the Letters Received by the Confederate Adjutant and Inspector General and by the Confederate Quartermaster General, 1861–1865. 41 rolls. DP. 16mm.

M416 Union Provost Marshals' File of Papers Relating to Two or More Civilians. 94 rolls. DP.

M437 Letters Received by the Confederate Secretary of War, 1861–1865. 151 rolls. DP.

M469 Letters Received by the Confederate Quartermaster General, 1861–1865. 14 rolls. DP.

M474 Letters Received by the Confederate Adjutant and Inspector General, 1861–1865. 164 rolls. DP.

M522 Letters Sent by the Confederate Secretary of War, 1861–1865. 10 rolls. DP.

M523 Letters Sent by the Confederate Secretary of War to the President, 1861–1865. 2 rolls. DP.

M524 Telegrams Sent by the Confederate Secretary of War, 1861–1865. 1 roll. DP.

M598 Selected Records of the War Department Relating to Confederate Prisoners of War, 1861–1865. 145 rolls. DP.

M618 Telegrams Received by the Confederate Secretary of War, 1861–1865. 19 rolls. DP.

M627 Letters and Telegrams Sent by the Confederate Adjutant and Inspector General, 1861–1865. 6 rolls.

M628 Letters and Telegrams Sent by the Engineer Bureau of the Confederate War Department, 1861–1864. 5 rolls. DP.

M836 Confederate States Army Casualties: Lists and Narrative Reports, 1861–1865. 7 rolls. DP.

M861 Compiled Records Showing Service of Military Units in Confederate Organizations. 74 rolls. DP.

M900 Letters and Telegrams Sent by the Confederate Quartermaster General, 1861–1865. 8 rolls. DP.

M901 General Orders and Circulars of the Confederate War Department, 1861–1865. 1 roll. DP.

M909 Papers Pertaining to Vessels of or Involved With the Confederate States of America: "Vessel Papers." 32 rolls. DP.

M921 Orders and Circulars Issued by the Army of the Potomac and the Army and Department of Northern Virginia, C.S.A., 1861–1865. 4 rolls. DP.

M935 Inspection Reports and Related Records Received by the Inspection Branch in the Confederate Adjutant and Inspector General's Office. 18 rolls. DP.

M998 Records of the Virginia Forces, 1861. 7 rolls. DP.

*M1781 Muster Rolls and Lists of Confederate Troops Paroled in North Carolina. 7 rolls. DP.

*M2063 Selected Military Service Records Relating to Robert E. Lee. 1 roll.

*M2072 Lists of Confederates Captured at Vicksburg, Mississippi, July 4, 1863. 1 roll.

T731 Copies of Letters and Telegrams Received and Sent by Governor Zebulon B. Vance of North Carolina, 1862–1865. 1 roll.

T1025 Correspondence and Reports of the Confederate Treasury Department, 1861–1865. 2 rolls.

RG 110 Records of the Provost Marshal General's Bureau (Civil War)

M621 Reports and Decisions of the Provost Marshal General, 1863-1866. 1 roll. DP.

M1163 Historical Reports of the State Acting Assistant Provost Marshal General and District Provost Marshals, 1865. 5 rolls. DP.

RG 111 Records of the Office of the Chief Signal Officer

T252 The Mathew B. Brady Collection of Civil War Photographs. 4 rolls.

RG 115 Records of the Bureau of Reclamation

M96 Project Histories and Reports of Reclamation Bureau Projects, 1905-1925. 141 rolls.

RG 120 Records of the American Expeditionary Forces (World War I), 1917–1923

M819 Records of the 27th Division of the American Expeditionary Forces (World War I), 1917-1919. 60 rolls. DP.

M923 Records of the American Section of the Supreme War Council, 1917-1919. 21 rolls. DP.

M924 Historical Files of the American Expeditionary Forces, North Russia, 1918-1919. 2 rolls. DP.

M930 Cablegrams Exchanged Between General Headquarters, American Expeditionary Forces, and the War Department, 1917-1919. 19 rolls. DP.

M990 Gorrell's History of the American Expeditionary Forces Air Service, 1917-1919. 58 rolls. DP.

T900 Index to Correspondence of the Office of the Commander in Chief, American Expeditionary Forces, 1917-1919. 132 rolls. 16mm.

RG 121 Records of the Public Buildings Service

*M1117 Letters Sent, Chiefly by the Supervising Architect, 1855-1930. 1,119 rolls.

RG 122 Records of the Federal Trade Commission

*C0013 Federal Trade Commission Docket No. 5253, National Lead Company. 6 rolls.

RG 123 Records of the U.S. Court of Claims

M1104 Eastern Cherokee Applications of the U.S. Court of Claims, 1906-1909. 348 rolls. DP.

*M2007 U.S. Court of Claims Docket Cards for Congressional Case Files, ca. 1884-1943. 5 rolls.

RG 125 Records of the Office of the Judge Advocate General (Navy)

M273 Records of General Courts-Martial and Courts of Inquiry of the Navy Department, 1799-1867. 198 rolls. 16mm.

RG 126 Records of the Office of the Territories

*T834 U.S. Antarctic Service Pictures File. 7 rolls.

*T835 U.S. Antarctic Service Daily Logs and Scientific Reports, 1939-41. 2 rolls.

RG 127 Records of the U.S. Marine Corps

*T977 Muster Rolls of Officers and Enlisted Men of the U.S. Marine Corps, 1893-1940. 461 rolls.

T1118 Muster Rolls of the U.S. Marine Corps, 1798-1892. 123 rolls.

RG 129 Records of the Bureau of Prisons

M1619 McNeil Island Penitentiary Records of Prisoners Received, 1887-1951. 4 rolls.

RG 134 Records of the Interstate Commerce Commission

T913 Annual Reports by Common Carriers to the Interstate Commerce Commission, 1888-1914. 1,348 rolls. 16mm.

RG 147 Records of the Selective Service System, 1940–

T1002 Method for Preservation of Selective Service Records, 1944-1945 (P.I. 27, Entry 56). 2 rolls.

RG 148 Records of Exposition, Anniversary, and Memorial Commissions

T271 Card Index to Pictures Collected by the George Washington Bicentennial Commission. 1 roll.

RG 153 Records of the Office of the Judge Advocate General (Army)

See also Records of U.S. Army Commands, 1942- (RG 338).

M592 Proceedings of a Court of Inquiry Concerning the Conduct of Maj. Marcus A. Reno at the Battle of the Little Big Horn River on June 25 and 26, 1876. 2 rolls.

M599 Investigation and Trial Papers Relating to the Assassination of President Lincoln. 16 rolls. DP.

M1105 Registers of the Records of the Proceedings of the U.S. Army General Courts-Martial, 1809-1890. 8 rolls. DP.

M1536 United Nations War Crimes Commission List, 1944-1948. 164 cards (microfiche).

M1739 Col. Charles L. Decker's Collection of Records Relating to Military Justice and the Revision of Military Law, 1948-1956. 31 rolls. DP.

*M2031 Selected Military Service Records Relating to Edgar Allan Poe. 1 roll.

T1027 Records Relating to the Army Career of Henry Ossian Flipper, 1873-1882. 1 roll.

T1103 General Court Martial of Gen. George Armstrong Custer, 1867. 1 roll.

RG 155 Records of the Wage and Hour Division

T950 Wage Data on Wage and Hour Cases, Region 5, 1938-1944. 9 rolls.

RG 159 Records of the Office of the Inspector General (Army)

M624 Inspection Reports of the Office of the Inspector General, 1814-1842. 3 rolls. DP.

RG 162 General Records of the Federal Works Agency

T1028 Checklist of Historical Records Survey Publications, Apr. 1943. 1 roll.

RG 163 Records of the Selective Service System (World War I)

*M1509 World War I Selective Service System Draft Registration Cards. 4,277 rolls.

*M1860 Boundary Maps of Selected Cities and Counties of World War I Selective Draft Registration Boards, 1917-1918. 1 roll.

RG 165 Records of the War Department General and Special Staffs

M912 Indexes to Records of the War College Division and Related General Staff Offices, 1903-1919. 49 rolls. DP.

M995 Papers and Minutes of Meetings of Principal World War II Allied Military Conferences, 1941-1945. 4 rolls. DP.

M1023 Record Cards to the Correspondence of the War College Division, Related General Staff, and Adjutant General Offices, 1902-1919. 37 rolls. DP.

M1080 Name and Subject Index to the General Correspondence of the War Plans Division, 1921-1942. 18 rolls. DP.

M1194 Name Index to Correspondence of the Military Intelligence Division of the War Department Staff, 1917-1941. DP.

M1216 Correspondence of the Military Intelligence Division Relating to General, Political, Economic, and Military Conditions in Japan, 1918-1941. 31 rolls. DP.

M1271 Registers of Communication Received from Military Attaches and Other Intelligence Officers ("Dispatch Lists"), 1889-1941. 5 rolls. DP.

M1440. Correspondence of the Military Intelligence Division Correspondence Relating to "Negro Subversion," 1917-1941. 6 rolls. DP.

M1443 Correspondence of the Military Intelligence Division Relating to General, Political, Economic, and Military Conditions in Russia and the Soviet Union, 1918-1941. 23 rolls. DP.

M1444 Correspondence of the Military Intelligence Division Relating to General, Political, Economic, and Military Conditions in China, 1918-41. 19 rolls. DP.

M1445 Correspondence of the Military Intelligence Division Relating to General, Political, Economic, and Military Conditions in Spain, 1918-1941. 12 rolls. DP.

M1446 Correspondence and Record Cards of the Military Intelligence Division Relating to General, Political, Economic, and Military Conditions in Italy, 1918-1941. 26 rolls. DP.

M1474 Geographic Index to Correspondence of the Military Intelligence Division of the War Department General Staff, 1917-41. 17 rolls. DP.

M1488 Correspondence and Record Cards of the Military Intelligence Division Relating to General, Political, and Military Conditions in Central America, 1918-1941. 12 rolls. DP.

M1497 Correspondence of the Military Intelligence Division Relating to General, Political, and Military Conditions in Scandinavia and Finland, 1918-1941. 12 rolls. DP.

M1507 Correspondence and Record Cards of the Military Intelligence Division Relating to General, Political, Economic, and Military Conditions in Cuba and the West Indies, 1918-1941. 10 rolls. DP.

M1508 Correspondence and Record Cards of the Military Intelligence Division Relating to General, Political, Economic, and Military Conditions in Poland and the Baltic States, 1918-1941. 10 rolls. DP.

M1513 The Military Intelligence Division Regional File Relating to China, 1922-1944. 58 rolls. DP.

T251 List of Photographs and Photographic Negatives Relating to the War for the Union (War Department Subject Catalogue No. 5, 1897). 1 roll.

RG 174 General Records of the Department of Labor

T4 Reports of the U.S. Commission on Industrial Relations, 1912-1915. 15 rolls.

RG 179 Records of the War Production Board

M185 Press Releases of the Advisory Commission to the Council of National Defense, June 3, 1940-Jan. 15, 1941. 1 roll. DP.

M186 Progress Reports of the Advisory Commission to the Council of National Defense, July 24, 1940-May 28, 1941. 1 roll. DP.

M187 Numbered Document File of the Advisory Commission to the Council of National Defense, 1904-1941. 2 rolls. DP.

M195 Numbered Document File of the Council of the Office of Production Management, 1940-1942. 1 roll. DP.

M196 Numbered Document File of the Supply Priorities and Allocations Board, Sept. 2, 1941-Jan. 15, 1942. 1 roll. DP.

M911 Index to the War Production Board Policy Documentation File, 1939-1947. 86 rolls. DP.

M1200 Applications for Certificates of Necessity, 1941-1945. 1,095 rolls.

M1239 War Production Board Press Releases and Indexes, 1940-1947. 53 rolls.

RG 181 Records of Naval Districts and Shore Establishments

T1015 Activity Location Cards of the Fleet Post Office, San Francisco, California, 1940-1945. 2 rolls.

T1017 Historical Records of the Newport Naval Training Station, Rhode Island, 1883-1948. 1 roll.

RG 186 Records of the Spanish Governors of Puerto Rico

T1120 Expediente sobre la rebelion de Lares, 1868-1869 (Case File on the Rebellion of Lares). 6 rolls.

T1121 Registro central de esclavos, 1872 (Slave Schedules). 8 rolls.

T1122 Reales ordenes, 1792-1793, y reales ordenes y decretos, 1767-1854 (Royal Orders and Decrees). 1 roll.

T1170 Extranjeros (Foreigners) in Puerto Rico, 1872-1880. 19 rolls.

RG 187 Records of the National Resources Planning Board

M120 Reports of the National Resources Planning Board, 1936-1943. 5 rolls. DP.

RG 188 Records of the Office of Price Administration

M164 Studies and Reports of the Office of Price Administration, 1941-1946. 2 rolls.

RG 204 Records of the Office of the Pardon Attorney

*M2022 Pardon Case File No. 39-242, Relating to Industrial Workers of the World Members Convicted in the U.S. District Court for the District of Kansas, December 18, 1919. 1 roll.

RG 210 Records of the War Relocation Authority

M1342 Community Analysis Reports and Community Analysis Trend Reports of the War Relocation Authority, 1942-1946. 29 rolls. DP.

*C0053 Field Basic Documentation of the War Relocation Authority, 1942-1946. 115 rolls.

RG 217 Records of the Accounting Officers of the Department of the Treasury

M235 Miscellaneous Treasury Accounts of the First Auditor (Formerly the Auditor) of the Treasury Department, September 6, 1790-1840. 1,170 rolls.

M497 Letters Sent by the Commissioner of Customs Relating to Smuggling, 1865-1869. 1 roll.

M498 Letters Sent by the Commissioner of Customs Relating to Captured and Abandoned Property, 1868-1875. 1 roll.

M520 Records of the Board of Commissioners for the Emancipation of Slaves in the District of Columbia, 1862-1863. 6 rolls. DP.

M1658 Southern Claims Commission Approved Claims, 1871-1880: Georgia. 761 cards (microfiche). DP.

*M1678 Accounts and Claims Settled by the Second Auditor of the Treasury Department Relating to the Arsenal at Harper's Ferry, 1817-1851. 62 rolls.

*M1745 Claims for Georgia Militia Campaigns Against Indians on the Frontier, 1792-1827. 5 rolls. DP.

*M1746 Final Revolutionary War Pension Payment Vouchers: Georgia. 6 rolls. DP.

*M2062 Southern Claims Commission Approved Claims, 1871-1880: Alabama. 36 rolls.

*M2079 Final Revolutionary War Pension Payment Vouchers: Delaware. 1 roll. DP.

T135 Selected Records of the General Accounting Office Relating to the Fremont Expeditions and the California Battalion, 1818-1890. 3 rolls.

T227 Civil War Direct Tax Assessment Lists: Tennessee. 6 rolls.

T718 Ledgers of Payments, 1818-1872, to U.S. Pensioners Under Acts of 1818 Through 1858, from Records of the Office of the Third Auditor of the Treasury. 23 rolls.

T964 Day Book of the Register's Office of the Treasury, 1789-1791. 1 roll.

T899 Register of Audits of "Miscellaneous Treasury Accounts" (First Auditor's Office). 1 roll.

RG 218 Records of the U.S. Joint Chiefs of Staff

T826 German and Japanese Surrender Documents of World War II and the Korean Armistice Agreements. 1 roll.

T1174 Capt. Tracy B. Kittredge's "The Evolution of Global Strategy." 1 roll.

RG 220 Records of Temporary Committees, Commissions, and Boards

M1293 Public Hearings of the Commission on Wartime Relocation and Internment of Civilians. 6 rolls.

M1496 *Challenger* Commission P.C. Numbered Documents, 1986. 73 rolls. 16mm.

M1501 Indexes to Records of the Presidential Commission on the Space Shuttle *Challenger* Accident, 1986. 30 cards (microfiche).

*C0005 Records of the Subversive Activities Control Board, 1950-72, Part I: Communist Party USA. 30 rolls.

*C0006 Records of the Subversive Activities Control Board, 1950-72, Part II: Communist-Action and Communist Front Organizations. 77 rolls.

RG 225 Records of Joint Army and Navy Boards and Committees

M1421 Records of the Joint Board, 1903-1947. 21 rolls. DP.

RG 226 Records of the Office of Strategic Services

M1499 Records of the Research and Analysis Branch, Office of Strategic Services ("Regular" Series), 1941-1945. 389 rolls.

M1623 History of the London Office of the OSS. 10 rolls. DP.

M1642 Records of the Office of Strategic Services, Washington Director's Office Administrative Files, 1941-1945. 136 rolls.

M1656 Strategic Services Unit Intelligence Reports, 1945-1946. 5 rolls.

M1740 The Boston Series, 1941-1945 (Intelligence Files, Office of the Director, OSS). 3 rolls.

*C0002 OSS Foreign Nationalities Branch Files, 1942-45. 2450 fiche.

RG 227 Records of the Office of Scientific Research and Development

M1392 Bush-Conant File Relating to the Development of the Atomic Bomb, 1940-1945. 14 rolls. DP.

T1012 Reports of the Office of Scientific Research and Development, 1941-1947. 487 rolls.

RG 233 Records of the U.S. House of Representatives

M1264 Journals of the U.S. House of Representatives, 1789-1817. 17 rolls. DP.

M1265 Bill Books of the U.S. House of Representatives, 1814-1817. 1 roll. DP.

M1266 Petition Books of the U.S. House of Representatives, 1789-1817. 2 rolls. DP.

M1267 Transcribed Reports of the Committees of the U.S. House of Representatives, 1789-1841. 15 rolls. DP.

M1268 Transcribed Reports and Communications Transmitted by the Executive Branch to the U.S. House of Representatives, 1789-1819. 15 rolls. DP.

M1407 Barred and Disallowed Case Files of the Southern Claims Commission, 1871-1880. 4,829 cards (microfiche). DP.

M1167 Hearings of the House Select Committee That Investigated the Race Riots in East St. Louis in 1917. 7 rolls. DP.

M1705 Unbound Records of the U.S. House of Representatives, Fifth Congress, 1797-1799. 1 roll. DP.

M1707 Unbound Records of the U.S. House of Representatives, Sixth Congress, 1799-1801. 4 rolls. DP.

M1404 Unbound Records of the House of Representatives for the Eighth Congress, 1803-1805. 5 rolls. DP.

*P2000 Unbound Records of the U.S. House of Representatives, Seventh Congress, 1803-1805. 6 rolls (rolls 6-11).

RG 234 Records of the Reconstruction Finance Corporation

M1637 Minutes of the Defense Plant Corporation, 1940-1945. 105 rolls.

T948 German Reports on Synthetic Rubber, 1937-1945. 13 rolls.

T949 Agreements and Subject Files of the Office of Synthetic Rubber, 1941-1953. 41 rolls. 16mm.

RG 238 National Archives Collection of World War II War Crimes Records

U.S. Nuernberg War Crimes Trials

See also Records of the U.S. Army Commands, 1942-(RG 338).

M887 Records of the U.S. Nuernberg War Crimes Trials: *United States of America* v. *Karl Brandt et al.* (Case I), Nov. 21, 1946-Aug. 20, 1947. 46 rolls. DP.

M888 Records of the U.S. Nuernberg War Crimes Trials: *United States of America* v. *Erhard Milch* (Case II), Nov. 13, 1946-Apr. 17, 1947. 13 rolls. DP.

M889 Records of the U.S. Nuernberg War Crimes Trials: *United States of America* v. *Josef Altstoetter et al.* (Case III), Feb. 17-Dec. 4, 1947. 53 rolls. DP.

M890 Records of the U.S. Nuernberg War Crimes Trials: *United States of America* v. *Oswald Pohl et al.* (Case IV), Jan. 13, 1947-Aug. 11, 1948. 38 rolls. DP.

M891 Records of the U.S. Nuernberg War Crimes Trials: *United States of America* v. *Friedrich Flick et al.* (Case V), Mar. 3-Dec. 22, 1947. 42 rolls. DP.

M892 Records of the U.S. Nuernberg War Crimes Trials: *United States of America* v. *Carl Krauch et al.* (Case VI), Aug. 14, 1947-July 30, 1948. 113 rolls. DP.

M893 Records of the U.S. Nuernberg War Crimes Trials: *United States of America* v. *Wilhelm List et al.* (Case VII), July 8, 1947-Feb. 19, 1948. 48 rolls. DP.

M894 Records of the U.S. Nuernberg War Crimes Trials: *United States of America* v. *Ulrich Greifelt et al.* (Case VIII), Oct. 10, 1947-Mar. 10, 1948. 38 rolls. DP.

M895 Records of the U.S. Nuernberg War Crimes Trials: *United States of America* v. *Otto Ohlendorf et al.* (Case IX), Sept. 15, 1947-Apr. 10, 1948. 38 rolls. DP.

M896 Records of the U.S. Nuernberg War Crimes Trials: *United States of America* v. *Alfried Krupp et al.* (Case X), Aug. 16, 1947-July 31, 1948. 69 rolls. DP.

M897 Records of the U.S. Nuernberg War Crimes Trials: *United States of America* v. *Ernst von Weizsaecker et al.* (Case XI), Dec. 20, 1947-Apr. 14, 1949. 173 rolls. DP.

M898 Records of the U.S. Nuernberg War Crimes Trials: *United States of America* v. *Wilhelm von Leeb et al.* (Case XII), Nov. 28, 1947-Oct. 28, 1948. 69 rolls. DP.

M936 Records of the U.S. Nuernberg War Crimes Trials: NM Series, 1874-1946. 1 roll. DP.

M942 Records of the U.S. Nuernberg War Crimes Trials: NP Series, 1934-1946. 1 roll. DP.

M946 Records of the U.S. Nuernberg War Crimes Trials: WA Series, 1940-1945. 1 roll. DP.

M978 Records of the U.S. Nuernberg War Crimes Trials: Guertner Diaries, Oct. 5, 1934-Dec. 24, 1938. 3 rolls. DP.

M1019 Records of the U.S. Nuernberg War Crimes Trials: Interrogations, 1946-1949. 91 rolls. DP.

M1270 Interrogation Records Prepared for War Crimes Proceedings at Nuernberg, 1945-1947. 31 rolls. DP.

M1278 Nuernberg Trials Records: Register Cards to the NG Document Series, 1946-1949. 3 rolls. DP.

M1291 Nuernberg Trials Records: Register Cards to the NOKW Document Series, 1946-1949. 2 rolls. DP.

M1397 Nuernberg Trials Records: Register Cards to the NI Document Series, 1946-1949. 8 rolls. DP.

T1119 Records of the U.S. Nuernberg War Crimes Trials: NOKW Series. 47 rolls.

T1139 Records of the U.S. Nuernberg War Crimes Trials: NG Series, 1933-1948. 70 rolls.

T301 Records of the U.S. Nuernberg War Crimes Trials: NI Series, 1933-1948. 164 rolls.

Other World War II Crimes Records

T918 Court Papers, Journal, Exhibits, and Judgments of the International Military Tribunal for the Far East, 1900-1948. 61 rolls.

T988 Prosecution Exhibits Submitted to the International Military Tribunal. 54 rolls.

T989 War Diaries and Correspondence of Gen. Alfred Jodl. 2 rolls.

T990 Mauthausen Death Books. 2 rolls.

T991 U.S. Trial Brief and Document Books. 1 roll.

T992 Diary of Hans Frank. 12 rolls. 16mm.

RG 241 Records of the Patent and Trademark Office

T280 Patent Drawings, 1792-1833. 2 rolls.

T1239 Patent Drawings, 1791-1877. 320 rolls.

RG 242 National Archives Collection of Foreign Records Seized

The National Archives recently acquired approximately 40,000 rolls of microfilm from the bibliographic collections of the Berlin Documents Center. Some collections are still being processed at this time, and the final number of rolls is undetermined. The documents consist of personnel and related records of the Nazi Party and affiliated organizations during the Third Reich. Finding aids to these records, including series descriptions and extant roll lists, are maintained in the Textual Research Room at Archives II. For general information on these collections, contact the Textual Reference Branch at 301-713-7250.

M129 An Exhibit of German Military Documents from the Heeresarchiv Potsdam, 1679-1935. 2 rolls.

M132 Papers of Gen. Hans von Seeckt, 1866-1936. 28 rolls.

M137 Papers of Gen. Wilhelm Groener, 1867-1939. 27 rolls.

M207 Papers of Herman von Boyen, ca. 1787-1849. 12 rolls.

M211 Papers of August von Gneisenau, ca. 1785-1831. 43 rolls.

M953 Papers of Hans Karl von Winterfeldt, 1707-1757. 2 rolls.

M954 Papers of August Wilhelm Herzog von Braunschweig-Bevern, 1717-1781. 1 roll.

M955 Papers of Friedrich Wilhelm III of Prussia, 1770-1840. 1 roll.

M956 Papers of Albrecht Graf von Roon, 1803-1879. 2 rolls.

M957 Papers of Lieutenant General Heinrich Scheüch, 1864-1946. 1 roll.

M958 Papers of Christoph Emanuel Hermann Ritter Mertz von Quirnheim, 1866-1947. 2 rolls.

M959 Papers of Gerhard Johann David von Scharnhorst, 1775-1813. 12 rolls.

M960 Papers of Graf Helmuth Carl Bernhard von Moltke, 1800-1891. 6 rolls.

M961 Papers of Alfred Graf von Schlieffen, 1833-1913. 8 rolls.

M962 Prussian Mobilization Records, 1866-1918. 5 rolls.

M963 Records of the Royal Bavarian War Ministry and Other Bavarian Military Authorities, 1866-1913. 7 rolls.

M1743 Guide to the Records of the German Navy, 1850-1945. 1 roll.

T70 Records of the Reich Ministry for Public Enlightenment and Propaganda, 1936-1944. 133 rolls.

T71 Records of the Reich Ministry of Economics. 149 rolls.

T73 Records of the Reich Ministry for Armaments and War Production. 193 rolls.

T74 Records of the Office of the Reich Commissioner for the Strengthening of Germandom. 20 rolls.

T75 Records of the Office of the Deputy for Serbian Economy. 89 rolls.

T76 Records of the Todt Organization. 7 rolls.

T77 Records of the Headquarters of the German Armed Forces High Command. 1,687 rolls.

T78 Records of the Headquarters of the German Army High Command. 882 rolls.

T79 Records of German Army Areas. 315 rolls.

T81 Records of the National Socialist German Labor Party. 732 rolls.

T82 Records of Nazi Cultural and Research Institutions. 549 rolls.

T83 Records of Private Austrian, Dutch, and German Enterprises. 248 rolls.

T84 Miscellaneous German Records Collection. 440 rolls.

T87 Records of the All-Union (Russian) Communist Party (Smolensk Archives), 1917-1941. 69 rolls.

T88 Miscellaneous Russian Records Collection. 4 rolls.

T120 Records of the German Foreign Office Received by the Department of State. 5,055 rolls.

T136 Records of the German Foreign Office Received by the Department of State from St. Antony's College. 144 rolls.

T139 Records of the German Foreign Office Received by the Department of State from the University of California (Project I). 445 rolls.

T149 German Foreign Ministry Archives, 1867-1920, Filmed by the American Historical Association. 434 rolls.

T175 Records of the Reich Leader of the SS and Chief of the German Police. 678 rolls.

T176 Data Sheets to Microfilmed Captured German Records. 34 rolls.

T177 Records of the Reich Air Ministry (Reichsluftfahrtministerium). 52 rolls.

T178 Fragmentary Records of Miscellaneous Reich Ministries and Offices, 1919-1945. 28 rolls.

T179 Records of German and Japanese Embassies and Consulates, 1890-1945. 78 rolls.

*T249 Miscellaneous Records of the German Foreign Office Received by the Department of State. 7 rolls.

T253 Records of Private Individuals (Captured German Records). 62 rolls.

T264 Records of the German Foreign Office Received by the Department of State from the British Museum. 2 rolls.

T283 German Military and Technical Manuals, 1910-1945. 162 rolls.

T290 Archives of the German Embassy at Washington (American Historical Association Project I). 52 rolls.

T291 Papers of German Diplomats (Nachlasse and Asservate), 1833-1927 (American Historical Association Project II). 25 rolls.

T311 Records of German Field Commands: Army Groups. 304 rolls.

T312 Records of German Field Commands: Armies. 1,696 rolls.

T313 Records of German Field Commands: Panzer Armies. 489 rolls.

T314 Records of German Field Commands: Corps. 1,670 rolls.

T315 Records of German Field Commands: Divisions. 3,256 rolls.

T321 Records of the Headquarters of the German Air Force High Command (Oberkommando der Luftwaffe-OKL). 274 rolls.

T322 A Catalog of Files and Microfilms of the German Foreign Ministry Archives, 1867-1920. 1 roll.

T354 Miscellaneous SS Records—The Einwandererzentralstelle Waffen-SS, and SS Oberabschnitte. 799 rolls.

T355 Name Index of Jews Whose German Nationality Was Annulled by the Nazi Regime (Berlin Documents Center). 9 rolls.

T401 Reich Office for Soil Exploration (Reichsamt fur Bodenforschung). 7 rolls.

T405 German Air Force Reports: Luftgaukommandos, Flak, Deutsche Luftwaffenmission in Rumanien. 64 rolls.

T407 Index of Microfilmed Records of the German Foreign Ministry and the Reich's Chancellery Covering the Weimar Period. 1 roll.

T454 Records of the Reich Ministry for the Occupied Eastern Territories, 1941-1945 (Reichsministerium fur die besetzten Ostgebiete). 107 rolls.

T457 Documents Concerning Jews in the Berlin Documents Center. 14 rolls. 16mm and 35mm.

T459 Records of the Reich Commissioner for the Baltic States (Reichskommissar fur das Ostland), 1941-1945. 45 rolls.

T501 Records of German Field Commands: Rear Areas, Occupied Territories, and Others. 363 rolls.

T580 Captured German Records Filmed at Berlin (American Historical Association), 1960. 986 rolls.

T586 Personal Papers of Benito Mussolini. Also, Some Official Records of the Italian Foreign Office and the Ministry of Culture, 1922-1944. 318 rolls.

T608 Records of the Headquarters of the German Navy High Command (OKM). 8 rolls.

T611 Captured German Documents Filmed at Berlin (University of Nebraska). 49 rolls.

T816 Papers of Count Ciano (Lisbon Papers) Received from the Department of State. 3 rolls.

T821 Collection of Italian Military Records, 1935-1943. 514 rolls.

T971 The Von Rhoden Collection of Research Materials on the Role of the German Air Force in World War II, 1911-1947. 73 rolls.

T972 Collection of Correspondence of Herbert von Bismarck, 1881-1883. 1 roll.

T973 Collection of Hungarian Political and Military Records, 1909-1945. 21 rolls.

T976 Records of the Economic Enterprises of the SS (Econombetriebe, SS Wirtschafts-Verwaltungshauptamt), 1936-1945. 37 rolls.

T1022 Records of the German Navy, 1850-1945, Received from the United States Naval History Division. 4,268 rolls.

T1026 Records of the German Foreign Office Filmed for the University of London. 25 rolls.

T1141 Records of the German Foreign Ministry Pertaining to China, 1919-1935. 31 rolls.

T1173 Transcript of Cossman v. Gruber (Dolchstoss-Prozess), Munich, Oct. 19-Nov. 17, 1925. 2 rolls.

RG 243 Records of the U.S. Strategic Bombing Survey

M1013 Final Reports of the U.S. Strategic Bombing Survey, 1945-1947. 25 rolls. DP.

M1159 Tactical Mission Reports of the 20th and 21st Bomber Commands, 1945. 6 rolls.

M1169 Joint Army-Navy Intelligence Studies (JANIS), 1944-1945. 20 rolls.

M1199 Japanese Resources Reference Notebooks, 1945-1947. 6 rolls.

M1205 Statistical Reports Covering Allied and U.S. Air Force Attack Data, 1945-1946. 11 rolls.

M1651 Twentieth Air Force Damage Assessment Cards, 1945. 1 roll.

M1652 U.S. Strategic Bombing Survey (Pacific): Intelligence Library, 1932-47. 118 rolls.

M1653 Japanese Air Target Analyses, Objective Folders, and Aerial Photographs, 1942-1945. 7 rolls.

M1654 Interrogation of Japanese Leaders and Responses to Questionnaires, 1945-1946. 9 rolls.

M1655 U.S. Strategic Bombing Survey (Pacific): Reports and Other Records, 1928-1947. 507 rolls.

M1720 Land-Based Navy and Marine Corps Aircraft Action Reports, 1944-1945. 36 rolls.

M1721 Damage Assessment Reports, 1945. 17 rolls.

M1738 Miscellaneous Documents Relating to the Atomic Bombing of Japan, Allied and Japanese Military Operations in the Pacific, and Japanese Reports on the Chinese Communist Party. 8 rolls.

RG 249 Records of the Commissary General of Prisoners

M1303 Selected Records of the War Department Commissary General of Prisoners Relating to Federal Prisoners of War Confined at Andersonville, Georgia, 1864-1865. 6 rolls. DP.

RG 256 Records of the American Commission to Negotiate Peace

M820 General Records of the American Commission to Negotiate Peace, 1918-1931. 563 rolls. DP.

M1107 "Inquiry Documents" (Special Reports and Studies), 1917-1919. 47 rolls.

RG 260 Records of United States Occupation Headquarters, World War II

M1075 Minutes of the Division Staff Meetings of the U.S. Group Council for Germany and the Office of Military Government for Germany (U.S.) (OMGUS), Nov. 1944-Aug. 1949. 4 rolls. DP.

RG 261 Records of Former Russian Agencies

M11 Records of the Russian-American Company, 1802-1867. 77 rolls. DP.

M1486 Records of the Imperial Russian Consulates in the United States, 1862-1922. 180 rolls. DP.

M1742 Records of Imperial Russian Consulates in Canada, 1898-1922. 83 rolls. DP.

RG 263 Records of the Central Intelligence Agency

M1750 Records of the Shanghai Municipal Police, 1894-1949. 1 roll.

RG 267 Records of the Supreme Court of the United States

M162 The Revolutionary War Prize Cases: Records of the Court of Appeal in Cases of Capture, 1776-1787. 15 rolls. DP.

M214 Appellate Case Files of the U.S. Supreme Court, 1792-1831. 96 rolls. DP.

M215 Minutes of the U.S. Supreme Court, 1790-1950. 41 rolls. DP.

M216 Dockets of the U.S. Supreme Court, 1791-1950. 27 rolls. DP.

M217 Attorney Rolls of the U.S. Supreme Court, 1790-1951. 4 rolls. DP.

M408 Index to Appellate Case Files of the U.S. Supreme Court, 1792-1909. 20 rolls. DP. l6mm.

*M1843 Appellate Case File No. 1631, *Charles River Bridge Co.* v. *Warren River Bridge Co.*, 36 U.S. 420 (11 Peters 420), Decided February 14, 1837, and Related Records. 1 roll. DP.

*M2012 Appellate Case File No. 2161, *United States* v. *The Amistad*, 40 U.S. 518 (15 Peters 518), Decided March 9, 1841, and Related Lower Court and Department of Justice Records. 1 roll. DP.

*M2013 Appellate Case File No. 3230, *Dred Scott* v. *Sandford*, 60 U.S. 393 (19 Howard 383), Decided March 6, 1857, and Related Records. 1 roll.

*M2023 Appellate Case File No. 13879, *Thomas Cunningham, Sheriff of the Country of San Joaquin, California* v. *David Neagle*, and Related Department of Justice Records. 2 rolls

T57 Original Opinions of the Justices of the U.S. Supreme Court Delivered at the January Term 1832; and Opinions and Other Case Papers of Chief Justice Marshall, 1834 and 1835 Terms. 1 roll.

RG 272 Records of the President's Commission on the Assassination of President Kennedy

M1124 Numbered Documents of the President's Commission on the Assassination of President Kennedy. 42 rolls. DP.

M1289 "Key Persons" Files of the President's Commission on the Assassination of President Kennedy, 1963-1964. 34 rolls.

M1402 "Other Individuals and Organizations" File of the President's Commission on the Assassination of President Kennedy, 1963-1964. 39 rolls. DP.

M1758 Report and Hearings of the President's Commission on the Assassination of President Kennedy. 11 rolls.

RG 273 Records of the National Security Council

M1534 Natural Security Council Policy Papers, 1947-1961. 322 cards. DP.

RG 284 Records of the Government of American Samoa

T1182 Records of the Government of American Samoa, 1900-1958. 62 rolls.

RG 287 Publications of the U.S. Government

M1506 *The Stars and Stripes*: Newspaper of the U.S. Armed Forces in Europe, the Mediterranean, and North Africa, 1942-1964. 138 rolls. DP.

M1624 *Stars and Stripes*: Newspaper of the U.S. Armed Forces in the Pacific, 1945-1963. 166 rolls. DP.

M1641 Indexes and Lists to Army Technical and Administrative Publications, 1940-1979. 29 rolls. DP.

*T1219 State Department Transcripts of Passenger Lists, ca. October 1819-ca. December 1832. 2 rolls.

RG 295 Records of the Office of Price Stabilization

T460 Defense History Program Studies Prepared During the Korean War Period. 3 rolls.

RG 306 Records of the U.S. Information Agency

M1149 New York Times Paris Bureau Photographs, 1900-1940 (A Series). 1 roll.

M1150 New York Times Paris Bureau Photographs, 1900-1940 (B Series). 2 rolls.

M1151 New York Times Paris Bureau Photographs, 1900-1940 (Letterless Series). 95 rolls.

M1152 New York Times Paris Bureau Photographs, 1900-1940 (C Series). 28 rolls.

M1153 New York Times Paris Bureau Photographs, 1924-1940 (D Series). 7 rolls.

M1154 New York Times Paris Bureau Photographs, 1940–1945 (E Series). 1 roll.

M1155 New York Times Paris Bureau Photographs, 1945–1950 (V Series). 33 rolls.

RG 331 Records of Allied Operational and Occupation Headquarters, World War II

M1112 Reviews of the Yokohama Class B and Class C War Crimes Trials by the 8th Army Judge Advocate, 1946–1949. 5 rolls. DP.

M1190 Subject File Headings for the Records of the Allied Control Commission (Italy), 1943–1947. 5 rolls. DP.

M1660 Copies of Judgments of the International Military Tribunal for the Far East, 1948. 7 rolls.

M1661 Transcripts from the Case of the *United States of America* v. *Soemu Toyoda and Hiroshi Tamura*, 1946–1948. 4 rolls.

M1662 Studies, Reports, and Other Reference Documents of the Allied Operational and Occupation Headquarters, World War II, Supreme Commander Allied Powers, International Prosecution Section, 1944–1948. 44 rolls.

M1663 International Prosecution Section Staff: Historical Files Relating to Cases Tried Before the International Military Tribunal for the Far East, 1945–1948. 66 rolls.

M1664 Miscellaneous Records of the Allied Operational and Occupation Headquarters, World War II, Supreme Commander Allied Powers, International Prosecution Section, 1945–1948. 9 rolls.

M1665 Prosecution and Defense Summations for Cases Tried Before International Military Tribunal for the Far East, 1948. 21 rolls.

M1666 Narrative Summary and Transcripts of Court Proceedings for Cases Tried Before the International Military Tribunal for the Far East, 1946–1948. 64 rolls.

M1667 Transcripts of Proceedings in Chambers for Cases Tried Before the International Military Tribunal for the Far East, 1946–1948. 1 roll.

M1668 Records of the Chief Prosecutor Relating to Preparation for and Conduct of Cases Tried by the International Prosecution Section Before the International Military Tribunal for the Far East, 1946–1948. 18 rolls.

M1669 Records of the International Prosecution Section: Prosecution's Opening Statements, Summary of Evidence, and Copies of Indictments, 1946. 2 rolls.

M1679 War Crimes Trial Documents Collected by the International Prosecution Section for Use Before the International Military Tribunal for the Far East, 1945–1947. 1 roll.

M1680 Documents Assembled by the International Prosecution Section for Use as Exhibits Before the International Military Tribunal for the Far East, 1945–1947. 34 rolls.

M1681 Reports, Orders, Studies, and Other Background Documents Gathered by the International Prosecution Section, 1945–1947. 9 rolls.

M1682 Indexes to Numerical Case Files Relating to Particular Incidents and Suspected War Criminals, International Prosecution Section, 1945–1947. 4 rolls.

M1683 Numerical Case Files Relating to Particular Incidents and Suspected War Criminals, International Prosecution Section, 1945–1947. 73 rolls.

M1684 International Prosecution Section Documents Relating to Witnesses for the Prosecution and the Defense, 1946–1947. 21 rolls.

M1685 Indexes of Exhibits of the Prosecution and of the Defense, Introduced as Evidence Before the International Military Tribunal for the Far East, 1945–1947. 2 rolls.

M1686 Exhibits of the Prosecution and of the Defense Introduced as Evidence Before the International Military Tribunal for the Far East, 1945–1947. 17 rolls.

M1687 Index to Court Exhibits in English and Japanese, International Prosecution Section, 1945–1947. 1 roll.

M1688 Court Exhibits in English and Japanese, International Prosecution Section, 1945–1947. 48 rolls.

M1689 Indexes to Numerical Evidentiary Documents Assembled by the Prosecution for Use as Evidence Before the International Military Tribunal for the Far East, 1945–1947. 8 rolls.

M1690 Numerical Evidentiary Documents Assembled as Evidence by the Prosecution for Use Before the International Military Tribunal for the Far East, 1945–1947. 477 rolls.

M1691 Indexes to Documents Presented as Evidence by the Defense and Defense Documents Rejected as Evidence Before the International Military Tribunal for the Far East, 1945–1947. 2 rolls.

M1692 Documents Presented as Evidence by the Defense Before the International Military Tribunal for the Far East, 1945–1947. 19 rolls.

M1693 Defense Documents Rejected as Evidence Before the International Military Tribunal for the Far East, 1946–1947. 16 rolls.

M1694 Alphabetical Series of Defense Documents Presented for Evidence and Rejected by the International Military Tribunal for the Far East, 1945–1947. 3 rolls.

M1695 Index to Names of Witnesses and Suspected War Crimes Perpetrators Who Appeared Before the International Military Tribunal for the Far East, 1945–1947. 1 roll.

M1696 Indexes to Files Showing the Receipt and Distribution of Defense Documents and the Receipt of Affidavits from Prisoners of War and Other Sources, 1946–1948. 2 rolls.

M1697 Analyses of the Documentary Evidence Introduced by the Prosecution Before the International Military Tribunal for the Far East, 1946–1948. 6 rolls.

M1698 Indexes to Court Documents Including Orders, Rules of Procedure, and Copies of the Indictment and Motions of the Defense, 1946–1948. 1 roll.

M1699 Court Documents Including Orders, Rules of Procedure, and Copies of the Indictment and Motions of the Defense, 1946–1948. 3 rolls.

M1700 Indexes and Lists of Witnesses for the Defense and for the Prosecution Before the International Military Tribunal for the Far East, 1946–1948. 1 roll.

M1701 Numeric Records of the Prosecution Attorneys Relating to the Prosecution's Evidence Before the International Military Tribunal for the Far East, 1946–1948. 4 rolls.

M1722 Records Pertaining to Rules and Procedures Governing the Conduct of Japanese War Crimes Trials, Atrocities Committed Against Chinese Laborers, and Background Investigations of Major Japanese War Criminals. 17 rolls.

M1723 Miscellaneous Documents Relating to Japan's Economic, Industrial, Military, and Diplomatic Activities Used as Background Materials by the International Prosecution Section, 1929–1945. 7 rolls.

M1724 Nuremberg Transcripts Used as Reference Documents by the International Prosecution Section for the International Military Tribunal for the Far East, 1945–1947. 8 rolls.

M1725 Supreme Commander for the Allied Powers: Report on the Summation of U.S. Army Military and Non-Military Activities in the Far East, 1945–1947. 3 rolls.

M1726 Records of Trials and Clemency Petitions for Accused Japanese War Criminals Tried at Yokohama, Japan, by a Military Commission Appointed by the Commanding General, Eighth Army, 1946–1948. 59 rolls.

M1727 Records of Trials of Accused Japanese War Criminals Tried at Manila, Philippines, by a Military Commission Convened by the Commanding General of the United States Army in the Western Pacific, 1945–1947. 34 rolls.

M1728 Records of the Trial of Accused War Criminal Hiroshi Tamura, Tried by a Military Tribunal Appointed by the Supreme Commander of the Allied Powers, Tokyo, Japan, 1948–1949. 3 rolls.

M1729 Records of the Trial of Accused War Criminal Soemu Toyoda, Tried by a Military Tribunal Appointed by the Supreme Commander of the Allied Powers, Tokyo, Japan, 1948–1949. 7 rolls.

M1730 Miscellaneous Documents Relating to the Japanese Attack on Pearl Harbor and Other Japanese Military Activities, 1941–1945. 1 roll.

M1731 Photostatic Copies of Newspaper Articles Relating to Japanese War Crimes and War Crimes Trials, 1943–1948. 1 roll.

M1732 Miscellaneous International Prosecution Documents Used as Background in Preparation for the International Military Tribunal for the Far East, 1940–1948. 19 rolls.

M1733 Photographs of Japanese Soldiers and of Allied Prisoners of War, 1942–1945. 1 roll.

RG 332 Records of U.S. Theaters of War, World War II

M1419 "Eyes Alone" Correspondence of General Joseph W. Stilwell, January 1942–October 1944. 5 rolls. DP.

RG 333 Records of International Military Agencies

T1152 United Nations Command Korean Armistice Negotiations, 1951–1953. 11 rolls.

RG 338 Records of U.S. Army Commands, 1942–

U.S. Army Investigation and Trial Records of War Criminals

Some records in these publications are from RG 153.

See also National Archives Collection of World War II War Crimes Records (RG 238)

M1078 U.S. Army Investigation and Trial Records of War Criminals: *United States of America* v. *Alfons Klein et al.*, Oct. 8–15, 1945 (Case No. 12-449 and 000-12-31). 3 rolls. DP.

M1079 U.S. Army Investigation and Trial Records of War Criminals: *United States of America* v. *Kurt Andrae et al.*, Apr. 27, 1945–June 11, 1958 (Case No. 12-481 and 000-50-37). 16 rolls. DP.

M1093 U.S. Army Investigation and Trial Records of War Criminals: *United States of America* v. *Franz Auer et al.*, Nov. 1943–July 1958. 13 rolls. DP.

M1095 U.S. Army Investigation and Trial Records of War Criminals: *United States of America* v. *Juergen Stroop et al.*, Mar. 29, 1945–Aug. 21, 1957. 10 rolls. DP.

M1100 U.S. Army Trials and Post-trial Records of War Criminals: *United States of America* v. *Ernest Dura et al.*, June 9–23, 1947. 2 rolls. DP.

M1103 U.S. Army Investigation and Trial Records of War Criminals: *United States of America* v. *Kurt Goebell et al.*, Feb. 6–Mar. 21, 1946, and *United States of America* v. *August Haesiker*, June 26, 1947. 7 rolls. DP.

M1106 U.S. Army Investigation and Trial Records of War Criminals: *United States of America* v. *Otto Skorzeny et al.*, July 13, 1945–Dec. 13, 1948. 24 cards (microfiche). DP.

M1139 Records of the U.S. Army War Crimes Trials: *United States of America* v. *Johann Haider et al.*, Sept. 3–12, 1947. 2 rolls. DP.

M1173 Records of the U.S. Army War Crimes Trials: *United States of America* v. *Michael Vogel et al.*, July 8–15, 1947. 2 rolls. DP.

M1174 U.S. Army Investigation and Trial Records of War Criminals: *United States of America* v. *Gottfried Weiss et al.*, Nov. 15–Dec. 13, 1945. 6 rolls. DP.

M1191 Records of the U.S. Army War Crimes Trials: *United States of America* v. *Hans Joachim Georg Geiger et al.*, July 9–Aug. 5, 1947. 2 rolls.

M1204 Records of the U.S. Army War Crimes Trials: *United States of America* v. *Friedrich Becker et al.*, July 5, 1945–June 11, 1958. 15 rolls. DP.

M1210 Records of the U.S. Army War Crimes Trials: *United States of America* v. *Ernest Angerer et al.*, Nov. 26–Dec. 3, 1946. 1 roll. DP.

M1217 Reviews of U.S. Army War Crimes Trials in Europe, 1945–1948. 5 rolls. DP.

T1021 German Documents Among the War Crimes Records of the Judge Advocate Division, Headquarters, U.S. Army, Europe. 20 rolls.

RG 341 Records of Headquarters U.S. Air Force (Air Staff)

T1206 Project *Bluebook*. 94 rolls.

RG 350 Records of the Bureau of Insular Affairs

M24 Index to Official Published Documents Relating to Cuba and the Insular Possessions of the United States, 1876–1906. 3 rolls. DP.

RG 351 Records of the Government of the District of Columbia

M605 Records of the City of Georgetown (District of Columbia), 1800–1879. 49 rolls. DP.

M1116 District of Columbia Building Permits, 1877–1949, and Index, 1877–1958.* 695 rolls, 1877–June 25, 1912 and index (35mm); 681 rolls, July 1, 1915–Sept. 7, 1949. 16mm.

*These records continue to be filmed. Contact Research Support Branch (NWCC2) for current information on availability.

RG 353 Records of Interdepartmental and Intra-departmental Committees (State Department)

M1195 State-War-Navy Coordinating Committee (SWNCC) and State-Army-Navy-Air Force Coordinating Committee (SANACC) Decimal Subject Files, 1944–1949. 12 rolls.

T1194 Minutes of Meetings of the State-War-Navy Coordinating Committee (SWNCC), 1944–1947. 1 roll.

T1198 Minutes of Meetings of the Subcommittee for the Far East, 1945–1947. 1 roll.

T1205 Records of the Subcommittee for the Far East, 1945–1948. 14 rolls.

M1054 Records of the Secretary of State's Staff Committee, 1944–1947. 5 rolls. DP.

RG 360 Records of the Continental and Confederation Congresses and the Constitutional Convention

M247 Papers of the Continental Congress, 1774–1789. 204 rolls. DP.

M332 Miscellaneous Papers of the Continental Congress, 1774–1789. 10 rolls. DP.

M866 Records of the Constitutional Convention of 1787. 1 roll. DP.

RG 365 Treasury Department Collection of Confederate Records

M499 Letters Received by the Confederate Secretary of the Treasury, 1861–1865. 57 rolls. DP.

M500 Letters Sent by the Confederate Secretary of the Treasury, 1861, 1864–1865. 1 roll. DP.

T1129 Records of the Cotton Bureau of the Trans-Mississippi Department of the Confederate War Department, 1862–1865. 50 rolls.

RG 374 Records of the Defense Threat Reduction Agency

A1218 Manhattan Engineer District History. 14 rolls.

RG 393 Records of the U.S. Army Continental Commands, 1821–1920

M210 Records of the Tenth Military Department, 1846–1851. 7 rolls. DP.

M989 Headquarters Records of Fort Dodge, Kansas, 1866–1882. 25 rolls. DP.

M1072 Letters Sent by the Ninth Military Department, Department of New Mexico, and District of New Mexico, 1849–1890. 7 rolls. DP.

M1076 Headquarters Records of Fort Verde, Arizona, 1866–1891. 11 rolls. DP.

M1077 Headquarters Records of Fort Scott, Kansas, 1869–1873. 2 rolls. DP.

M1081 Headquarters Records of Fort Cummings, New Mexico, 1863–1873, 1880–1884. 8 rolls. DP.

M1084 Letters Sent, Registers of Letters Received, and Letters Received by Headquarters, Troops in Florida, and Headquarters, Department of Florida, 1850–1858. 10 rolls. DP.

M1088 Letters Received by Headquarters, District of New Mexico, Sept. 1865–Aug. 1890. 65 rolls. DP.

M1090 *Memoir of Reconnaissances With Maps During the Florida Campaign*, Apr. 1854–Feb. 1858. 1 roll. DP.

M1096 Letters Sent by the Department of Florida and Successor Commands, Apr. 18, 1861–Jan. 1869. 2 rolls. DP.

M1097 Registers of Letters Received by Headquarters, District of New Mexico, Sept. 1865–Aug. 1890. 11 rolls. DP.

M1102 Register of Letters Received, and Letters Received by Headquarters, Ninth Military Department, 1848–1853. 7 rolls. DP.

M1114 Letters Sent by Headquarters, Department of Texas, 1870–1898. 10 rolls. DP.

M1120 Registers of Letters Received, and Letters Received by Headquarters, Department of New Mexico, 1854–1865. 30 rolls. DP.

M1165 Letters Sent by the Department of Texas and the Fifth Military District, 1856–1858, 1865–1870. 3 rolls. DP.

M1188 Correspondence of the Office of Civil Affairs of the District of Texas, the 5th Military District, and the Department of Texas, 1867–1870. 40 rolls. DP.

M1189 Headquarters Records of Fort Stockton, Texas, 1867–1886. 8 rolls. DP.

M1193 Registers of Letters Received and Letters Received of the Department of Texas, the District of Texas, and the 5th Military District, 1865–1870. 33 rolls. DP.

M1302 Records of Headquarters, Army of the Southwestern Frontier, and Headquarters, Second and Seventh Military Departments, 1835–1853. 8 rolls. DP.

M1381 Headquarters Records of the District of the Pecos, 1878–1881. 5 rolls. DP.

M1466 Headquarters Records of Fort Gibson, Indian Territory, 1830–1857. 6 rolls. DP.

M1475 Correspondence of the Eastern Division Pertaining to Cherokee Removal, April–December 1838. 2 rolls. DP.

M1495 "Special Files" of Headquarters, Division of the Missouri, Relating to Military Operations and Administration, 1863-1885. 16 rolls. DP.

M1512 Headquarters Records of Fort Sumner, New Mexico, 1862-1869. 5 rolls. DP.

*M1734 Letters Received by Headquarters, Department of Dakota, 1866-1877. 23 rolls. DP.

*M2031 Selected Military Service Records Relating to Edgar Allan Poe. 1 roll.

T320 Letters Sent by the Post Commander at Fort Bayard, New Mexico, 1888-1897. 3 rolls.

*T713 Records of Fort Hays, Kansas (Army Post), 1866-1889. 22 rolls.

T838 Letters Sent, Fort Mojave, Arizona Territory, 1859-1890. 2 rolls.

T912 Brief Histories of U.S. Army Commands (Army Posts) and Descriptions of Their Records. 1 roll.

RG 395 Records of U.S. Army Overseas Operations and Commands, 1898–1942

M917 Historical Files of the American Expeditionary Forces in Siberia, 1918-1920. 11 rolls. DP.

RG 404 Records of the U.S. Military Academy

M1089 Letters Sent By the Superintendent of the United States Military Academy, 1838-1902. 5 rolls. DP.

*M2047 Engineer Department Letters Received Relating to the United States Military Academy, 1819-1866. 46 rolls. DP.

*M2048 War Department Letters and Telegrams Sent Relating to the United States Military Academy, 1867-1904. 4 rolls.

RG 405 Records of the U.S. Naval Academy

M1018 Registers of Letters Received and Letters Received by the Superintendent of the U.S. Naval Academy, 1888-1906. 89 rolls. DP.

M949 Letters Received by the Superintendent of the U.S. Naval Academy, 1845-1887. 11 rolls. DP.

M945 Letters Sent by the Superintendent of the U.S. Naval Academy, 1845-1865. 3 rolls. DP.

M994 Letters Sent by the Superintendent of the U.S. Naval Academy (Main Series), 1865-1907. 53 rolls. DP.

M991 U.S. Naval Academy Registers of Delinquencies, 1846-1850, 1853-1882, and Academic and Conduct Records of Cadets, 1881-1908. 45 rolls. DP.

RG 407 Records of the Adjutant General's Office, 1917–

*M2035 Selected Military Service and Pension Records Relating to Ulysses S. Grant. 1 roll.

*M2063 Selected Military Service Records Relating to Robert E. Lee. 1 roll.

T822 Cross Index to the Central Files of the Adjutant General's Office, 1917-1939. 1,956 rolls.

T978 U.S. Army Regulations, Aug. 10, 1920-Dec. 31, 1945. 15 rolls.

Donated Materials in the National Archives

Donated materials are grouped into collections and receive a collection designator instead of a record group number.

Collection Designator: LOS

M1608 Naturalization Index of the Superior Court for Los Angeles County, California, 1852-1915. 1 roll.

M1614 Naturalization Records of the Superior Court of Los Angeles County, California, 1876-1915. 28 rolls.

Collection Designator: SAN

M1609 Index to Citizens Naturalized in the Superior Court of San Diego, California, 1853-1956. 1 roll.

M1612 Index to Declarations of Intention in the Superior Court of San Diego County, California, 1853-1956. 1 roll.

M1613 Naturalization Records in the Superior Court of San Diego County, California, 1883-1958. 19 rolls.

M1526 Naturalization Index Cards from the Superior Court of San Diego County, California, 1929-1956. 5 rolls.

Miscellaneous

Microfilm publications in this section are copies of records that belong to no Record Group or are compilations from many Record Groups.

M1036 Military Operations of the Civil War: A Guide Index to the Official Records of the Union and Confederate Armies, 1861-1865, Volume I, Conspectus. 1 roll. DP.

M1815 Military Operations of the Civil War: A Guide-Index to the Official Records of the Union and Confederate Armies, 1861-1865, Volumes II-V. 18 cards (microfiche). DP.

*M1858 *Historical Register and Dictionary of the United States Army from its Organization, September 29, 1789, to March 2, 1903,* by Francis B. Heitman. Washington, GPO, 1903. 1 roll. 35mm.

*M1859 *Records of Living Officers of the United States Army,* by William H. Powell. Philadelphia, Hamersley & Co., 1890. 1 roll. 35mm.

*M2009 Work Projects Administration Transcript of Passenger Lists of Vessels Arriving at New Orleans, Louisiana, 1813-1849. 2 rolls.

M262 Official Records of the Union and Confederate Armies, 1861-1865. 128 rolls. 16mm.

M275 Official Records of the Union and Confederate Navies, 1861-1865. 31 rolls. 16mm.

M867 Selected Photographs of Calvin Coolidge, 1917-1943. 1 roll. DP.

M865 Selected Photographs of Franklin D. Roosevelt, 1913-1945. 1 roll. DP.

M835 Selected Photographs of Harry S. Truman, 1885-1953. 2 rolls. DP.

M868 Selected Photographs of Dwight D. Eisenhower, 1943-1961. 1 roll. DP.

M721 The Territorial Papers of the United States. 16 rolls. DP.

*M2078 General Register of the United States Navy and Marine Corps, 1782-1882. 1 roll.

M325 The Territorial Papers of the United States: Iowa, 1838-1846. 102 rolls. DP.

*M1050 The Territorial Papers of the United States: Minnesota, 1849-1858. 19 rolls.

M1049 The Territorial Papers of the United States: Oregon, 1848-1859. 12 rolls.

M236 The Territorial Papers of the United States: Wisconsin, 1836-1848. 122 rolls. DP.

T325 Examples of Records in the National Archives Frequently Used in Genealogical Research. 1 roll.

T911 Compilation of Tennessee Census Reports, 1820. 1 roll.

M1809 Wisconsin Territorial Censuses of 1836, 1838, 1842, 1846, and 1847. 3 rolls.

T987 National Archives Teaching Aids: Selected State Department Records. 6 rolls.

T1105 Historical Sketches for Jurisdictional and Subject Headings Used for the Letters Received by the Office of Indian Affairs, 1824-1880. 1 roll.

A1176 The Papers of Henry William Ellsworth, 1845-1849. 4 rolls.

T1203 Subject-Author-Title Catalog of Selected Publications of the Federal Government, ca. 1900-ca. 1950. 64 rolls.

Papers Relating to the Administration of the U.S. Patent Office During the Superintendency of William Thornton, 1802-1828: A Guide to Accompany Federal Documentary Microfilm Edition No. 1. 5 rolls. DP.

M939 General Correspondence of the Alaskan Territorial Governor, 1909-1958. 378 rolls. DP.

M1012 Records of the Alaskan Territorial Legislature, 1913-1953. 21 rolls. DP.

T1200 Chronological Files of the Alaskan Governor, 1884-1919. 44 rolls.

T1201 Correspondence of the Secretary of Alaska, 1900-1913. 20 rolls.

Belgian Foreign Ministry.

T125 Records Relating to North America, 1834-1899, from the Archives of the Belgian Ministry of Foreign Affairs. 9 rolls.

T294 Papers of R. Dorsey Mohun, 1892-1913. 3 rolls.

Republic of the Philippines.

M254 Philippine Insurgent Records, 1896-1901, With Associated Records of the U.S. War Department, 1900-1906. 643 rolls. DP.

Records from More Than One Record Group.

RG 15, 94, and 407

M2035 Selected Military Service and Pension Records Relating to Ulysses S. Grant. 1 roll.

RG 24 and 94

T732 Records Relating to Military Service in the Civil War of Medal of Honor Winners from Michigan. 5 rolls.

RG 36 and 287

*T1219 State Department Transcripts of Passenger Lists, ca. October 1819-ca. December 1832. 2 rolls.

RG 38, 80, and 313

M964 Records Relating to U.S. Navy Fleet Problems I to XXII, 1923-1941. 36 rolls. DP.

RG 39 and 53

M1004 Central Treasury Records of the Continental and Confederation Governments Relating to Foreign Affairs, 1775-1787. 3 rolls. DP.

RG 39, 53, and 217

M1014 Central Treasury Records of the Continental and Confederation Governments, 1775-1789. 23 rolls. DP.

M1015 Central Treasury Records of the Continental and Confederation Governments Relating to Military Affairs, 1775-1789. 7 rolls. DP.

RG 45 and 80

M984 Navy Department General Orders, 1863-1948. 3 rolls. DP.

RG 45, 71, and 80

M977 Navy Department General Orders and Circulars, 1798-1862. 2 rolls. DP.

RG 48 and 75

M1070 Reports of Inspections of the Field Jurisdictions of the Office of Indian Affairs, 1873-1900. 60 rolls. DP.

RG 77, 94, and 407

M2063 Selected Military Service Records Relating to Robert E. Lee. 1 roll.

RG 92, 93, and 94

M927 Letters, Orders for Pay, Accounts, Receipts, and Other Supply Records Concerning Weapons and Military Stores, 1776-1801. 1 roll. DP.

RG 94, 153, 393, and 407.

M2031 Selected Military Service Records Relating to Edgar Allan Poe. 1 roll.

RG 94 and 393

M903 Descriptive Commentaries from the Medical Histories of Posts. 5 rolls. DP.

RG 94 and 391

M744 Returns from Regular Army Cavalry Regiments, 1833-1916. 117 rolls. DP.

RG 24, 25, 94, 107, 153, 391, and 393

M929 Documents Relating to the Military and Naval Service of Blacks Awarded the Congressional Medal of Honor from the Civil War to the Spanish American War. 4 rolls. DP.

M997 Annual Reports of the War
Department, 1822–1907. 164 rolls. DP.

RG 94 and 149

M1002 Selected Documents Relating to
Blacks Nominated for Appointment to the
U.S. Military Academy During the 19th
Century, 1870–1887. 21 rolls. DP.

RG 156 and 159

M1281 Summary Statements of Quarterly
Returns of Ordnance and Ordnance
Stores on Hand in Regular and Volunteer
Army Organizations, 1862–1867,
1870–1876. 8 rolls. DP.

RG 21, 60, 206, and 267

*M2012 Appellate Case File No. 2161,
United States v. *The Amistad*, 40 U.S. 518
(15 Peters 518), Decided March 9, 1841,
and Related Lower Court and Department
of Justice Records. 1 roll. DP.

RG 60 and 267

*M2023 Appellate Case File No. 13879,
*Thomas Cunningham, Sheriff of the
Country of San Joaquin, California* v.
David Neagle, and Related Department of
Justice Records. 2 rolls.

Each listing is shown with corresponding page number/column

A Publications			C0043	32.1		M40	35.1		M93	18.2
A1150	39.2		C0044	32.3		M41	18.2		M94	5.3
A1151	41.2		C0045	30.3		M42	18.2		M95	15.1
A1154	10.3		C0046	30.3		M43	18.3		M96	51.1
A1176	62.1		C0047	30.3		M44	18.2		M97	18.2
A1188	41.2		C0048	33.1		M45	18.3		M98	27.3
A1218	60.2		C0049	33.1		M46	18.3		M99	28.3
A3361	41.3		C0050	32.1		M47	27.2		M100	19.1
A3363	42.1		C0051	32.2		M48	27.2		M101	20.1
			C0052	33.3		M49	27.3		M102	20.3
C Publications			C0053	53.2		M50	27.3		M103	20.3
C0002	54.1					M51	27.3		M104	20.3
C0003	32.1		M Publications			M52	27.3		M105	21.2
C0004	32.1		M1	38.3		M53	27.3		M106	22.1
C0005	53.3		M2	38.3		M54	28.1		M107	22.1
C0006	53.3		M3	34.2		M55	28.2		M108	22.2
C0007	32.1		M4	37.3		M56	28.1		M109	23.1
C0008	32.1		M5	38.3		M57	28.2		M110	23.3
C0009	32.1		M6	49.1		M58	27.3		M111	24.1
C0010	32.1		M7	49.1		M59	28.2		M112	26.1
C0011	32.1		M8	15.2		M60	28.2		M113	26.2
C0012	30.1		M9	20.2		M61	18.1		M114	26.3
C0013	51.2		M10	18.2		M62	15.1		M115	24.1
C0014	33.3		M11	57.1		M63	5.3		M116	34.2
C0015	34.1		M12	34.3		M64	48.1		M117	26.3
C0016	34.1		M13	34.3		M65	39.1		M118	13.3
C0017	4.1		M14	39.3		M66	39.1		M119	50.2
C0018	32.2		M15	37.3		M67	28.2		M120	53.1
C0019	32.2		M16	37.3		M68	15.2		M121	18.1
C0020	47.3		M17	35.1		M69	18.1		M122	1.3
C0021	47.3		M18	37.3		M70	20.1		M123	1.2
C0022	47.3		M19	6.2		M71	23.3		M124	13.2
C0023	47.3		M20	39.3		M72	25.2		M125	13.2
C0024	47.3		M21	37.3		M73	27.3		M126	15.1
C0025	47.3		M22	48.3		M74	37.3		M127	49.1
C0026	31.3		M23	19.1		M75	12.3		M128	18.3
C0027	30.3		M24	60.1		M76	25.1		M129	55.1
C0028	30.3		M25	15.2		M77	18.1		M130	13.1
C0029	33.1		M26	34.3		M78	18.1		M131	23.3
C0030	33.1		M27	15.2		M79	18.3		M132	55.2
C0031	33.1		M28	18.1		M81	25.2		M133	18.2
C0032	33.1		M29	46.2		M82	18.2		M134	18.2
C0033	30.2		M30	18.2		M83	35.1		M135	22.2
C0034	34.2		M31	18.3		M84	22.3		M136	27.2
C0035	33.2		M32	6.1		M85	34.3		M137	55.2
C0036	13.2		M33	6.2		M86	35.1		M138	23.3
C0037	30.2		M34	18.2		M87	16.3		M139	24.2
C0038	32.2		M35	18.3		M88	13.3		M140	20.1
C0039	33.2		M36	35.1		M89	13.2		M141	23.1
C0040	31.1		M37	35.1		M90	18.2		M142	37.3
C0041	31.1		M38	28.3		M91	46.2		M143	18.3
C0042	32.2		M39	28.2		M92	18.2		M144	22.2

M145	15.2	M205	13.3	M264	44.1	M322	50.1
M146	27.1	M206	14.1	M265	12.2	M323	50.1
M147	13.3	M207	55.2	M266	50.1	M324	50.1
M148	13.3	M208	37.3	M267	50.1	M325	62.1
M149	13.3	M209	13.3	M268	50.1	M326	12.1
M152	17.1	M210	60.2	M269	50.1	M327	12.2
M153	27.1	M211	55.2	M270	50.1	M328	24.1
M154	22.3	M213	1.1	M271	37.3	M329	30.1
M155	20.1	M214	57.1	M272	12.2	M330	5.2
M156	17.1	M215	57.2	M273	51.2	M331	49.3
M157	17.2	M216	57.2	M274	32.2	M332	60.2
M158	10.3	M217	57.2	M275	61.3	M333	33.3
M159	23.2	M218	34.2	M276	45.2	M334	12.2
M160	15.1	M219	18.2	M277	12.2	M335	31.3
M161	21.2	M220	49.1	M278	45.2	M336	31.1
M162	57.1	M221	48.3	M279	10.3	M337	1.1
M163	28.1	M222	49.1	M280	24.1	M338	1.1
M164	53.1	M223	18.3	M281	23.2	M339	30.1
M165	23.3	M224	36.3	M282	22.3	M340	33.3
M166	28.1	M225	49.2	M283	24.1	M341	30.1
M167	26.1	M226	49.2	M284	22.1	M342	34.2
M168	19.3	M227	49.3	M285	18.3	M343	31.3
M169	23.3	M228	34.3	M286	20.1	M344	31.3
M170	18.2	M229	43.2	M287	23.2	M345	50.2
M171	21.3	M230	49.3	M288	20.1	M346	50.2
M172	18.3	M231	49.3	M289	20.3	M347	49.3
M173	26.2	M232	49.2	M290	21.2	M348	37.3
M174	16.3	M233	46.2	M291	21.2	M349	32.3
M175	16.3	M234	37.3	M292	22.1	M350	28.2
M176	16.3	M235	53.2	M293	22.1	M351	45.2
M177	12.3	M236	62.1	M294	22.2	M352	10.3
M178	16.3	M237	12.2	M295	23.2	M353	34.1
M179	35.1	M238	35.1	M296	23.2	M354	31.1
M180	14.1	M239	43.3	M297	23.2	M355	31.1
M181	39.2	M240	45.1	M298	23.3	M356	34.3
M182	46.2	M241	43.3	M299	24.2	M357	33.3
M183	27.1	M242	44.3	M300	25.3	M358	34.2
M184	20.3	M243	43.3	M301	25.3	M359	50.2
M185	52.3	M244	43.3	M302	25.3	M360	12.2
M186	52.3	M245	43.3	M303	26.2	M361	34.2
M187	52.3	M246	43.1	M304	26.3	M362	34.2
M188	16.3	M247	60.1	M305	26.3	M363	34.1
M189	14.3	M248	37.1	M306	27.1	M364	14.3
M190	37.1	M250	43.2	M307	27.2	M365	34.1
M191	14.3	M251	50.1	M308	20.3	M366	34.2
M192	14.3	M252	6.2	M309	34.2	M367	35.1
M193	18.1	M253	49.2	M310	14.3	M368	34.2
M194	27.2	M254	62.2	M311	49.3	M369	34.2
M195	52.3	M255	12.2	M313	1.2	M370	49.1
M196	52.3	M256	43.3	M314	32.2	M371	13.2
M198	36.3	M257	42.3	M315	32.3	M372	18.1
M199	25.3	M258	49.3	M316	33.2	M374	49.2
M200	14.1	M259	12.2	M317	49.3	M375	49.2
M201	28.2	M260	50.2	M318	49.3	M376	49.2
M202	28.1	M261	12.2	M319	50.1	M377	49.2
M203	15.2	M262	61.3	M320	50.1	M378	49.2
M204	14.3	M263	44.1	M321	50.1	M379	49.2

M380	49.3	M438	34.3	M495	48.3	M553	44.3
M381	49.3	M439	34.3	M496	7.2	M554	44.3
M382	49.3	M440	1.3	M497	53.2	M555	44.3
M383	44.1	M441	13.3	M498	53.2	M556	45.1
M384	45.3	M442	25.3	M499	60.2	M557	45.1
M385	44.1	M443	31.2	M500	60.2	M558	45.1
M386	44.2	M444	49.1	M502	16.3	M559	45.1
M387	44.2	M445	34.2	M503	17.1	M560	31.1
M388	44.2	M446	19.1	M504	49.1	M561	33.1
M389	44.2	M447	19.1	M505	39.1	M562	33.1
M390	44.2	M448	19.2	M506	39.1	M563	33.2
M391	44.3	M449	19.2	M507	45.1	M564	48.3
M392	44.3	M450	20.1	M508	46.1	M565	43.2
M393	44.3	M451	21.1	M509	30.1	M566	43.2
M394	45.1	M452	22.1	M510	30.2	M567	43.2
M395	46.1	M453	22.2	M511	28.2	M568	31.1
M396	45.3	M454	23.1	M512	28.2	M569	31.1
M397	45.3	M455	23.2	M513	17.1	M570	35.2
M398	46.1	M456	23.3	M514	28.3	M571	30.2
M399	45.2	M457	23.3	M515	29.1	M572	30.2
M400	45.3	M458	24.1	M516	29.1	M573	30.3
M401	46.1	M459	24.1	M517	13.3	M574	37.3
M402	46.1	M460	24.2	M518	13.3	M575	12.2
M403	45.3	M461	24.2	M519	29.2	M576	14.3
M404	45.3	M462	24.3	M520	53.2	M577	32.3
M405	45.3	M463	25.2	M521	16.2	M578	32.3
M406	34.3	M464	26.1	M522	50.2	M579	32.3
M407	7.2	M465	26.2	M523	50.2	M580	31.1
M408	57.2	M466	27.1	M524	50.2	M581	31.1
M409	50.2	M467	27.2	M525	29.3	M582	31.2
M410	50.2	M468	27.2	M526	29.3	M583	29.3
M411	30.3	M469	50.2	M527	31.3	M584	29.3
M412	30.3	M470	34.3	M528	13.3	M585	29.3
M413	45.1	M471	34.3	M529	31.3	M586	35.2
M414	18.1	M472	13.3	M530	31.3	M587	35.2
M415	16.3	M473	49.1	M531	34.3	M588	35.2
M416	50.2	M474	50.2	M532	44.1	M589	45.1
M417	39.1	M475	31.2	M533	44.1	M590	17.2
M418	34.3	M476	31.2	M534	44.1	M591	39.3
M419	34.3	M477	15.2	M535	44.1	M592	51.3
M420	48.3	M478	15.2	M536	44.1	M593	6.2
M421	49.1	M479	15.2	M537	44.1	M594	46.2
M422	32.1	M480	13.3	M538	44.1	M595	37.3
M423	32.1	M481	19.1	M539	44.2	M596	12.2
M425	12.2	M482	19.2	M540	44.2	M597	10.2
M426	32.2	M483	22.1	M541	44.2	M598	50.2
M427	46.1	M484	25.1	M542	44.2	M599	51.3
M428	14.3	M485	25.1	M543	44.2	M600	28.3
M429	14.3	M486	27.1	M544	44.2	M601	6.1
M430	14.3	M487	30.1	M545	44.2	M602	43.2
M431	14.3	M488	30.1	M546	44.2	M603	17.3
M432	6.2	M489	30.1	M547	44.3	M604	37.1
M433	2.3	M490	30.1	M548	44.3	M605	60.1
M434	2.3	M491	48.3	M549	44.3	M606	15.1
M435	4.3	M492	49.1	M550	44.3	M607	33.1
M436	3.3	M493	48.3	M551	44.3	M608	33.1
M437	50.2	M494	49.1	M552	44.3	M609	33.1

M610	31.2	M672	29.3	M733	17.1	M802	12.3
M611	31.2	M673	29.3	M734	38.3	M803	48.1
M612	31.2	M674	30.1	M735	17.1	M804	1.2
M613	32.2	M675	29.2	M736	17.1	M805	1.2
M614	32.2	M676	29.2	M737	17.1	M808	14.3
M616	43.3	M677	29.2	M738	17.1	M809	48.1
M617	46.2	M678	45.2	M739	13.3	M810	48.1
M618	50.3	M679	35.2	M740	37.3	M814	15.1
M619	43.2	M680	36.3	M741	17.1	M815	15.2
M620	15.1	M681	36.3	M742	48.1	M816	47.3
M621	51.1	M682	32.3	M743	35.2	M817	47.3
M622	17.2	M683	32.3	M744	62.3	M818	49.2
M623	17.2	M684	32.3	M745	42.3	M819	51.1
M624	52.1	M685	37.3	M746	33.2	M820	57.1
M625	14.1	M686	46.2	M748	33.2	M821	48.3
M626	30.2	M687	35.1	M749	17.1	M822	48.3
M627	50.3	M688	46.2	M750	15.1	M823	46.3
M628	50.3	M689	43.2	M752	48.1	M824	15.2
M629	43.2	M690	46.2	M753	42.3	M825	15.2
M630	43.3	M691	46.3	M754	17.2	M826	48.2
M631	43.3	M692	46.1	M755	17.2	M827	14.3
M632	32.3	M693	14.3	M756	17.2	M828	14.3
M633	32.3	M694	43.2	M757	17.2	M829	15.3
M634	32.3	M695	29.1	M758	17.2	M830	15.1
M635	1.2	M696	29.1	M759	17.2	M831	15.1
M636	45.1	M697	29.1	M760	17.2	M832	38.3
M637	6.1	M698	43.1	M761	17.2	M833	38.3
M638	45.2	M699	36.1	M762	17.2	M834	38.3
M639	34.3	M700	36.1	M763	17.2	M835	61.3
M640	38.3	M701	36.1	M764	17.3	M836	50.3
M641	5.3	M702	36.2	M765	17.3	M837	38.3
M642	5.2	M703	36.2	M766	17.3	M838	13.1
M644	29.2	M704	6.2	M767	17.3	M839	37.1
M646	29.2	M705	33.2	M768	17.3	M840	16.2
M647	31.3	M708	29.1	M769	17.3	M841	6.1
M648	31.3	M709	29.1	M770	17.3	M842	38.3
M650	35.1	M710	29.1	M771	17.3	M843	48.2
M652	43.2	M711	43.2	M773	17.3	M844	48.2
M653	6.2	M712	29.3	M774	17.3	M845	10.3
M654	46.2	M713	29.3	M775	17.3	M846	10.3
M655	31.2	M715	33.2	M776	17.3	M847	43.1
M656	31.2	M716	33.2	M777	17.3	M848	15.2
M657	31.2	M717	33.2	M779	17.3	M849	15.1
M658	30.3	M719	46.3	M780	17.3	M850	1.2
M659	30.3	M720	5.1	M782	17.3	M851	46.3
M660	30.3	M721	62.1	M784	17.3	M852	46.3
M661	46.2	M722	29.1	M787	17.3	M853	43.1
M662	13.2	M723	29.1	M788	17.3	M854	3.2
M663	28.3	M724	29.1	M789	18.1	M855	3.2
M664	28.3	M725	43.2	M791	18.1	M856	38.3
M665	46.2	M726	17.1	M792	18.1	M857	49.1
M666	43.2	M727	46.3	M793	18.1	M858	46.3
M667	18.1	M728	46.3	M795	18.1	M859	43.1
M668	1.1	M729	33.3	M797	46.3	M860	42.3
M669	30.1	M730	33.3	M798	48.2	M861	50.3
M670	30.1	M731	33.3	M799	48.2	M862	35.2
M671	30.1	M732	14.3	M800	35.2	M863	45.2

No.	Val.	No.	Val.	No.	Val.	No.	Val.
M864	1.1	M928	3.2	M988	4.1	M1064	46.3
M865	61.3	M929	62.3	M989	60.2	M1065	2.1
M866	60.2	M930	51.1	M990	51.1	M1066	12.2
M867	61.3	M931	3.1	M991	61.2	M1067	39.2
M868	61.3	M932	4.1	M992	4.1	M1069	37.1
M869	48.2	M933	3.2	M993	4.1	M1070	62.3
M871	45.1	M934	3.2	M994	61.2	M1072	60.2
M872	45.1	M935	50.3	M995	52.1	M1073	36.3
M873	35.1	M936	54.3	M996	36.2	M1074	37.1
M874	47.3	M937	3.2	M997	63.1	M1075	57.1
M875	14.1	M938	3.3	M998	50.3	M1076	60.2
M876	14.1	M939	62.1	M999	48.2	M1077	60.2
M879	42.3	M940	36.2	M1000	48.3	M1078	59.2
M880	43.1	M941	37.3	M1002	63.1	M1079	59.2
M881	43.1	M942	54.3	M1003	46.3	M1080	52.1
M882	3.2	M945	61.2	M1004	62.2	M1081	60.2
M883	3.2	M946	54.3	M1005	16.2	M1082	3.1
M884	3.2	M947	36.2	M1006	16.2	M1084	60.2
M885	3.2	M948	3.3	M1007	16.2	M1085	37.2
M886	3.2	M949	61.2	M1008	16.1	M1086	45.2
M887	54.2	M950	15.1	M1010	3.1	M1087	46.2
M888	54.2	M951	39.1	M1011	38.1	M1088	60.3
M889	54.2	M953	55.2	M1012	62.1	M1089	61.1
M890	54.2	M954	55.2	M1013	56.3	M1090	60.3
M891	54.2	M955	55.2	M1014	62.2	M1091	14.1
M892	54.2	M956	55.2	M1015	62.3	M1092	39.2
M893	54.2	M957	55.2	M1016	38.3	M1093	59.2
M894	54.3	M958	55.2	M1017	46.2	M1094	46.3
M895	54.3	M959	55.2	M1018	61.1	M1095	59.2
M896	54.3	M960	55.2	M1019	54.3	M1096	60.3
M897	54.3	M961	55.2	M1021	2.3	M1097	60.3
M898	54.3	M962	55.2	M1022	15.1	M1098	46.3
M899	22.1	M963	55.2	M1023	52.1	M1099	37.2
M900	50.3	M964	62.2	M1025	47.3	M1100	59.3
M901	50.3	M965	3.3	M1026	48.2	M1102	60.3
M902	14.1	M966	4.1	M1027	48.2	M1103	59.3
M903	62.3	M967	35.1	M1028	45.2	M1104	51.2
M904	46.3	M968	35.1	M1029	13.3	M1105	51.3
M905	45.2	M969	4.1	M1030	5.2	M1106	59.3
M907	43.3	M970	36.2	M1031	3.1	M1107	57.1
M908	43.3	M971	39.2	M1033	15.1	M1108	39.1
M909	50.3	M972	12.3	M1034	14.1	M1109	39.1
M910	1.2	M973	28.3	M1036	61.3	M1110	15.3
M911	52.3	M974	35.2	M1037	33.1	M1111	3.1
M912	52.1	M975	12.3	M1048	48.3	M1112	58.1
M913	43.1	M976	30.1	M1049	62.1	M1113	39.1
M917	61.1	M977	62.3	M1050	62.1	M1114	60.3
M918	42.3	M978	54.3	M1051	42.3	M1115	3.1
M919	3.2	M979	48.1	M1052	39.2	M1116	60.1
M920	42.3	M980	48.1	M1053	48.3	M1117	51.2
M921	50.3	M981	14.1	M1054	60.1	M1118	1.1
M922	43.1	M982	35.2	M1055	48.1	M1119	14.3
M923	51.1	M983	46.3	M1056	48.2	M1120	60.3
M924	51.1	M984	62.3	M1057	4.2	M1121	38.1
M925	16.1	M985	4.1	M1058	15.1	M1124	57.2
M926	43.1	M986	4.1	M1059	38.1	M1125	47.1
M927	62.3	M987	4.1	M1062	49.1	M1126	6.1

M1127	47.3	M1196	14.1	M1259	14.2	M1350	38.1
M1128	47.3	M1197	33.2	M1260	14.2	M1352	36.2
M1131	6.1	M1198	33.2	M1261	14.2	M1356	36.2
M1134	34.2	M1199	56.3	M1264	54.1	M1357	40.1
M1135	35.2	M1200	52.3	M1265	54.1	M1358	40.1
M1136	47.1	M1202	31.3	M1266	54.1	M1359	41.1
M1137	37.1	M1203	34.2	M1267	54.1	M1360	2.3
M1139	59.3	M1204	59.3	M1268	54.1	M1362	36.2
M1140	39.2	M1205	56.3	M1270	54.3	M1364	41.3
M1141	39.2	M1206	31.3	M1271	52.2	M1365	42.2
M1144	42.2	M1207	29.3	M1272	30.2	M1366	37.2
M1145	51.1	M1208	4.2	M1273	32.3	M1367	37.2
M1146	11.1	M1209	29.1	M1274	1.2	M1368	3.1
M1147	11.2	M1210	59.3	M1275	28.3	M1369	34.1
M1148	37.2	M1211	28.3	M1276	28.3	M1370	32.2
M1149	57.3	M1212	4.2	M1277	30.2	M1371	35.3
M1150	57.3	M1213	4.3	M1278	54.3	M1372	35.3
M1151	57.3	M1214	4.3	M1279	1.2	M1373	5.3
M1152	57.3	M1215	4.3	M1280	31.2	M1375	1.3
M1153	57.3	M1216	52.2	M1281	63.1	M1378	30.2
M1154	58.1	M1217	59.3	M1282	38.1	M1379	6.1
M1155	58.1	M1218	30.2	M1283	11.1	M1380	2.1
M1157	2.1	M1219	28.3	M1284	35.2	M1381	60.3
M1159	56.3	M1220	29.2	M1285	42.2	M1382	15.3
M1160	6.1	M1221	35.2	M1288	15.3	M1383	41.3
M1162	12.3	M1222	2.1	M1289	57.2	M1385	15.3
M1163	51.1	M1223	34.1	M1290	44.1	M1387	42.2
M1164	3.3	M1224	34.1	M1291	54.3	M1389	40.2
M1165	60.3	M1229	38.1	M1292	34.1	M1390	33.1
M1166	38.3	M1230	28.3	M1293	53.3	M1391	1.2
M1167	54.1	M1231	31.3	M1294	30.1	M1392	54.1
M1168	3.1	M1232	4.3	M1299	42.2	M1395	47.1
M1169	56.3	M1233	5.1	M1300	4.3	M1397	54.3
M1170	30.3	M1234	5.1	M1301	38.1	M1398	41.3
M1171	35.2	M1235	5.1	M1302	60.3	M1399	42.1
M1172	3.1	M1236	3.2	M1303	57.1	M1401	4.3
M1173	59.3	M1237	5.1	M1304	38.1	M1402	57.2
M1174	59.3	M1238	5.1	M1306	22.1	M1403	14.2
M1176	2.1	M1239	52.3	M1314	38.1	M1404	54.1
M1177	32.2	M1241	2.1	M1320	40.3	M1406	32.3
M1178	32.2	M1242	4.1	M1321	41.1	M1407	54.1
M1179	31.2	M1243	13.2	M1322	28.3	M1410	41.3
M1180	4.2	M1244	35.2	M1323	15.3	M1411	41.3
M1181	4.2	M1245	14.3	M1325	15.3	M1412	41.3
M1182	4.2	M1246	31.2	M1326	1.1	M1413	42.2
M1183	4.2	M1247	1.1	M1327	36.2	M1414	41.3
M1184	3.1	M1248	4.2	M1328	5.2	M1416	42.1
M1185	29.2	M1249	2.1	M1329	15.3	M1417	40.2
M1186	38.1	M1250	36.2	M1330	29.3	M1418	36.2
M1188	60.3	M1251	14.1	M1331	1.1	M1419	59.2
M1189	60.3	M1252	14.1	M1332	13.1	M1421	53.3
M1190	58.1	M1253	14.2	M1333	38.1	M1423	31.3
M1191	59.3	M1254	14.2	M1334	38.1	M1424	34.1
M1192	2.3	M1255	14.2	M1339	13.1	M1425	3.3
M1193	60.3	M1256	14.2	M1340	13.1	M1426	3.3
M1194	52.2	M1257	14.2	M1342	53.1	M1427	3.3
M1195	60.1	M1258	14.2	M1345	36.2	M1428	4.1

M1429	4.1	M1504	41.3	M1570	9.2	M1629	15.3
M1430	4.1	M1505	45.2	M1571	9.2	M1630	15.3
M1435	29.3	M1506	57.3	M1572	9.2	M1631	17.3
M1436	42.1	M1507	52.2	M1573	9.2	M1632	13.1
M1437	40.2	M1508	52.3	M1574	9.2	M1633	12.3
M1438	41.3	M1509	52.1	M1575	9.2	M1635	49.1
M1439	42.2	M1511	29.3	M1576	9.2	M1637	54.2
M1440	52.2	M1512	61.1	M1577	9.2	M1638	42.2
M1442	31.1	M1513	52.3	M1578	9.2	M1639	4.2
M1443	52.2	M1514	40.1	M1579	9.2	M1640	3.1
M1444	52.2	M1515	29.2	M1580	9.3	M1641	57.3
M1445	52.2	M1518	1.1	M1581	9.3	M1642	53.3
M1446	52.2	M1520	39.3	M1582	9.3	M1643	5.1
M1447	29.2	M1522	4.2	M1583	9.3	M1644	2.3
M1448	33.1	M1523	47.1	M1584	9.3	M1645	4.3
M1449	36.2	M1524	2.2	M1585	9.3	M1646	4.3
M1452	30.2	M1525	2.2	M1586	9.3	M1647	4.3
M1455	31.1	M1526	61.3	M1587	9.3	M1648	4.3
M1457	34.1	M1527	31.2	M1588	9.3	M1649	2.3
M1461	40.2	M1528	10.2	M1589	9.3	M1650	38.2
M1462	42.2	M1530	3.1	M1590	9.3	M1651	56.3
M1463	40.2	M1531	37.2	M1591	9.3	M1652	56.3
M1464	41.2	M1534	57.3	M1592	9.3	M1653	56.3
M1465	41.2	M1535	36.2	M1593	9.3	M1654	56.3
M1466	60.3	M1536	51.3	M1594	9.3	M1655	56.3
M1468	30.2	M1537	4.2	M1595	9.3	M1656	54.1
M1470	33.2	M1538	3.2	M1596	9.3	M1658	53.2
M1471	36.2	M1539	2.1	M1597	10.1	M1659	47.1
M1472	29.2	M1540	4.1	M1598	10.1	M1660	58.1
M1473	38.1	M1541	5.1	M1599	10.1	M1661	58.1
M1474	52.2	M1542	5.1	M1600	10.1	M1662	58.1
M1475	60.3	M1543	5.1	M1601	10.1	M1663	58.1
M1476	42.2	M1545	3.1	M1602	10.1	M1664	58.1
M1478	40.3	M1546	14.2	M1603	10.1	M1665	58.1
M1479	40.3	M1547	5.1	M1604	10.1	M1666	58.1
M1481	40.3	M1548	9.1	M1605	10.1	M1667	58.1
M1482	41.1	M1549	9.1	M1606	2.2	M1668	58.2
M1483	48.2	M1550	9.1	M1607	2.2	M1669	58.2
M1484	41.2	M1551	9.1	M1608	61.2	M1674	3.3
M1485	41.3	M1552	9.1	M1609	61.2	M1675	3.3
M1486	57.1	M1553	9.1	M1610	4.3	M1676	3.3
M1487	29.2	M1554	9.1	M1611	4.3	M1677	3.3
M1488	52.2	M1555	9.1	M1612	61.2	M1678	53.2
M1489	29.3	M1556	9.1	M1613	61.3	M1679	58.2
M1490	35.3	M1557	9.1	M1614	61.2	M1680	58.2
M1491	36.3	M1558	9.1	M1615	2.1	M1681	58.2
M1492	29.2	M1559	9.1	M1616	2.1	M1682	58.2
M1493	39.2	M1560	9.1	M1618	5.1	M1683	58.2
M1494	41.3	M1561	9.1	M1619	51.2	M1684	58.2
M1495	61.1	M1562	9.1	M1620	15.3	M1685	58.2
M1496	53.3	M1563	9.2	M1621	15.3	M1686	58.2
M1497	52.2	M1564	9.2	M1622	15.3	M1687	58.2
M1499	53.3	M1565	9.2	M1623	53.3	M1688	58.2
M1500	42.2	M1566	9.2	M1624	57.3	M1689	58.3
M1501	53.3	M1567	9.2	M1626	4.2	M1690	58.3
M1502	40.3	M1568	9.2	M1627	15.3	M1691	58.3
M1503	41.2	M1569	9.2	M1628	15.3	M1692	58.3

M1693	58.3	M1766	41.1	M1843	57.2	M2035	47.1
M1694	58.3	M1767	41.3	M1844	42.1	M2035	61.2
M1695	58.3	M1768	41.1	M1845	42.3	M2035	62.2
M1696	58.3	M1770	41.2	M1848	35.3	M2037	47.1
M1697	58.3	M1771	41.1	M1849	42.1	M2038	37.1
M1698	58.3	M1778	41.1	M1850	41.3	M2039	38.2
M1699	58.3	M1780	42.3	M1851	41.2	M2040	41.1
M1700	58.3	M1781	50.3	M1852	42.2	M2041	41.1
M1701	59.1	M1783	12.1	M1853	38.2	M2042	40.3
M1702	39.1	M1784	1.3	M1854	38.2	M2043	38.2
M1703	39.2	M1785	1.3	M1858	61.3	M2047	47.1
M1704	14.2	M1786	1.3	M1859	61.3	M2047	61.1
M1705	54.1	M1787	46.1	M1860	52.1	M2048	47.2
M1706	14.2	M1788	2.1	M1898	45.3	M2048	61.1
M1707	54.1	M1789	46.1	M1945	39.3	M2061	47.2
M1720	56.3	M1791	10.3	M1959	41.3	M2062	53.2
M1721	56.3	M1792	10.2	M1960	45.3	M2063	39.2
M1722	59.1	M1793	10.1	M1961	45.3	M2063	47.2
M1723	59.1	M1794	10.1	M1966	2.1	M2063	50.3
M1724	59.1	M1795	10.1	M1967	2.1	M2063	61.2
M1725	59.1	M1796	10.2	M1971	38.2	M2063	62.3
M1726	59.1	M1797	10.3	M1973	41.3	M2064	41.1
M1727	59.1	M1798	10.3	M2005	42.1	M2066	10.3
M1728	59.1	M1799	10.2	M2007	51.2	M2067	10.3
M1729	59.1	M1801	45.3	M2008	41.2	M2068	11.1
M1730	59.1	M1802	10.2	M2009	61.3	M2069	10.3
M1731	59.1	M1803	11.1	M2010	36.3	M2070	11.1
M1732	59.2	M1804	11.1	M2011	2.3	M2071	42.1
M1733	59.2	M1805	10.2	M2012	2.3	M2072	50.3
M1734	61.1	M1806	10.2	M2012	36.3	M2073	7.2
M1735	2.2	M1807	10.3	M2012	57.2	M2073	11.1
M1736	2.2	M1808	11.1	M2012	63.1	M2074	3.1
M1737	2.2	M1809	11.1	M2013	57.2	M2075	6.1
M1738	56.3	M1809	62.1	M2014	42.3	M2076	6.1
M1739	51.3	M1810	10.2	M2015	36.3	M2077	6.1
M1740	54.1	M1811	11.1	M2016	40.3	M2078	62.1
M1741	2.2	M1813	11.1	M2017	41.3	M2079	53.2
M1742	57.1	M1814	11.1	M2018	40.3		
M1743	55.2	M1815	61.3	M2019	47.1	**P Publications**	
M1744	2.2	M1816	46.1	M2020	16.1	P2000	14.2
M1745	53.2	M1817	45.3	M2021	41.2	P2000	54.2
M1746	53.2	M1818	46.2	M2022	53.1	P2186	38.3
M1747	47.1	M1819	46.1	M2023	36.3	P2187	38.3
M1749	1.2	M1820	46.1	M2023	57.2	P2280	14.2
M1750	57.1	M1825	12.3	M2023	63.1	P2282	47.2
M1751	35.3	M1827	2.3	M2024	42.1	P2289	14.2
M1752	13.1	M1828	47.1	M2025	35.3		
M1753	2.3	M1829	47.1	M2027	42.1	**T Publications**	
M1754	40.3	M1830	47.1	M2028	36.3	T1	24.2
M1755	41.1	M1831	38.2	M2030	40.3	T4	52.3
M1756	41.1	M1832	47.1	M2031	51.3	T9	6.2
M1757	41.1	M1833	38.2	M2031	61.1	T10	13.1
M1758	57.2	M1834	35.3	M2031	62.3	T12	14.1
M1759	40.3	M1836	47.1	M2032	35.3	T17	34.3
M1761	40.2	M1838	10.3	M2032	42.1	T21	38.3
M1763	40.2	M1840	41.2	M2034	13.1	T23	25.1
M1764	40.2	M1842	41.1	M2035	1.3	T24	27.2

T25	22.3	T109	22.2	T192	20.2	T264	56.1
T27	19.1	T110	19.3	T193	21.1	T265	5.1
T30	18.2	T111	19.1	T194	21.1	T268	6.1
T31	22.2	T114	27.1	T195	21.1	T271	51.3
T32	47.2	T115	26.3	T196	21.1	T274	5.2
T33	18.2	T116	19.3	T197	21.1	T275	38.2
T34	27.3	T119	35.3	T199	21.1	T276	21.3
T35	25.3	T120	55.3	T200	21.1	T279	1.1
T36	47.2	T121	19.2	T201	21.2	T280	55.1
T37	13.2	T122	20.3	T202	21.2	T282	17.2
T38	13.2	T125	62.2	T203	21.2	T283	56.1
T39	16.3	T127	22.2	T204	21.2	T285	20.1
T41	20.1	T129	25.2	T205	21.2	T286	35.3
T42	43.1	T130	27.1	T206	21.3	T288	1.3
T45	19.1	T132	6.2	T207	21.3	T289	1.3
T47	19.3	T133	22.2	T208	21.3	T290	56.1
T49	19.2	T135	53.2	T209	22.1	T291	56.1
T50	18.2	T136	55.3	T211	22.1	T292	13.1
T51	18.1	T139	55.3	T212	22.1	T294	62.2
T52	18.3	T142	48.3	T213	22.1	T296	5.2
T54	39.2	T145	25.1	T214	22.3	T297	14.1
T55	26.1	T148	27.1	T215	22.3	T298	6.1
T56	26.1	T149	55.3	T216	23.1	T301	55.1
T57	57.2	T151	21.3	T217	23.1	T303	27.1
T58	38.2	T152	25.3	T218	23.1	T305	26.3
T59	26.2	T153	26.3	T219	23.1	T307	39.3
T60	26.3	T156	26.3	T220	23.2	T308	39.3
T61	26.3	T157	18.1	T222	23.3	T311	56.1
T62	23.2	T158	18.2	T223	23.3	T312	56.1
T64	21.3	T159	18.2	T224	23.3	T313	56.1
T70	55.2	T160	28.1	T225	24.1	T314	56.1
T71	55.2	T163	19.3	T226	24.2	T315	56.1
T73	55.2	T164	19.3	T227	53.2	T316	1.3
T74	55.2	T165	19.3	T228	24.3	T317	1.3
T75	55.2	T166	20.1	T229	24.3	T318	1.3
T76	55.3	T168	23.1	T230	26.2	T319	14.1
T77	55.3	T169	23.1	T231	25.1	T320	61.1
T78	55.3	T170	23.2	T232	25.1	T321	56.1
T79	55.3	T171	23.1	T233	25.2	T322	56.1
T81	55.3	T172	25.1	T234	25.2	T325	62.1
T82	55.3	T173	25.2	T235	20.3	T326	35.3
T83	55.3	T174	27.1	T236	25.2	T327	19.1
T84	55.3	T175	55.3	T237	25.3	T328	19.1
T87	55.3	T176	55.3	T238	26.1	T329	19.1
T88	55.3	T177	55.3	T239	26.2	T330	19.2
T89	20.1	T178	55.3	T242	26.3	T331	19.2
T90	24.3	T179	55.3	T243	27.1	T332	21.1
T91	24.1	T180	23.1	T247	19.3	T333	19.2
T92	24.1	T181	19.1	T248	26.1	T334	19.3
T93	28.3	T183	19.3	T249	56.1	T335	20.3
T94	37.1	T184	19.3	T251	52.3	T336	21.3
T98	18.3	T185	19.3	T252	51.1	T337	22.1
T101	22.3	T186	20.1	T253	56.1	T338	22.3
T102	23.2	T187	20.1	T255	12.3	T339	23.2
T103	25.1	T188	18.3	T260	34.3	T341	23.2
T104	24.2	T190	20.1	T261	23.3	T342	24.1
T108	22.3	T191	20.2	T262	19.3	T343	25.1

T344	24.2	T413	19.3	T479	24.2	T543	20.2
T346	24.3	T414	25.3	T480	24.3	T544	20.2
T348	25.3	T415	23.3	T481	24.3	T545	20.2
T350	25.3	T416	24.1	T482	25.1	T546	20.2
T351	26.1	T417	24.1	T483	25.3	T547	20.3
T352	26.3	T418	24.1	T484	25.2	T548	20.3
T353	27.1	T419	24.1	T485	25.2	T549	20.3
T354	56.1	T420	24.2	T486	25.2	T550	20.3
T355	56.1	T421	24.3	T487	25.3	T551	20.3
T356	18.3	T422	24.3	T488	26.1	T552	20.3
T357	19.1	T424	25.1	T490	26.2	T553	20.3
T358	19.1	T425	25.1	T491	26.3	T554	25.3
T359	19.1	T426	25.1	T492	27.2	T555	21.1
T361	19.2	T427	26.1	T493	35.3	T556	21.1
T362	19.1	T428	25.2	T494	38.2	T557	21.1
T363	19.2	T429	25.2	T495	35.3	T558	21.1
T364	19.2	T430	25.2	T496	38.2	T559	21.1
T365	19.2	T431	25.3	T498	11.1	T560	21.1
T366	19.2	T432	26.1	T500	38.2	T561	21.1
T367	19.2	T433	26.1	T501	56.2	T562	21.2
T368	19.2	T434	26.1	T502	18.3	T563	21.2
T369	19.3	T435	26.1	T503	18.3	T564	25.3
T370	19.3	T436	26.1	T504	19.1	T565	21.2
T371	19.3	T438	26.1	T505	19.1	T566	21.2
T372	22.1	T439	26.2	T508	5.2	T567	24.3
T373	20.1	T440	26.2	T509	19.2	T568	21.2
T374	20.1	T441	26.2	T510	19.2	T569	21.2
T375	20.2	T442	26.2	T511	19.2	T570	21.3
T376	20.2	T443	26.2	T512	19.2	T571	21.3
T377	20.2	T444	26.3	T513	19.3	T572	21.3
T378	20.2	T446	27.1	T514	19.3	T573	21.3
T379	20.2	T447	27.1	T517	40.1	T574	21.3
T380	20.3	T449	27.1	T518	40.2	T575	21.3
T381	20.3	T450	21.1	T519	40.1	T576	5.2
T382	21.1	T451	27.2	T520	40.1	T577	36.3
T383	21.1	T452	27.2	T521	40.1	T578	22.1
T384	21.3	T454	56.2	T522	40.1	T579	22.1
T385	21.3	T455	27.1	T523	40.1	T580	56.2
T387	21.3	T457	56.2	T524	40.2	T582	23.2
T388	21.3	T458	42.1	T525	18.2	T583	20.2
T390	22.1	T459	56.2	T526	40.2	T584	25.3
T391	22.2	T460	57.3	T527	12.2	T585	23.1
T393	22.3	T461	35.3	T528	19.3	T586	56.2
T394	22.3	T462	20.2	T529	15.2	T587	48.1
T395	22.3	T463	21.1	T530	19.3	T588	24.1
T396	22.3	T465	21.2	T531	20.1	T589	19.1
T397	22.3	T466	21.2	T532	19.3	T590	19.1
T398	23.2	T467	21.3	T533	20.1	T591	22.2
T399	23.2	T468	21.3	T534	24.2	T592	19.1
T400	39.3	T469	22.1	T535	20.1	T593	22.2
T401	56.1	T470	22.1	T536	24.2	T594	22.2
T402	39.3	T472	22.2	T537	20.1	T595	22.2
T403	39.3	T473	23.3	T538	20.2	T596	22.2
T405	56.1	T474	22.3	T539	21.3	T597	22.2
T407	56.1	T475	24.1	T540	20.2	T598	22.3
T410	5.1	T477	24.1	T541	20.2	T599	20.2
T412	36.3	T478	24.2	T542	24.2	T600	24.2

T601	22.3	T672	25.2	T736	6.2	T797	28.1
T602	21.2	T673	25.2	T737	6.2	T798	27.3
T603	22.3	T674	25.2	T738	6.2	T799	27.3
T604	23.1	T675	25.2	T739	6.2	T800	27.3
T605	23.1	T676	25.3	T740	6.2	T801	27.3
T606	39.1	T678	25.1	T741	6.2	T802	28.2
T607	23.1	T679	26.1	T742	6.2	T803	28.1
T608	56.2	T680	26.1	T743	6.3	T804	28.2
T611	56.2	T681	26.1	T744	6.3	T805	28.2
T612	40.2	T682	26.1	T745	6.3	T806	28.1
T613	23.2	T683	26.2	T746	6.3	T807	28.1
T614	28.1	T684	26.2	T747	6.3	T808	27.3
T617	40.1	T685	26.2	T748	6.3	T809	28.2
T618	40.1	T686	26.2	T749	6.3	T810	27.3
T621	40.2	T687	26.2	T750	6.3	T811	28.1
T623	7.2	T688	26.2	T751	6.3	T812	28.1
T624	8.2	T689	21.2	T752	6.3	T813	28.2
T625	9.1	T690	26.3	T753	6.3	T814	28.1
T630	18.3	T691	26.3	T754	6.3	T815	28.2
T631	16.2	T692	1.1	T755	6.3	T816	56.2
T632	23.1	T693	39.3	T756	6.3	T817	47.2
T633	23.1	T694	16.1	T757	6.3	T819	4.2
T634	23.1	T695	16.2	T758	6.3	T820	37.1
T635	23.2	T696	16.2	T759	6.3	T821	56.2
T636	23.3	T697	16.1	T760	7.1	T822	61.2
T637	23.3	T698	16.2	T761	7.1	T825	11.1
T638	23.3	T699	26.3	T762	7.1	T826	53.3
T639	20.2	T700	26.3	T763	7.1	T829	14.1
T640	35.3	T701	27.1	T764	7.1	T834	51.2
T641	24.1	T702	27.2	T765	7.1	T835	51.2
T642	24.2	T704	27.2	T766	7.1	T838	61.1
T643	24.2	T705	27.2	T767	7.1	T840	41.2
T645	35.3	T706	27.2	T768	7.1	T841	36.1
T646	48.1	T707	27.2	T769	7.1	T842	3.3
T647	24.2	T708	27.2	T770	7.1	T843	40.3
T648	24.2	T709	27.2	T771	7.1	T844	40.3
T649	24.2	T711	20.1	T772	7.1	T845	11.2
T650	24.3	T712	17.1	T773	7.1	T846	11.2
T651	24.3	T713	61.1	T774	7.1	T847	11.2
T652	16.2	T715	41.2	T775	7.1	T848	11.2
T653	16.2	T716	39.1	T776	7.1	T849	11.2
T654	16.1	T717	2.2	T777	7.2	T850	11.2
T655	10.3	T718	53.2	T778	7.2	T851	11.2
T656	24.3	T719	16.2	T779	7.2	T852	11.2
T657	24.3	T720	5.3	T780	7.2	T853	11.2
T658	24.3	T723	13.1	T781	39.3	T854	11.2
T659	24.3	T724	39.3	T783	16.1	T855	11.2
T660	24.3	T725	18.2	T784	16.1	T856	11.2
T661	24.3	T726	18.3	T786	16.2	T857	11.2
T662	25.1	T727	18.3	T787	16.2	T858	11.2
T663	24.3	T728	18.3	T788	16.1	T859	11.2
T664	22.3	T730	36.1	T790	40.1	T860	11.2
T666	25.1	T731	50.3	T791	40.2	T861	11.2
T667	25.1	T732	62.2	T792	40.2	T862	11.2
T668	25.1	T733	37.1	T793	40.2	T863	11.2
T669	20.3	T734	6.2	T795	27.3	T864	11.2
T670	25.3	T735	6.2	T796	28.1	T865	11.2

T866	11.3	T939	42.1	T1044	7.3	T1103	52.1
T867	11.3	T940	41.1	T1045	7.3	T1104	47.2
T868	11.3	T941	42.1	T1046	7.3	T1105	62.1
T869	11.3	T942	42.1	T1047	7.3	T1107	47.2
T870	11.3	T943	41.3	T1048	7.3	T1108	47.2
T871	11.3	T944	41.2	T1049	7.3	T1109	47.2
T872	11.3	T947	47.3	T1050	7.3	T1114	47.2
T873	11.3	T948	54.2	T1051	7.3	T1115	47.2
T874	11.3	T949	54.2	T1052	7.3	T1116	47.2
T875	11.3	T950	52.1	T1053	7.3	T1117	47.2
T876	11.3	T952	16.3	T1054	7.3	T1118	51.2
T877	11.3	T953	28.1	T1055	7.3	T1119	54.3
T878	11.3	T954	13.2	T1056	8.1	T1120	53.1
T879	11.3	T957	16.1	T1057	8.1	T1121	53.1
T880	11.3	T964	53.2	T1058	8.1	T1122	53.1
T881	11.3	T967	36.1	T1059	8.1	T1128	10.2
T882	11.3	T971	56.2	T1060	8.1	T1129	60.2
T883	11.3	T972	56.2	T1061	8.1	T1130	10.2
T884	11.3	T973	56.2	T1062	8.1	T1132	10.3
T885	11.3	T976	56.2	T1063	8.1	T1133	10.1
T886	12.1	T977	51.2	T1064	8.1	T1134	10.3
T887	12.1	T978	61.2	T1065	8.1	T1135	10.3
T888	12.1	T985	38.2	T1066	8.1	T1136	10.2
T889	12.1	T987	62.1	T1067	8.1	T1137	10.1
T890	12.1	T988	55.1	T1068	8.1	T1138	10.2
T891	12.1	T989	55.1	T1069	8.1	T1139	55.1
T892	12.1	T990	55.1	T1070	8.1	T1141	56.3
T893	12.1	T991	55.1	T1071	8.1	T1152	59.2
T894	12.1	T992	55.1	T1072	8.1	T1156	10.1
T895	12.1	T1002	51.3	T1073	8.2	T1157	10.2
T896	12.1	T1008	16.1	T1074	8.2	T1159	10.2
T897	12.1	T1012	54.1	T1075	8.2	T1163	10.2
T898	39.3	T1015	53.1	T1076	8.2	T1164	10.2
T899	53.3	T1017	53.1	T1077	8.2	T1167	37.1
T900	51.1	T1021	59.3	T1078	8.2	T1169	16.1
T903	36.1	T1022	56.2	T1079	8.2	T1170	53.1
T904	36.1	T1023	37.3	T1080	8.2	T1171	36.1
T905	41.2	T1024	36.1	T1081	8.2	T1173	56.3
T907	6.1	T1025	50.3	T1082	8.2	T1174	53.3
T908	36.1	T1026	56.2	T1083	8.2	T1175	10.3
T910	15.3	T1027	52.1	T1085	47.2	T1177	34.1
T911	62.1	T1028	52.1	T1087	5.2	T1178	32.2
T912	61.1	T1029	38.2	T1088	5.2	T1179	33.3
T913	51.3	T1030	7.2	T1089	5.2	T1180	31.3
T915	42.2	T1031	7.2	T1090	5.2	T1181	34.1
T917	42.2	T1032	7.2	T1091	5.2	T1182	57.3
T918	55.1	T1033	7.2	T1092	5.2	T1183	37.2
T919	5.3	T1034	7.2	T1093	5.2	T1184	30.3
T920	5.3	T1035	7.2	T1094	5.2	T1185	30.3
T921	5.3	T1036	7.2	T1095	5.2	T1186	31.1
T925	5.3	T1037	7.2	T1096	5.3	T1187	39.1
T926	5.3	T1038	7.2	T1097	14.1	T1189	12.3
T928	3.2	T1039	7.3	T1098	5.3	T1190	29.2
T935	37.2	T1040	7.3	T1099	5.3	T1191	29.2
T936	37.2	T1041	7.3	T1100	5.3	T1192	29.1
T937	37.2	T1042	7.3	T1101	5.3	T1193	29.1
T938	42.1	T1043	7.3	T1102	5.3	T1194	60.1

T1195	37.2		T1272	8.3
T1196	1.3		T1273	8.3
T1197	36.1		T1274	8.3
T1198	60.1		T1275	8.3
T1200	62.1		T1276	8.3
T1201	62.1		T1277	8.3
T1203	62.1		T1278	8.3
T1204	10.2		T1279	8.3
T1205	60.1			
T1206	59.3			
T1207	2.3			
T1208	17.2			
T1209	17.2			
T1212	36.1			
T1214	2.3			
T1215	2.3			
T1216	2.2			
T1219	12.3			
T1219	57.3			
T1219	62.2			
T1220	2.2			
T1221	36.1			
T1222	36.1			
T1223	1.1			
T1224	11.1			
T1234	16.1			
T1239	55.1			
T1240	16.1			
T1241	33.3			
T1242	33.3			
T1243	30.2			
T1244	30.2			
T1245	34.1			
T1246	34.2			
T1247	33.3			
T1248	33.3			
T1249	33.2			
T1250	33.2			
T1251	30.2			
T1252	31.2			
T1253	31.1			
T1256	17.1			
T1257	16.3			
T1258	16.3			
T1259	8.2			
T1260	8.2			
T1261	8.2			
T1262	8.2			
T1263	8.3			
T1264	8.3			
T1265	8.3			
T1266	8.3			
T1267	8.3			
T1268	8.3			
T1269	8.3			
T1270	8.3			
T1271	8.3			

Index

Each listing is shown with corresponding page number/column

MICROFILM ORDER

Microfilm publication numbers (preceded by an "M" or "T") are assigned to each microfilm publication. Please enter the microfilm publication number and roll number(s) in the proper columns. Because we accept orders for individual rolls, as well as for complete microfilm publications, we must know which rolls you wish to purchase.

Effective May 15, 1996, the price for each roll of microfilm is $34 for U.S. orders. The price is $39 per roll for foreign orders. Shipping is included. These prices are subject to change without notice. For current price information, write to National Archives Customer Service Center (NWCC2), 8601 Adelphi Road, College Park, MD 20740; or call 1-800-234-8861 (in the Washington, DC, metropolitan area, 202-501-5235).

Sample of correctly completed form.

MICRO. PUB. NUMBER	ROLL NUMBER(S)	PRICE
T624	1138	$34.
T1270	88 - 89	$68.

Additional order forms are available upon request.

ORDERED BY (Include organization if shipping to a business address.)	Name	
	Organization *(if applicable)*	
	Address *(Number and Street)*	
	City, State & ZIP Code	
	Daytime Telephone Number *(Include area code)*	

PAYMENT TYPE

SEND YOUR ORDER TO:

CREDIT CARD

Check one and enter card number below. ☐ VISA ☐ MasterCard ☐ American Express ☐ Discover

Exp. Date

Signature

National Archives Trust Fund Cashier (NAT) 8601 Adelphi Road College Park, MD 20740 (Credit card orders may be faxed to 301-713-6169)

OTHER

☐ Check ☐ Money Order

Make payable to: National Archives Trust Fund.

Amount Enclosed $

National Archives Trust Fund P.O. Box 100793 Atlanta, GA 30384-0793

IDENTIFY THE ROLLS YOU WISH TO ORDER

MICRO. PUB. NUMBER	ROLL NUMBER(S)	PRICE	MICRO. PUB. NUMBER	ROLL NUMBER(S)	PRICE
					Subtotal (this column)
					Subtotal from first column
	Subtotal (this column)				**TOTAL PRICE**

MICROFILM ORDER

Microfilm publication numbers (preceded by an "M" or "T") are assigned to each microfilm publication. Please enter the microfilm publication number and roll number(s) in the proper columns. Because we accept orders for individual rolls, as well as for complete microfilm publications, we must know which rolls you wish to purchase.

Effective May 15, 1996, the price for each roll of microfilm is $34 for U.S. orders. The price is $39 per roll for foreign orders. Shipping is included. These prices are subject to change without notice. For current price information, write to National Archives Customer Service Center (NWCC2), 8601 Adelphi Road, College Park, MD 20740; or call 1-800-234-8861 (in the Washington, DC, metropolitan area, 202-501-5235).

Sample of correctly completed form.

MICRO. PUB. NUMBER	ROLL NUMBER(S)	PRICE
T624	1138	$34.
T1270	88 - 89	$68.

Additional order forms are available upon request.

ORDERED BY *(Include organization if shipping to a business address.)*	Name
	Organization *(if applicable)*
	Address *(Number and Street)*
	City, State & ZIP Code
	Daytime Telephone Number *(Include area code)*

PAYMENT TYPE

SEND YOUR ORDER TO:

CREDIT CARD

Check one and enter card number below. ☐ VISA ☐ MasterCard ☐ American Express ☐ Discover

Exp. Date

Signature

National Archives Trust Fund Cashier (NAT)
8601 Adelphi Road
College Park, MD 20740
(Credit card orders may be faxed to 301-713-6169)

OTHER ☐ Check ☐ Money Order
Make payable to: National Archives Trust Fund.

Amount Enclosed $

National Archives Trust Fund
P.O. Box 100793
Atlanta, GA 30384-0793

IDENTIFY THE ROLLS YOU WISH TO ORDER

MICRO. PUB. NUMBER	ROLL NUMBER(S)	PRICE		MICRO. PUB. NUMBER	ROLL NUMBER(S)	PRICE
					Subtotal (this column)	
					Subtotal from first column	
	Subtotal (this column)				**TOTAL PRICE**	

GUIDE TO
FEDERAL RECORDS
in the
NATIONAL ARCHIVES
of the
UNITED STATES

GUIDE
to
FEDERAL
RECORDS
in the
NATIONAL ARCHIVES
of the
UNITED STATES

VOLUME 2
RECORD GROUPS
171 THROUGH 515

$\mathcal{T}$his essential three-volume reference work introduces users to the archival records of the Federal Government—executive, legislative, and judicial. Two volumes describe nearly 1.7 million cubic feet of records in the custody of the Archivist of the United States, and the third is an index.

All types of records—textual, electronic, audiovisual, and cartographic—are covered. The information is organized into 400 "record groups," each of which generally includes the records of a Government agency. The text for each record group begins with an administrative history of the agency and an overview of the extent and location of its archival records, whether the records are in the Washington, DC, area or in a regional Federal archival repository. Detailed descriptions of the types of records, dates covered, and range of agency activities documented are included. The extensive index enables users to trace connections between related records described in separate chapters.

The *Guide* is an invaluable source of information about the resources of the National Archives of the United States and an ideal addition to the collections of libraries, archival and historical institutions, and individual researchers.

8¾ x 11⅜, 3 volumes, 2,428 pages

National Archives and Records Administration, 1996

#100009–Three-volume hardcover set–$95

To order the *Guide*, a check (payable to the National Archives Trust Fund) must accompany each order unless payment is made by credit card. VISA, MasterCard, American Express, and Discover are accepted; simply provide the account number, expiration date, and cardholder signature. Please add $5 shipping and handling for orders up to $100 and add 5% of merchandise total for for orders over $100. Please specify exact title and order number. Send payment, with your name, address, and daytime telephone number to: National Archives Trust Fund, NWCC2, Dept. MCG, P.O. Box 100793, Atlanta, GA 30384-0793. Persons placing credit card orders can call toll free 1-800-234-8861. Orders can also be faxed to 301-713-7170.